Fact Investigation:
A Practical Guide to Interviewing,
Counseling, and Case Theory
Development

Fact Investigation:
A Practical Guide to Interviewing, Counseling, and Case Theory Development

Paul J. Zwier
Director of the Center for Advocacy
and Dispute Resolution
University of Tennessee College of Law

Anthony J. Bocchino
Jack E. Feinberg Professor of Litigation
Temple University Beasley School of Law

© 2000 National Institute for Trial Advocacy
PRINTED IN THE UNITED STATES OF AMERICA
ALL RIGHTS RESERVED

Zwier, Paul J., Anthony J. Bocchino, *Fact Investigation: A Practical Guide to Interviewing, Counseling, and Case Theory Development* (NITA, 2000).

ISBN 1-55681-532-8

Library of Congress Cataloging-in-Publication Data
Zwier, Paul J., 1954-
  Fact investigation : a practical guide to interviewing, counseling, and case theory development / Paul J. Zwier, Anthony J. Bocchino.
    p. cm.
  Includes index.
  ISBN 1-55681-532-8
    1. Trial practice--United States. 2. Interviewing in law--United States. 3. Attorney and client--United States. 4. Law and fact--United States. I. Bocchino, Anthony J. II. Title

  KF8915 .Z89 2000
  347.73'504--dc21   00-046279

To the faculty and participants in NITA's many law skills programs, especially those in the in-house programs at Jones, Day, Reavis & Pogue. And to the founders of the University of Tennessee Center for Advocacy and Dispute Resolution, and my students and faculty colleagues at the University of Tennessee, College of Law.

PJZ

To NITA, its faculty and students

AJB

Table of Contents

Acknowledgments

I would like to name here a number of the NITA teachers I have worked with over the years who have taught me most if not all of what I know about lawyering. Of course, any mistakes or perversions in what I say are mine. Maude Pervere and Janeen Kerper have been particularly inspiring resources for helping me learn the importance of listening and problem solving. Anthony Bocchino is the best and brightest lawyer/teacher I know. Don Beskind, Jo Anne Epps, Jean Cary, M. J. Tocci, Frank Rothchild, and many more of the NITA greats have encouraged and challenged me in more ways than they can ever know.

My good friends and colleagues Joe Harbaugh and Tom Guernsey from the University of Richmond Law School and Jerry Black, Doug Blaze, and Janice McAlpine from the University of Tennessee College of Law have also contributed and inspired me in so many ways. My heartfelt thanks to them.

— Paul Zwier

With the exception of this Bocchino character, I share in Paul's acknowledgments. All those NITA teachers mentioned, to which I add Lou Natali, have been generous to me in providing their time, talent, and assistance.

Sam Solomon and Deanne Siemer have been particularly helpful in providing insight on developing effective case theory.

Finally, I thank generations of NITA and Temple students who taught me whatever I know.

I, too, am a fan of my coauthor, who is yet another example of the student exceeding the teacher.

— Anthony Bocchino

Chapter 1

Preliminary Perspectives

Establishing the right balance between truth seeking and advocacy is key to the lawyer's role in representing any client. The lawyer's ethics require that the client be zealously represented while the lawyer also serves as an officer of the court. The lawyer is expected to be the client's champion—to speak forcefully and passionately on the client's behalf. But that doesn't mean that the lawyer is to follow the client's apparent interest blindly. Not every statement of fact by the client need be presumed accurate. Not every legal position or remedy sought by the client need be pursued. To do so would not serve the interests of the lawyer, client, or legal system well. The lawyer's zealous representation of the client requires advocacy at the highest level. Such advocacy, in turn, requires judgment and the wisdom of experience. And that experience teaches lawyers that in order to truly represent a client zealously and well, it is necessary to look behind client statements of facts and desired remedies to the facts as they are likely to be perceived by the legal decision makers—judges and juries, and to the ramifications to the client of taking legal positions beyond those articulated by the client.

To accomplish this goal the lawyer must discover the risks the client's behavior entails and present these risks in a clear, objective, and balanced way. If there is a linchpin to the attorney-client relationship, it can be found in Model Rule of Professional Conduct 1.4, which provides:

> Rule 1.4 Communication
>
> (b) A lawyer shall explain a matter to the extent reasonably necessary to permit the client to make informed decisions regarding the representation.

This rule requires that the lawyer learn the facts of the matter from the perspective of all those whose interests are at issue. To do so, what the client says and what the client wants must be thoroughly informed by the complete facts of the matter from all sources, no matter whether conflicting, so that the client, in the end, can make informed decisions.

To provide the explanation necessary in Rule 1.4, the lawyer must be skilled at exploring options for the client's future behavior, and not only the legal and economic implications of such options, but also their social, psychological, ethical and moral ones. In the end the clients who will be best served are the ones, whose entire legal matter, are considered in the plain light of all those other considerations that inform his worldview. The only way, then, that the lawyer can be the zealous advocate the client deserves is to develop skills as a comprehensive fact investigator.

Today we more often hear complaints that lawyers are overlooking their clients' real needs and goals when they attempt to solve their clients' "legal" problems. Perhaps the blame lies with traditional legal education, which develops persuasive skills at the expense of excellence in fact-finding skills. Also, in the process of training about the law the education fails to properly concern its students with factors other than legal that go to resolution of client desires through litigation or otherwise.

Yet there are good reasons for emphasizing strenuous advocacy skills—reasons tied up in the assumptions that undergird our traditional adversarial system. Lawyers are forbidden from circumventing the legitimate goals and aims of the client in order to promote *their own or society's goals.* That is not to say the lawyers should ignore factors other than legal in assisting a client in decision making. What is difficult is separating the social, psychological, moral, and ethical goals of the lawyer or society in general, from the social, psychological, moral, and ethical goals of the client. It would be wrong for a lawyer to guide a client based solely on the lawyer's worldview or the lawyer's view of how the rest of society would react to certain decisions or behaviors. What is necessary is for the lawyer to assist the client to find the client's comfort level in a conclusion to a legal matter that meets the client's social, psychological, moral, and ethical goals. A difficult task, to be sure. How, then, should the lawyer deal with such paradoxical roles?

Brown and Dauer, in their book *Planning for Lawyers*, argue that although the lawyer serves a public function as an officer of the court in the legal system, ultimately the interests of both the lawyer and society are subjugated to those of the client and that is the essence of the adversarial system. By taking the position of the client and the client alone, when faced with lawyer opponents performing the same function for their clients, the *truth* will be known.[1]

The premise underlying Brown and Dauer's point is that the truth-seeking power of our system is ultimately found in the requirement that loyalty to the client overrides the lawyer's loyalty to self or society. And this book, or "practical guide," agrees, ultimately, with these sentiments. However, loyalty to the client does not mean blindly following the client's stated preferences but rather informing and counseling the client so that the client makes an informed authentic choice, considering all those factors in making decisions in his legal matter that he uses in all other matters. It demands that the client also be given the information necessary to make informed choices about both the objectives *and* the means by which the client's legal matters are pursued and resolved. Such is the mandate of MRPC 1.2.[2]

Loyalty to the client is an obligation more easily assented to than lived and realized. How does one best serve the client? Does he always take the client's word regarding what the client wants? Should he play psychiatrist or psychologist to determine who the client really is and what it is that he really wants? Some suggest that lawyers should do exactly that: become sufficiently trained in psychology and psychiatry to ferret out what the client's "real" desires are. Or will such a process ultimately become a subversion of the client's will to that of the lawyer, or society's broader mores and biases? Take for example a client who initially says she wants a divorce from her physically abusive spouse. During the course of the interview, she is at times scared, conflicted, angry, still in love, and ready to end it. She is influenced by her father, who says she should leave him; her mother, who says she shouldn't; and her pastor, who says she should wait it out.

The lawyer turns psychiatrist and determines that "what is really going on" is that the client doesn't want to leave her husband, that the husband needs "anger management," and that all will work out once the husband finishes school and gets a new job.

We are very troubled by the preceding notion. First, it is true that a lawyer needs to be concerned about "what is really going on." Granted, what people first say is not always what they really want. On the other hand, how can anyone know what he really wants, especially when what he wants is in a constant state of change? Whether when divorcing, or selling a business, or going bankrupt, or pressing or defending a lawsuit, clients are always deeply conflicted and emotionally distraught. And is it possible for us to become either sufficiently trained or sufficiently clairvoyant to actually perform the calculus suggested by this position? Aren't we destined, as armchair mental health professionals, to merely see in our clients a reflection of our own values, and inflict them on our clients through our "legal" representation? The whole process is dangerous and destined for ultimate failure. In addition, there are some real justice concerns that require a lawyer's training and advice. After all, some clients who seek a divorce do so for valid and well-considered reasons that need not be second-guessed by well-meaning but ill-trained legal professionals attempting to perform a medical function. In most cases aren't we better off performing the tasks for which we have been trained? Unfortunately we don't view the problem as that simple.

The solution we propose is one of process. We suggest that we take the phrase "attorney *and* counselor at law" seriously. We would define the profession as including not only adversary skills, but skills in assisting the client in getting what the client truly wants. To do so we suggest that the attorney/counselor needs to develop abilities in three separate but related functions.

First, the lawyer as attorney/counselor must be a skilled researcher, which involves the ability to seek facts appropriately and through listening skills appreciate what is discovered. The lawyer needs to "find out" the way things were and are. The researcher tries to discover what happened; what people's actions and behavior were; what they said and didn't say; knew and didn't know; intended or didn't intend; and what they remember or perceived as opposed to reconstructed from memories and perceptions filtered through experience and desire.

Second, and simultaneously, the lawyer as attorney/counselor must be a skilled storyteller and producer. The lawyer must be able to produce a story from the raw materials of clients' lives and relationships that will maximize the clients' options for resolution of the matter at hand. In this role, lawyers are concerned with how what actually happened can be formulated into a persuasive story they can tell to maximize the potential benefit to their clients. The story as told by the lawyer seeks to fashion the facts gained as a researcher into an understandable whole for consumption by the ultimate decision maker, be it judge, jury, or business partner entering into an agreement with the client. The story, in turn, must be produced in whatever venue and using whatever devices are necessary whether it be written advocacy in a brief or motion, oral advocacy at motion practice or appeal, trial advocacy before a judge or jury using computer graphics, or merely the persuasion necessary to get a deal done in the client's best interest.

It can be fairly said that these first two roles are traditionally recognized, and for the most part, successfully practiced by lawyers. We recognize these functions, are comfortable with them, and to a greater or lesser extent practice them with skill for our clients' benefit. The third function is harder for us, although every bit as necessary to attain the goals of professional representation of our clients.

Third, the attorney/counselor must take the title seriously and become a creative and caring counselor. The lawyer is more than a neutral presenter of legal information who walks away from moral discourse with the client and neither cares that the client understands the ramifications of his choices, nor cares that he can live with these ramifications, but only that he pay his legal bills on time. The client needs to be involved in the decision making regarding the legal matter brought to the lawyer. The lawyer must appreciate what to research, and what other "stories" and impacts of client decision making ought to be explored. In order to do so, the lawyer must develop the skills of counseling to the effect that clients are given the opportunity to know and tell about their decisions regarding the lawyer's representation. It is this skill that is the hardest as it requires the lawyer to do what we are usually, by temperament, ill equipped to do: give up control. For it is the essence of counseling that the control of the matter is given to someone else. The counselor must provide to the client the options, coupled with appropriate advice, for *client* decision making. And that, of course, is the way it should be. It is the clients who must live with the resolution of their legal matters while the lawyer moves on to the next one. So, after considering all perspectives, including the lawyer's, it must be the client who makes ultimate decisions.

And all of these skills are necessary to implement an effective case theory. Case theory depends upon and is informed by the lawyer's research, storytelling/persuasion, and client selection, and counseling.

So much for the part of the title of this book—"Fact Investigation: Interviewing, Counseling, and Case Theory Development."

But what explanation can we give for the "Practical Guide" part of the title?

Over the years, law professor types have been loath to write anything that can be entitled "practical." After all, law school is where lawyers came apart and thought about "the truth." Law professors aren't supposed to be concerned with producing skilled lawyers. Skilled lawyers who serve clients need not be concerned with truth. They need only be concerned with rhetorical skills and business skills that would allow them to make a living. Law professors are more scholarly. They are involved in studying the way law "is" and works in order to advise legislatures and courts about the way things ought to be.

Yet, more frequently, as scholars study the way the law works they discover that key to its adequate functioning is the relationship between lawyer and client. Whether in studying Rule 11 and the problem of frivolous lawsuits, or corporate governance issues and the role of shareholder litigation, or sexual harassment in the workplace and the inadequacies of mediated settlements, or punitive damages and the question of adequate deterrence of greedy corporate actors, legal scholars are finding that various dispute resolution systems break down at the point where lawyer and client interact with each other. And key to understanding how that relationship functions (and fails to function) is to study and write about how "practical wisdom" is gained and imparted to clients about what is or is not in their "long-term best interests." After all, how will the law students communicate to the clients what they have learned or the underlying values and assumptions bound up in the law? How will they communicate law's moderating effect on a free market economy if the lawyer divorces their substantive training from the skills of lawyering? And so there is a need to look once again at *Fact Investigation: A Practical Guide to Interviewing, Counseling, and Case Theory Development*.

What models—organizational frameworks or prima facie thinking steps—are out there from which the lawyer can choose in order to best serve the clients' legitimate needs and wants? How best can lawyers gather, produce, and impart "practical wisdom" to their clients? These are the questions we attempt to address in this book.

Why should lawyers have a learning model in their heads when they are practicing law? Wouldn't it be better for lawyers to take each case as it comes and have no set preconceptions about what the case will require?

While there is certain rationale that learning models might restrict the creativity and spontaneity of the lawyer, the advantages of having a learning model greatly outweigh the disadvantages. The learning models that follow do not guarantee that the case will be handled in a particular way or style. Neither do they guarantee that opposing lawyers, clients, parties, or judges will behave in a certain way or respond in a particular order of doing things. Instead, they provide the lawyer with planning methods that facilitate making meaningful choices about how they conduct their tasks in carrying out the mandates of their client representation. They empower lawyers to prepare to meet the various obstacles that they will face with confidence. They will be more likely able to control their emotional reactions to the opposition's behavior, so that they respond most appropriately to the behavior. Learning models provide lawyers with the freedom that comes from being able to recognize, understand, and label both their and others' behavior.

This is not to say that learning models are disconnected from what works in the real world. These are learning models that have been developed from years of training lawyers in firm settings about the vagaries of case analysis and fact investigation. The models come from interviews with experienced lawyers and teachers who have trained their associates in successful practice planning and implementation. In addition, the models come from clinical teachers, who have tried and tested them. Finally, the models have been adapted from our amateur understanding of other fields: learning theory, clinical psychology, medicine, business, leadership theory, and sociology. They have been presented and adapted from programs conducted by the National Institute for Trial Advocacy (NITA) during the nearly thirty years of its existence. NITA has presented literally thousands of programs to litigators to help them be more effective in their advocacy techniques. These programs have been evaluated and critiqued by the participants in order to determine what these lawyers have found useful in their practice. While these models have not been sanctioned as official NITA learning models, we are proud to be counted as NITA teachers and have borrowed heavily from our NITA colleagues, teachers, and program directors, and their ideas and discussions of many of the models that are contained in these materials.

What follows are models tested by the reaction and experience of many lawyers and teachers. While they are not rigid and formulaic in nature, they are yet practical and tested real-world models for lawyer planning and decision making. And to keep our eyes on the practical use of the models we will use three NITA problems to show and integrate the models into overall case planning and ethical issues of day-to-day lawyering. The three problems we will use are *Quinlan v. Kane Electronics* (a business/contract matter), *Brown v. Byrd* (an auto accident, personal injury matter), and *State v. Lawrence* (a criminal matter). Case descriptions follow so that you may familiarize yourself with the facts.

QUINLAN v. KANE ELECTRONICS

Roberta Quinlan is a business broker who specializes in the buying and selling of electronics manufacturing and sales firms. Business brokers are agents for buyers or sellers of businesses, and generally work on a commission basis. Quinlan has been a broker in the industry for ten years. Kane Electronics was a family-owned chain of retail electronics outlets located throughout the state of Nita in twenty-six locations. Its president, founder, and sole shareholder was Brian Kane.

In September of YR-1, Kane Electronics was sold to Nita Computer World (NCW), a national retailer of computers and other electronic business equipment, for $10,000,000 of NCW stock. Roberta Quinlan claims that she served as the broker for this transaction and that she had an agreement with Brian Kane to do so. She claims that the agreement was set out in a June 16, YR-1 letter that she mailed to Kane on that date. She has sued Kane for $300,000.

Kane admits he had several conversations with Quinlan about the sale of his company, but says they were all preliminary and brainstorming in nature, and that there was no agreement between him and Quinlan. He also denies ever receiving a letter of agreement from Quinlan. He admits that when he was first contacted by phone by Cliff Fuller of NCW, Fuller said he had been referred by Roberta Quinlan. He also admits that he did not know Fuller or of NCW's interest in his company before the Fuller phone call. Nonetheless, Kane maintains he negotiated his own deal with NCW.

BROWN v. BYRD

Kenneth Brown has brought suit against Robert Byrd for damages arising out of a collision between their cars on April 20, YR-1 near the intersection of 12th Avenue and East Main Street in Nita City. He specifically alleges that Byrd was following too closely and failed to keep a proper lookout. The Plaintiff, Brown, is seeking to recover damages in excess of $50,000 for his neck and back injuries, which he claims were caused by the Defendant's negligence. The Defendant, Byrd, denies liability and asserts that the impact, even if it was his fault, was not sufficient to cause any physical injury to Brown.

STATE v. LAWRENCE

The Defendant, James Lawrence, has been charged with larceny and assault as a result of an alleged purse-snatching incident that occurred on October 1, YR-1. The victim of the purse snatching was Gale Fitzgerald. Ms. Fitzgerald reported the crime to the police on the evening it happened and gave a statement to Officer James Wright.

ENDNOTES

1. Elliot Evans Cheatham, *A Lawyer When Needed* (New York: Columbia University Press: 1963): 4: Louis M. Brown and Edward A. Dauer, *Planning by Lawyers: Materials on a Nonadversarial Legal Process,* vol.1 (Mineola: Foundations Press, 1978).

2. Model Rules 1.2 and 1.4 read in pertinent part,
    1.2(a) A lawyer shall abide by a client's decisions concerning the objectives of representation . . . and shall consult with the client as to the means by which they are to be pursued.
    1.4(b) A lawyer shall explain a matter to the extent reasonably necessary to permit the client to make informed decisions regarding the representation.

Chapter 2

Client Interviewing

The client interview is at the center of information gathering in any legal matter. While it is true that a lawyer will often have some information about the potential representation before meeting the client for the first time, this first meeting will likely determine: (1) whether the lawyer handles the legal matter for the client; (2) the relationship between the lawyer and the client; and (3) the factual basis for the representation. It is at this stage that the lawyer's role as researcher is paramount. Virtually everything that the lawyer does in the initial interview of the client is designed to facilitate the lawyer's ability as researcher to obtain all the relevant facts of the matter so that legal and other remedies for the client's problem can be pursued. While preliminary notions of the story to be told and how it will be produced can be obtained in this first meeting, it is generally too early in the process to make much headway on that note. Likewise, the lawyer's function as counselor is only implicated at this juncture in the relationship in the decision as to whether there will, in fact, be a further relationship with the client beyond the initial interview.

What follows, then, is some definition.[1] Interviewing can be defined as the task of gathering information through asking appropriate questions and listening actively to the client's answers. It assumes that the lawyer wants to know what the client knows, believes, and hopes about the matter. The lawyer wants information in the form of the client's perceptions, the existence of others who know about the matter, relevant documents, and other evidence having impact on the matter at hand. The skill of interviewing requires the ability to ask questions and listen to answers, thereby obtaining relevant information. Without expertise in both asking questions *and* listening, the lawyer as fact researcher is likely to fail.

> ## Forms of Information
>
> ◆ **Client's view of what happened**
> ◆ **Others who know about facts**
> ◆ **Relevant documents**
> ◆ **Other evidence having impact on the matter**

Before a lawyer can do an effective job of storytelling, producing, and counseling, the lawyer needs to know about the client's problem and the client's goals for its resolution. Because the professional skill of problem analysis is only as good as the professional's ability to gather relevant and complete information about the problem, the task of interviewing is our starting place. It is also the typical chronological beginning of the attorney-client relationship.

2.1 Goals of the Initial Client Interview[2]

2.1.1 The Goals of Clients and Lawyers Individually

Consider the goals or needs that the client and attorney each have at the outset of an interview. The client often has a much overlooked need—a need to tell someone, indeed anyone, about the problem he has. Clients want someone to listen to them, to hear their frustration and/or anger. As the psychologist knows, the very act of "telling" is crucial to the client. The telling is often therapeutic, as it can operate as a catharsis for the client. The client, then, wants to tell, to be heard, to be respected, and to be taken seriously.

In addition, in most cases the client wants the problem to go away. The client doesn't really even want to be in a lawyer's office. The client, at least the inexperienced consumer of legal services, is afraid and concerned that he is going to be evaluated by the attorney and found unworthy of the lawyer's time and effort. This client, then, wants acceptance and reassurance. The client wants to trust that the lawyer will have the client's best interests at heart. The client doesn't want "it" to cost much but at the same time wants his rights defended and pursued zealously. The experienced consumers of legal services usually have different needs. First and foremost, they want the lawyer to "take care" of the problem. Second, they want the problem taken care of as quickly as possible. And third, they want the problem taken care of without undue expense.

The lawyer, on the other hand, wants relevant information. When we use the term "relevant" here, we make no reference to the law of evidence. It is much too early in the process to decide the legalities. What the lawyer wants is any information that the client believes has something to do with the existence and resolution of the matter. Some would add that the lawyer wants the greatest amount of relevant information in the least amount of time and with the least amount of trouble. The lawyer also needs to evaluate the client in order to decide whether the client's cause is something he is interested in pursuing and is beneficial to both his personal and professional career goals and aspirations.

The lawyer is also, by necessity, interested in the economics of the relationship. The lawyer, if he charges by the hour, wants a low-maintenance, long-term relationship with predictable, manageable work in an area of the law in which the lawyer has interest and competence. He is interested in knowing what the retainer will be, what hourly rate is acceptable, and how quickly bills will be paid when presented. If billing on a contingent fee basis, the lawyer wants a short-term relationship with a favorable result—favorable meaning that the client wins a large liquid asset, usually cash.

Some argue that lawyers also have other goals. Particular lawyers may want the client's case to be interesting. Some lawyers may want the case to be "significant" in that it either involves an important societal goal or at least has a great deal of economic importance. Some lawyers may want to be "useful," that is, they want to be sure that service of the client's cause is on the side of "right" defined in any way that people determine what is right. For example, some lawyers will only represent individuals in personal injury matters against the oppressive insurance companies. Others may only work on behalf of insurance companies defending against frivolous claims.

2.1.2 Goals of the Client as Compared with Goals of the Lawyer

We can outline the goals of the client and lawyer as follows, with not every goal, obviously, applying to every client and every lawyer.

Client Goals	Lawyer Goals
Get and give information that can solve their problem	Get relevant information that is "valid," complete, and accurate
Get reassurance	Get information that is likely to lead to other relevant information
Get sympathy and/or an empathetic ear	Develop rapport
Get recognition	Begin to evaluate client as a possible witness
Find out cost	Provide for being paid for services
Assess the lawyer	
Catharsis	

2.2 Competing Motivations

There are a number of goals in conflict here. The need of the client for reassurance and sympathy (as opposed to empathy) may not be the lawyer's to give. (The lawyer's evaluation may be that the client is legally responsible and morally bankrupt.) Case finances may get in the way of discovering from the client, and otherwise, the complete information about the matter. (The matter may not be significant enough financially to merit taking every step available to ferret out the facts.) The lawyer's need to evaluate the client's case may also block the information exchange. (The lawyer may categorize the client's matter generally as being just like others he has handled, thereby interfering with individual discovery of the facts of *this* case.)

These and other goal conflicts create competing motivations, otherwise known as inhibitors and facilitators.[3]

2.2.1 Client Inhibitors

Inhibitors to client communication include:

1. Ego threat. Clients withhold information that threatens self-esteem. Because clients are embarrassed by the fact, they conceal it from their lawyers. Obviously, some embarrassing facts are often those that the lawyer most needs to know. For example, in the *Lawrence* case the defendant might not reveal that he had a criminal record, information relevant to any disposition of the matter, for fear that the lawyer would think less of him.

2. Case threat. Clients withhold information that threatens *their* view of the case and its result. Clients sometimes believe that all the lawyer wants to hear are those facts that clients believe are "good" for their position. Lawyers need to know all the relevant facts, and oftentimes clients are wrong in their evaluation about what facts are actually bad for their position. For example, in *Brown v. Byrd* the plaintiff who claims injury that prevents him from vigorous physical activity may keep from the lawyer the fact that he tried to play tennis once after the accident and although he was able to play, was laid up for a week afterwards. Brown may feel this hurts his case when in reality it is good evidence that he is trying to overcome his injuries.

3. Role expectations. Clients may expect that the lawyer is the professional and will ask directly about those matters that are relevant to the case. As a result, they will fail to volunteer information, believing that if a fact is important the lawyer will ask about it. For example, in *Brown v. Byrd* the plaintiff might not tell the lawyer about schoolchildren near the intersection where he was rear-ended without a direct question about bystanders.

4. Etiquette barrier. Clients and lawyers (albeit less frequently) may think that there are some things one just does not talk about. It is difficult for clients to speak to a virtual stranger about those things they consider intimate, including sexuality, religion, even finances, all of which may be important to a case. Likewise, lawyers may be hesitant to ask about such matters, not wanting to appear to be callous or offending in any way. For example, in the *Lawrence* case, Gale Fitzgerald may not tell the D.A. about a personal letter from a person with whom she has a romantic relationship because she feels embarrassed to talk about it with a stranger. Likewise, in a Dalkon Shield case a client may not tell a male lawyer about her difficulty in inserting the IUD, as such things are not spoken about in polite company.

5. Trauma. Clients may resist thinking and talking about unpleasant memories, anger, bad conduct, injury, or embarrassment. In so doing they may keep from their lawyers the most important information they have. This is often the case with personal injury plaintiffs who may avoid talking about the very matters that inform their properly collectible damages. For example, in the *Lawrence* case the victim, Gale Fitzgerald, may not be complete in her description of the assault and purse snatching as reliving the event is unpleasant.

6. Perceived irrelevance. Clients may feel there is no need to provide detailed information because in their view the details have nothing to do with the matter at hand. For example, again in *Lawrence*, Ms. Fitzgerald may not tell about the letter referred to earlier, even though that letter caused her to fight harder for her purse in her struggle with her assailant, thereby giving her a longer time to identify him.

7. Greater need. Clients may be unwilling or unable to listen carefully to lawyers' questions because they feel there is something more important that the lawyer needs to know that the lawyer hasn't asked about, or that the client has avoided saying. In this circumstance, the client has something on his mind that keeps him from giving full attention to the lawyer. Until the fact has gotten out on the table, this inhibitor can poison the rest of the interview. For this reason, until Quinlan in *Quinlan v. Kane Electronics* has the opportunity to tell all the reasons she believes she has been wronged by Kane, she will not be an effective provider of information in responding to lawyer questioning.

8. Forgetting. Memories fade over time. This is a special problem with clients and other witnesses who have no particular reason to recall an event if they merely saw it, but were not involved. Even with parties, over time there is a melding of memory, inference, and desire that leads to reconstruction of events that replaces whatever memory of the event existed. This process is sometimes referred to as inferential confusion and explains many of the circumstances where witnesses give conflicting reports of an event, while both witnesses believe they are telling the "truth." Again in *Quinlan*, if the lawsuit by Quinlan was not filed for eighteen months, Mr. Kane's recollections of the events would suffer from this inhibitor as the events of the sale of his business are remote enough that reconstruction of what happened is the best that he can provide in an interview.

9. Perception. People perceive things differently. What is fast for one person is slow for another. A tall man can be 5'10"or 6'10"(depending on the person looking and describing.

All perception is colored by experience and as a result perception evidence is almost inherently unreliable. For this reason, two people can see the same thing and report two apparently different events, even though both are telling the "truth" as they know it. This phenomenon is true in virtually every car accident case where both parties are likely to view fault in the other.

10. Chronological confusion. Clients recall events but are oftentimes unsure about their sequence. This creates enormous problems for a fact researcher, as often the key to an event is understanding its component parts in the order in which they occurred. The *Quinlan* case is a prime candidate for this inhibitor, especially when in conjunction with the passage of time.

Inhibitors to Communication

- Ego threat
- Case threat
- Role expectations
- Etiquette barrier
- Trauma
- Perceived irrelevance
- Greater need
- Forgetting
- Perception
- Chronological confusion

2.2.2 Lawyer Facilitators

It is the lawyer's job to anticipate the inhibitors to client communication and be prepared to overcome them. All of what the lawyer does in the interview will be designed to maximize client communication. There are, however, some well recognized facilitators to communication that every lawyer should bring to each interview. They include:

1. Promising confidentiality. All people are nervous about revealing information about themselves that might be embarrassing. When a client talks to a lawyer, the topics are almost always in that embarrassing category; lawyering is not a "good news" business. For example, the defendant Lawrence may be reluctant to tell where he was or who did the deed because he may want to protect someone or is worried about being a "rat." The lawyer needs to be sensitive to these possibilities and offer confidentiality to help the client assess the situation. The attorney-client privilege may ease the discomfort of the client in this regard. Of course, if the client admits the crime, the lawyer may still put the state to its burden. "Knowing" what happened may limit what the client can say on the stand, or whether the client can testify. Note also that proposed Model Rules of Professional Responsibility changes may mean that confidentiality may be forfeited if the lawyer knows that the client will defraud someone. In jurisdictions with such rules the lawyer should offer confidentiality, but with a "Miranda warning" that the lawyer can keep confidential only facts that don't involve future severe wounding, death, or substantial fraudulent financial injury to another. Although we list this facilitator first, it is not necessary to begin each interview with its recitation. Doing so may tell the client, indirectly, that you otherwise distrust the client's veracity. This is so because the client has some apparent difficulty in revealing information.

2. Empathetic understanding. Every client and every person want to be listened to. In the case of a client being interviewed by a lawyer, the need is even greater. One way to communicate interest in what a client is saying is by demonstrating listening by head nods and by use of phrases such as "I see," or "okay," or "go on." The use of such phrases communicates that the lawyer is listening, understanding, and appreciating what the client has to say.

Two additional active listening probes bear special mentioning here. Use silence. Silence gives the speakers time to gather their thoughts and put them into words. People who are very "verbal" sometimes forget that words may not come to others as easily. The importance of silence as a probe can't be overstated. It sends the message, "I've got the time for you. Don't rush. I am confident we will figure this all out together." Second, the lawyer needs to establish good eye contact with the client. The beginning of an interview is not the time to be scribbling notes or looking at papers or other work. Now is the time to "listen with your eyes."[4]

3. Fulfilling expectations. When clients come to a lawyer, they have certain expectations as to what will occur; and to the extent that those expectations can be fulfilled, communication will be enhanced. For that reason, lawyers should dress professionally, conduct themselves in a professional manner, and treat clients with courtesy and respect.

At the same time, some expectations must be exploded. For example, the client will often think that the lawyer will control the interview and dominate the conversation. Because the client has the information, the client must dominate the interview time. As a result, the lawyer should make clear that the client's information is paramount in the interview and that the lawyer can help only to the extent that the client provides the information necessary to that end. This is sometimes done directly, but more often through the use of questioning techniques designed to make the client the center of the interviewing process. Even when a client has difficulty remembering, the lawyer can raise the expectation that the client will be able to remember. The lawyer may say, "I understand how hard it is to recall; I've often had that difficulty myself. I find, however, that if I concentrate for a while and try to put myself back in time and place, things start to come back. So take your time and think a little more."

4. Recognition. Even though the client should dominate the interview, the client will still look to the lawyer to make sure everything is going according to form. One method of encouraging continued information flow from a client is for the lawyer to say such things as, "you're doing a good job," or "that's important—what you've said so far." By so doing, the client is assured that the interview is proceeding in a helpful way, and is further encouraged to continue to provide information.

5. Extrinsic reward. When a client provides information that is particularly relevant to the matter at hand, it is often appropriate for the lawyer to say something like, "This information will be very helpful." In this way the client is encouraged to search his memory for more information of the same sort, or from the same time period, or about the same topic, all of which will be helpful.

6. Catharsis. Where the lawyer determines that the client is inhibited by strongly held emotions, the lawyer might try to release them by encouraging their expression. In this way the client can bring them up, deal with them appropriately, and can put them behind and give more details about the event they are blocking.

7. Need for meaning. The lawyer might create cognitive dissonance by raising conflicting information, in order to spur the client into giving more information. If the lawyer uses this technique, the lawyer should raise the conflict as coming from the opposition, or the jury, or the judge, rather than from the lawyer, in order to protect the client from a feeling that the lawyer is not on the client's side. The lawyer might say, "You know, a judge might be curious about this letter? Doesn't it suggest you knew that the shipment was uninsured? How would we answer the judge's concern?"

Facilitators to Communication

- ◆ Promising confidentiality
- ◆ Empathetic understanding
- ◆ Fulfilling expectations
- ◆ Recognition
- ◆ Extrinsic reward
- ◆ Catharsis
- ◆ Need for meaning

2.3 An Overall Client Interview Strategy

The following interview model is offered so that the lawyers can start to control their behavior and make choices about what they do and ask about, rather than to simply react. Skills learning models are not meant to be cookbook tricks for successful client relationships, but are meant to allow the lawyers to ask questions not because they can't think of anything else to say, but because they have a reason for asking a question.

2.3.1 Pre-interview Planning

It is extremely helpful and efficient if the lawyer has some idea about the potential client's problem before the interview begins. For example, if the lawyer knows that the potential client's problem is outside the lawyer's area of expertise, both the lawyer and client can save time by a simple referral to a lawyer who does specialize in those matters. This basic problem is usually accounted for in that the client has already been directed to the lawyer by a friend or relative, by a court appointment, from a referral from another lawyer, or even through response to lawyer advertising.

Much can be done, however, through pre-interview information gathering that can make the time in the interview more productive for both the lawyer and the client. When the client makes an appointment, information about the client and the perceived problem can be obtained in a brief phone interview or by having the client respond by fax or e-mail to a brief questionnaire. In that way, the basic nature of the client's problem as well as necessary demographic material can be obtained before the interview begins. In addition, the client can be told to bring certain things with him. For example, when the plaintiff in *Brown v. Byrd* comes into the office he can bring with him his medical records or come armed with the names and addresses of treating physicians so that medical releases can be signed. In addition, copies of police reports and repair bills for property damage will also speed the process.

The lawyer, in turn, can review the information before the interview and if necessary, conduct some preliminary research in preparation for the interview. The lawyer may also determine that it would be more appropriate for the client's matter to be handled by someone else in the firm, or determine that a particular associate or paralegal be involved in the case so that he can attend the interview. Arrangements can also be made for interpreters if necessary. Moreover, the lawyer can begin thinking about the client's problem before the interview and plan for the use of the facilitators likely to overcome any apparent inhibitors that the potential client might have. In this way the lawyer is efficient and the client is made to feel important, which act as facilitators for communication.

2.3.2 Rapport/Icebreaking

If it is true that a willing interviewee provides better, more complete information faster than a reluctant interviewee, then taking the time to look to the client's comfort is worth some thought and preparation. Remember, the psychiatrist places the interviewee on the couch for good reasons. While the couch is a little much for the lawyer, picking a nonthreatening place (around the coffee table) may facilitate comfort and rapport. The setting of the interview can also help relax the client so that complete information can be easily and completely obtained. Lawyers often position themselves behind an imposing desk. They are elevated in big thronelike chairs; their clients are in front of the desk in smaller chairs, almost kneeling forward to the lawyer. If the lawyer wants more accurate and complete information, the client can't fear the lawyer. The lawyer has a number of choices in lessening their perceived status differences. The lawyer can move the client alongside the desk so that communication occurs over a corner rather than across the desk. The lawyer can move from behind the desk to a couch or to chairs arranged at a circular table or lower coffee table.

Office Setups

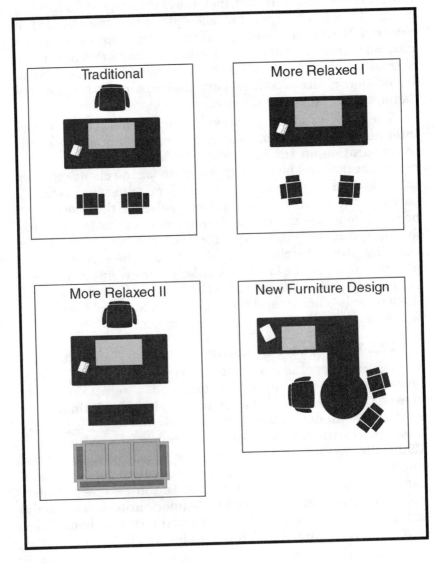

Asking about the person's health and welfare, seeing to a beverage, and talking weather or sports communicate far more than one might expect. If you pick the right icebreaker you can get valuable information about the case. (For example, "How's business?" or "You taking a vacation this summer?" can tell you much that may relate to the case.) Icebreaking also sends the message that this person is important to you, rather than some cog in a legal production assembly line.

Icebreakers and Conversation Starters

How's business?

Did you have any trouble finding our office?

Did you have any trouble finding parking?

Have you had a vacation this summer?

Did you see what the market did yesterday?

Did you see the game last night?

Family photographs

Travel souvenirs

Statistical or demographic information is best left to support staff either before or after the interview. In addition, although fees are important, that discussion is better left until the end of the interview once a decision has been made to accept the case.

In order to get legally relevant information and develop a good initial client relationship, the lawyer should plan carefully for client interviews starting from the very beginning icebreaker.

The lawyer needs information of a different sort than is usually sought in an initial interview. The lawyer needs to know what the client's goals are. The lawyer needs to hear how the client feels about his work, himself, his personal life, etc. In a way, the lawyer needs to manipulate the client until the client feels that he is not being judged or evaluated. That way, the lawyer can judge and evaluate whether he ought to represent this client. The last point is crucial. The judging is of the lawyer's values and beliefs and their compatibility with the client's values and beliefs in order that the client be zealously and enthusiastically served. The lawyer need not necessarily be wedded to the client's values, for often a true believer in a cause is too impassioned to see the cause's weaknesses and failings. On the other hand, if the lawyer takes all comers, the lawyer may be doing a serious disservice to the client by engaging in half-hearted and lukewarm advocacy of the client's cause.

Sometimes, however, despite the best-laid plans, an ice-breaker or "chitchat" period is inappropriate. For instance, if the client comes into the office, takes a chair, assumes a fetal position including crossing arms and legs and avoiding eye contact, the client will likely not be receptive to extensive icebreaking. In those cases it is best to read these nonverbal signals and get to the problem. In other words, lawyers need to be able to watch for and read nonverbal clues in order to respond most effectively to the client's needs.

2.3.3 Basic Questioning Technique

The following questioning techniques proceed from the perspective that it is much more efficient for the client to provide information about the matter in the first instance than for the lawyer to guess what and how "it" could have possibly happened. Playing the game "20 Questions" helps demonstrate this point. "20 Questions" forces a questioner to guess what the interviewee is thinking by allowing the interviewee to answer questions with *only* a yes or a no. The questioner must do all the work while the interviewee simply smiles and sits back and waits for the questioner to figure it all out. The questioner must ask narrow, leading questions or the interviewee won't be able to answer yes or no. It reminds the interviewer/lawyer how important the form of the question is to getting the witness to talk. Once freed of the restraints of the game, the questioner realizes that to get information it is much preferable to ask open-ended questions.

Open-Ended Questions

- ◆ What can I do for you?
- ◆ What happened?
- ◆ When did it happen?
- ◆ Explain that to me some more.
- ◆ How did it happen?
- ◆ Please tell me all you can about . . .
- ◆ Describe what happened.
- ◆ Why did this happen?
- ◆ Who was involved?
- ◆ Where did the events take place?

To guard against making false assumptions and creating too passive a role for the interviewee (making it too easy for him to fail to disclose threatening information and prolonging the interviewing process), basic interview questioning technique attempts open-ended questions first and saves more directive questions for follow-up, detail, confirmation, and theory verification. For example, the interview of the plaintiff in *Brown v. Byrd* after initial icebreaking might begin with a question as broad as "How can I help you?" if the nature of the client matter is unknown, or more likely if it's known that Brown has a potential case arising out of a car accident with a question like, "Tell me about the accident." The client is then encouraged to keep talking about the accident until he has exhausted his unaided memory. During this initial stage of questioning the only response of the lawyer to the client narrative will be head nods, questions like, "Go on," "Tell me more," or "What happened next?" or any other nondirective facilitator of continuing information. Only later will the lawyer fill in the gaps in the story with such matters as time, weather, witnesses, etc., through the use of more directive questioning.

2.4 The Three-Stage Interview

A three-stage interview is a flexible, useful model for thinking about the interview itself. First introduced in Binder and Price's groundbreaking book *Lawyer Interviewing and Counseling: A Client Centered Approach*, it balances conflicting goals and incorporates the basic interview questioning approach outlined above. First is a preliminary problem identification stage—what we call the "gush". Second is the problem overview. Third is the theory verification stage. These three steps in the initial fact investigation help the client efficiently and comprehensively cover the overall nature of the problem. Then there should be a structured review of the information the client has, arranged either chronologically or topically. Finally, there should be a time where the lawyer asks more pointed questions to verify certain legal theories that the lawyer has identified from the preliminary problem identification.

Taking the first part first, the client needs to be given an opportunity to gush, vent, emote, or simply tell what brings him to the lawyer's office at this time in his life.

2.4.1 The Gush

The gush is time for the witness to tell you what is most important to them for you to hear. It helps the lawyer get insight to what the client knows and how the client feels about the situation. It also helps the lawyer guard against making false assumptions and making inappropriate recommendations, comments, asking inartful questions, and becoming prematurely judgmental. Additionally, the lawyer can establish his empathy in what happened to the client, and his listening ability will further demonstrate client importance.

Open-ended questions are the order of the gush. And the idea is to prolong the gush at least until the client asks for input. The lawyer should interrupt as little as possible, hold off taking notes until the problem overview stage, and use nonverbal probes to try to exhaust the client's knowledge and feelings.

The following probes designed to provoke more from the client are arranged in order of directiveness. The more directive, the more the lawyer risks narrowing too quickly and making false assumptions. The lawyer should use the probes in descending order to keep the witness talking, facilitate the lawyer's role as a listener/information gatherer, and avoid the premature narrowing that can lead to misdiagnosis.

Silence

Mm-hm

Yes, okay, I see

These can be meant as "I hear you," but may communicate more.

● **Restatement.** Repeating the actual words of the interviewee is a technique used to communicate that the lawyer is listening, and encourages more information from the client. Client information is so important and the lawyer is listening so carefully that exact words can be repeated. For example, in the Brown case, the defense lawyer might ask Byrd, "You say that the Honda stopped short?" The implied unstated question that accompanies the restatement is, "Tell us more about why you say that."

● **Clarification.** Clarification is restatement, but the lawyer now risks using his own words, impliedly asking the client to correct his understanding or clarify what is being said. It is much more directive, since it involves interpretation. For example, when the client may have said the Honda stopped short, the lawyer might offer, "You're saying the Honda driver slammed on his brakes? . . ." The use of the lawyer's own words impliedly asks the client to listen and correct the lawyer's understanding with more detail.

● **Reflection.** Reflect the feelings and attitudes the client is feeling. ("I can understand you must have been angry.") As with clarification, reflection asks the client to revise the lawyer's guess at how the client feels as well as thinks about a subject. It is key to active listening, and often produces a more honest and complete response from the client. Lawyer: "You were surprised by the Honda's stopping short?" Client Byrd: "You bet; in fact, now that I think about it, I don't think the taillights came on." Or, after Byrd describes Brown as blaming him for the accident, the lawyer might say, "You must have been taken aback by what he said. . . ." Expect more emotion from the client in his response, and then urge him to give more details.

● **Explanation.** Tell the client how things are and how to respond. For example, you might say, "Mr. Byrd, you are now saying the taillights didn't work?" At trial, we would have to prove that. "Did you notice whether the taillights were broken . . . cracked or dented? Was Brown cited for a broken taillight?"

● **Assurance—Reassurance.** This is directive because it focuses the client's attention. ("I hear what you are saying and this is good stuff.")

It is also particularly important during the first gush to keep eye contact with the interviewee. Taking notes, especially in the gush stage of the interview, is probably unnecessary and may in fact interfere with the gush by focusing the client's attention on the matter about which the notes are apparently taken. There is too much going on and the interviewer must establish his empathy and listening ability. Notes can wait until the theory verification stage of the interview or after drafting an interview memo that summarizes facts, by confirming times and dates with the client. If a record of the interview is desired, it is usually preferable that the interview be tape-recorded. Of course, client consent to the recording is necessary. Failure to get consent in some jurisdictions amounts to illegal wiretapping. In most jurisdictions, such a recording would be protected work product and thus unavailable to opposing counsel. The downside to tape recording an interview is that many clients are inhibited by the recording device. Because most clients are not used to having what they say recorded, it is likely that at least for a short portion of the interview they may be inhibited in speaking while being recorded. For that reason, recording may be effective as a record-keeping device if it begins at the second stage of the interview, after the client is already comfortable with providing information. If and when tape recording begins, it should be done with a system that is out of sight of the client to minimize any inhibiting effect.

Open-ended questions and nonverbal probes will often prompt a gush, which is important for the psychological reasons (a need for catharsis) discussed earlier, and also so the lawyer can find out how best to structure the gathering of relevant information. Too many lawyers start off the interview by talking at the client with information about fees, their expertise, and the parameters of the relationship before they know what information the client needs and before the client is ready to hear it. In some cases, where the client is primarily concerned with cost, or where the client is more sophisticated, or where the client has already dealt with the lawyer before and the lawyer has already been given the parameters of the problem, this first gush is not as necessary. Still there are events that impact on a client's life that will get in the way of the lawyer's need for information if they are not discovered early. Spouses leave, people get sick, they lose their jobs, they get traffic tickets on the way to see the lawyer, they get into arguments. If the clients can describe where they are in their lives, the lawyer can more appropriately use their questions and counseling in a way that works best within that context. Without the gush, a lot of time is lost.

The lawyer needs to also make sure that the gush is over. Head nodding, silence, further open-ended questions like, "Tell me more," "Please explain," and "Is there anything else you're concerned with?" can get the lawyer to the different levels of the problem of the client's concerns quickly and efficiently. Questions like "So, how are you feeling about all this?" or "What are you looking to have happen next?" can also get the lawyer to understand what the client's goals are and get a glimpse at the client's value system.

2.4.2 Problem Overview

Once the gush is completed, the next interviewing stage is the problem overview. In this stage, the lawyer learns the scope and basic parameters of the problem. The second part of the interview needs a structure. The usual structure is a chronological overview. The client needs to tell a complete story with a beginning, middle, and end. There are a couple of pitfalls here to avoid.

Not getting the real beginning of the problem is a real problem. For instance, not finding out about the earlier business dealing, earlier conversations, or earlier life of the client out of which the problem arises can mislead the lawyer both as to the legal nature of the client problem and as to the value system of the client. The lawyer should first let the client tell where he thinks the problem began, but perhaps open the door to an earlier chapter with questions like "Was this the first time you dealt with this person?" or "What was going on in your life or business around this same time?"

Once a beginning is identified, the lawyer can then suggest the level of detail that is necessary and then simply ask a series of "What happened next?" or "Then what happened?" questions. This chronological overview is helpful not only to insure that the lawyer gets complete information, but also so that the client can feed into the story with the least interruption. When people relate information in the order that it occurred, it is more likely to be complete. It is much more likely that a lawyer will miss relevant information by proceeding in a reverse chronology or with some other organization tool. Most people are comfortable thinking chronologically. They also appreciate the concern that the lawyer get a complete picture of what happened.

During this second overview stage, it is important that the lawyer take the opportunity to ask a different type of question—one that focuses on the client's feelings. For instance, the lawyer should ask, "How did that make you feel?" or "Were you concerned, frustrated, angry, happy, etc., by that?"

Again, not only do these kind of questions get a better picture of the client's goals in order that the lawyer can solve the client's problem more efficiently, but also the lawyer can hear the potential value conflicts that could affect the lawyer's representation of the client.

During this part of the interview the lawyer should avoid being judgmental. Lawyers tend to signal their evaluative goals in the interview process too early, which has an effect on slowing the information flow and increasing the chances that the lawyer's impressions of the client's goals and values are wrong. For example, clients may sound angry and really be worried, may say they want a divorce when they really need money to pay medical bills, may say they want to fight when they really want respect, or may say they want money when they really want their child back. Excellent active listening skills are key to an accurate diagnosis of the client's problems, as well as an accurate picture of the client's values. If the lawyer says, "Well, I don't know" or "Why did you say that?" or "I wouldn't have done that" rather than, "Tell me more," or "What were your reasons?" or "How were you feeling when . . . ?" the lawyer is likely to cause the client to become defensive or inhibited in providing information. This is not to say that the client may not need to confront the harsh realities of his problems, but it does mean to say that there is a time for this to occur and a way that it should occur. The confrontation should not occur during the second part of an initial interview. Additionally, there is no need for the client to hear that the value judgment is the lawyer's, rather than the opponent's, or the judge's.

Lawyers who make personal moral judgments during an initial interview often make their clients very angry, whether or not they openly show the anger. When clients feel they are being judged, they often fight or are difficult and uncooperative. It is better that the client hear the judgment in the context of what the other side would argue, or what the judge or jury might think, rather than judgment that comes from the lawyer. More will be said about this issue in the chapter on counseling.

In some cases the lawyer may not choose a chronological organizational framework for an overview of the client's information. On some sorts of transactions or deals the lawyer might better try a topical approach to gather information. For instance, if a client is having trouble in his business raising money, it might be better to ask about the client's management structure for his company, his suppliers, his buyers, his financial structure, and his banking relationships in order to understand his or her problem. In order to decide a custody dispute, a lawyer might ask about the home, the school, the job, the church, the organizations the client belongs to, and the relationships the client has. Note that within each one of these topics is a potential story, but perhaps it is better to tell the client that you want information on a topic-by-topic basis, rather than by getting information about the chronological history of the problem.

Whether using a topical approach or a chronological approach, it is helpful to share the organizational framework with the client. The client then is comforted by the strategy and can concentrate on recalling the necessary information. If the client gets the feeling that the lawyer is bouncing all around, then the client also knows that the crucial pieces of the problem might be left out. Just as the doctor needs complete information for a diagnosis, the lawyer does so for good lawyering. Just as doctors have found that too early a decision leads to poor diagnosis, so too have lawyers.

An excellent mental image that many experienced lawyers have found helpful with this process is the picture of information gathering as a series of funnels. Lawyers use open-ended questions at the top of the funnel, move on to more direct or fact-specific questions in the middle of the funnel, and save the narrow, leading question to make sure they have heard correctly and to verify the information they feel is necessary to correctly diagnose the problem, aided by focused research. The key to a good understanding of a client's problem is to keep the funnel open for as long as the lawyer can. By narrowing too quickly, the lawyer risks misunderstanding the legal nature of the problem and may misunderstand the client's goals.

During this stage, find a beginning, middle, and end to the story. Create a time line, either physically or mentally, and then fill in the client's thoughts, feelings, and motivations before, during, and after each key event. Also be on the lookout for nonevents and lasting conditions. More will be said about this in the chapter on witness interviewing.[5]

2.4.3 Theory Verification

Though it is still very early in the process, you should seek to confirm your understanding of what has been told. Theory verification attempts to reach an understanding of the client's position by confirming what has been said. It also is the place where the lawyer can most safely move into the role of writer/producer. Your questioning technique now uses more leading questions. Typically, they will start with verbs: "Did you enter the intersection before you saw that Brown was stopping? Was the light still green when you entered the intersection?" Note that the questions call for yes or no answers. Pressure is applied through the question form to get the client to agree. Even more pressure can be applied by taking the question out of the question. For example, "So, you entered the intersection when the light was still green . . . right? You weren't drunk, you were alert, you were focused on your driving, you were not speeding?"

If the answers surprise you, you need to back up and ask the client to explain, describe, or elaborate on what happened. You should also use restatement of what the client says and reflection of what the client felt, in order to reach a good understanding and to guard against your wrong assumptions or conflicting values.[6]

Where appropriate, you can start to form your legal, factual, and persuasive theory of the case, which will be explored in the next chapter. One danger here! When the clients are hungry for assurance, they may hear these confirmations as advice about the success of their case. Also, if no legal research has been done, or the lawyer has no experience with potential statutes of limitations, defenses, or opposing conditions and facts, the lawyer has no business predicting the outcome of the case. It is better to involve the client in a process of gathering more facts, explaining that while it is premature to predict the outcome, the client can be assured of the lawyer's effort on the client's behalf. To avoid giving false assurances or unwarranted advice, the lawyer should also plan a closing statement. An example of a closing statement would be:

> It sounds like your case is one that we have the expertise to work on, and I would be pleased to take you on as a client. Before you decide, let me tell you that my fee for work on a case such as yours is [insert contingent fee or hourly rate]. Does that sound acceptable to you?

Assuming the client agrees to representation:

> Why don't you get me copies of the following documents and correspondence? In fact, let's make a list right now of these documents, where they are

located, and who has them. Also, let's make a list of other people I should talk to about the facts of this case. While you are getting me these materials I'm going to do some legal research, identify potential legal and factual theories for the case, and then prepare a fact investigation plan as to where we go from here. I would predict that this work will take approximately ten hours. If it will take longer than ten hours, I will get back to you to see what you want to do. Why don't we then get together in a week and I can look over what you have, and I can counsel you on where we should go from there.

Once the relationship is clearly established, lawyers should make clear the method to be used in keeping the client informed of the process of the case. The lawyer should copy the client on all correspondence, pleadings, and motions on the client's behalf. In addition, the lawyer might assign a contact person for the client to call if he has any questions. Explain the costs for these communications, but make clear that, if necessary, the client will always be able to get in touch with the lawyer.

2.5 Professional Responsibility Issues and the Initial Interview

2.5.1 The Onset of the Attorney-Client Relationship

The first professional responsibility issue facing a lawyer at the initial interview is when the formal relationship begins. Most lawyers would say that the formal relationship does not begin until there has been a mutual agreement between the lawyer and the client about the representation. In reality, the reported cases and the Restatement (Third) Of the Law Governing Lawyers would suggest that this view is only partially correct. The Restatement (Third) Of the Law Governing Lawyers Section 26(1), pfd no. 1 (1996) provides:

A relationship of client and lawyer arises when:

(1) a person manifests to a lawyer the person's intent that the lawyer provide legal services for the person; and <u>either</u>

(a) the lawyer manifests to the person consent to do so; or

> (b) the lawyer fails to manifest lack of
> consent to do so, and the lawyer knows or
> reasonably should know that the person
> reasonably relies on the lawyer to provide
> the services . . . (emphasis added)

Further, there exists case law that allows a finding of an attorney-client relationship sufficient to form the basis for a lawsuit based on professional negligence when a client consults a lawyer about representation and is told by the lawyer that he does not believe her potential case has merit but will check it with his partner. Under these circumstances, even though there was no further communication and no fee was charged, there was an attorney-client relationship formed. When it turned out the lawyer's opinion was wrong and no advice was given about the statute of limitations, the lawyer and his law firm were liable for what the client could have received if her lawsuit had been timely filed.[7]

These sources and other cases would seem to suggest that the test as to whether an attorney-client relationship has been formed is really based on the reasonable expectations of the client. Of course, lawyers are not required to take every case. Like other professionals, they can choose (at their own economic peril) the sorts of representations that they will undertake. The clear implication of MRPC Rule 1.16, Declining or Terminating Representation, is, however, that, as with terminating employment, a lawyer should decline only when it can be "accomplished without material adverse effect on the interests of the client." MRPC Rule 1.16(b).

In addition, lawyers have a special duty to the justice system to perform public service, and MRPC Rule 6.1, Voluntary Pro Bono Public Service, suggests that every lawyer should aspire to performing at least fifty hours of public service each year. One way that aspiration can be met is through accepting court-appointed representation. MRPC 6.2, Accepting Appointments, requires that lawyers not seek to avoid such appointment except for "good cause." Examples of "good cause" in the rule are representations that would require violation of other rules of the MRPC, representations that would cause unreasonable financial hardship, and representation of clients or causes so repugnant to the lawyer as to interfere with the ability to render competent representation.

Should a lawyer decide to decline employment by a potential client, it should be done clearly and in writing. In addition, the case law suggests at a minimum, even when declining employment the lawyer should inform the declined client that there may very well be other lawyers who may accept the employment, and specifically inform the potential client as to any applicable statute of limitations that might bar the potential lawsuit. This is especially true in circumstances where the reason for declining employment is lack of expertise in the matter presented by the potential client. In those cases, if lawyers with the required expertise are known, it is certainly appropriate to suggest their names and offer to make appropriate referrals.

2.5.2 Confidentiality of Communications and Other Information

Whether employment is accepted or declined, the duty to keep confidential the communications of potential clients attaches from the first time a person consults a lawyer for the purpose of obtaining legal representation. The duty of confidentiality springs from two sources, one with broader application than the other.

Although attorney-client privilege is a matter of statute, the Restatement (Third) Of the Law Governing Lawyers section 118, pfd no. 1 (1996) provides a generally accepted statement of the rule:

Except as otherwise provided in this Restatement, the attorney-client privilege may be invoked as provided in section 135 with respect to:

> (1) a communication

> (2) made between privileged persons

> (3) in confidence

> (4) for the purpose of obtaining or
> providing legal assistance for the client.

Whether or not employment by the potential client is accepted, statements made by that potential client in the initial interview fall clearly within the privilege. As a result, the lawyer cannot be compelled to reveal statements made by the client during the interview unless they fall within one of the exceptions to the rule of privilege, which typically include:

(1) If the client engages the lawyer for advice in the further-ance of a crime or fraud;

(2) If the client is deceased and there is a claim by parties through the deceased client;

(3) If the communication is relevant to a claimed breach of duty by either the lawyer or the client;

(4) If the communication is regarding an attested-to docu-ment where the lawyer is an attesting witness; and

(5) If the communication is relevant to a matter between two clients who jointly consulted the lawyer.

The MRPC Rule 1.6, Confidentiality of Information, pro-vides broader protection than the law of privilege. Rule 1.6 pre-cludes disclosure of not only communications, but any information, no matter what the source, regarding the repre-sentation unless the client consents to the disclosure after con-sultation. The only confidential information that can be disclosed is that necessary to prevent a criminal act likely to re-sult in at least substantial bodily harm or information neces-sary to establish a claim or defense on the part of the lawyer in a dispute with the client. For the purpose of Rule 1.6, potential but declined clients have the same protection as clients for whom representation is undertaken. Obviously, Rule 1.6 pro-tects matters not covered by privilege because its protection is not limited to communications, and further, it protects all com-munications except those narrowly proscribed in the rule.

Unlike privileged communications, however, confidential communications can be disclosed if they are the subject of a court order. Likewise, the MRPC provides in Rule 3.3, Candor Toward the Tribunal, for disclosure to the tribunal, notwith-standing Rule 1.6, of

(1) Facts necessary to avoid assisting a criminal or fraudu-lent act by the client;

(2) Legal authority that is contrary to the client's position (if not cited by the opponent);

(3) Facts necessary as a remedial measure for materially false information, including the fact or intention of the client to commit perjury.

2.5.3 Conflicts of Interest

In every representation there exists the potential for conflicts of interest that may preclude the representation. The issue of conflicts of interests is addressed in MRPC Rule 1.7, Conflict of Interest: General Rule; Rule 1.8, Conflict of Interest: Prohibited Transactions; Rule 1.9, Conflict of Interest: Former Client, and Rule 1.10, Imputed Disqualification: General Rule. Conflicts of interest take three basic forms:

1. Conflicts between the client's interest and the lawyer's personal interest;

2. Conflicts between two or more current clients; and

3. Conflicts between a current client and a former client.

The rules of conflicts of interest are based on two principles, loyalty and preservation of confidences. A client has the right to the undivided loyalty of his lawyer during the course of the representation. If a lawyer's personal interest or the interest of another client is in conflict with the interests of a current client, this loyalty principle will preclude representation. An example of a conflict of interest between a lawyer and a client in the *Lawrence* case would be if the potential lawyer for Lawrence was a friend of the complaining witness, Ms. Fitzgerald. An example of a conflict between two current clients in *Brown v. Byrd* would be if there was a passenger in Brown's car who also wanted to sue Byrd and wanted to be represented by Brown's lawyer. Depending on the state's guest statute, the passenger might have a potential lawsuit against both Byrd and Brown that could not be adequately prosecuted against Brown by Brown's lawyer. The client or clients may, however, waive the conflict of interest after full consultation. In criminal cases, codefendants usually have a conflict of interest as one codefendant is always a potential witness against the other codefendant.

Conflicts of interest between a current and former client rest on the principle of preservation of confidences. A former client cannot expect undivided loyalty from a lawyer once the representation has ended, but does have the right to expect that his or her confidential information will remain confidential. For that reason, if the former representation of a client is substantially related to the current representation, such that the confidences of the former client might be used to the detriment of that client, the representation of the current client will be precluded. An example of such a conflict of interest in the *Quinlan v. Kane Electronics* case would be if the potential lawyer for Quinlan had previously represented Kane Electronics in another matter and had learned facts that would be useful to Quinlan in the current matter against the company. Again, once the conflict is recognized, it can be waived by the former client after full consultation.

In modern practice, especially in the commercial area, conflicts of interest are inevitable. They are made more so by the fluidity of lawyers in changing law firms. For that reason, there are numbers of commercially available computer software programs that can track both the current and former clients of a firm for conflicts of interest. These "conflicts checks" can actually be performed based on pre-interview information provided by the client, but should be updated when the potential adversaries of the client are better known after the completion of the initial interview.

If a conflict of interest is discovered and the client or clients choose to waive the same, such waiver should be done in writing and reflect the nature of the consultation that led to the waiver. These waivers can be in a separate writing or made part of the fee agreement.

2.5.4 Conflicts with Other Clients and Former Clients

It is routine today for most large firms to do an immediate conflicts check to see whether any of their present or former clients have interests adverse to the prospective clients' interest. The motion to remove counsel for conflicts has been widely successful and brings with it costly incentive to do the conflicts check early. Despite attempts to create Chinese Walls and scrivener exceptions to the conflict rules, courts are still zealous in their protection of the confidentiality of other clients' communications. Loyalty to client still plays an important role in ethics enforcement.

Catching the conflict early is crucial to avoiding unethical behavior. If the lawyer has not yet put in the hours of research and preparation, he is not tempted as much to assume that the other client won't mind, and press on with the suit. Once the lawyer is also invested in the case, it becomes much harder to give it up.

Once the conflict is discovered, the lawyer always has the option of getting a waiver regarding the conflict. The waiver provisions of the Model Rules require that both clients receive full disclosure concerning the potential or existing conflicts before their consent to representation is binding. There are difficulties here about exactly what to disclose and whether waiver can ever be effective where the information concerning the conflicting interests is evolving. Yet again, the earlier the potential conflict is discovered, the more involvement the clients can have, and the less work biases the lawyers counseling of the clients and biases the information given to the clients in advance of their waiver. More will be said on this issue in chapter 6.

2.5.5 The Scope of Representation

When a lawyer undertakes the representation of a client, MRPC Rule 1.2, Scope of Representation, sets in Rule 1.2(a) the guiding principle of the relationship by providing that the lawyer is duty bound to "abide by a client's decisions concerning the objectives of the representation." This rule makes clear that it is the client's, not the lawyer's, case.

There are times, however, when a lawyer is willing to undertake the representation of a client only if the scope of that representation is limited. For example, a potential client who has been injured in the workplace may need representation in obtaining and maintaining workers' compensation benefits, and at the same time have a potential lawsuit for products liability if the injury was due to a defective product. In such a circumstance, one lawyer may not have the expertise to handle both matters. MRPC Rule 1.2(c) makes specific provision for limiting the scope of the representation so long as there is consultation with the client and client consent. Should a lawyer seek to limit the scope of the employment relationship, the limitation, the nature of the consultation had with the client regarding that limitation, and the client's consent should all be in writing and attested to by both the client and the lawyer. In that way, the agreement of the lawyer and client will be clear and the basis for the limitation of representation memorialized.

2.5.6 Fee Agreements

Once the lawyer and client agree to the representation, the financial aspects of the relationship must be settled. MRPC Rule 1.5, Fees, sets the professional responsibility parameters for fee agreements. The rule provides initially that the lawyer's fees have to be reasonable, but leaves to the lawyer and client the ability to negotiate any reasonable fee. Those factors taken into consideration on the reasonableness issue are virtually the same as would be considered in purchasing the services of any professional. They include whether the representation will require so much time as to preclude other employment, the customary fee charged for such services, time involved, results obtained, time exigencies in completing the work, whether there is a professional employment history between the lawyer and client, and the skill and talent of the lawyer. (See Rule 1.5(a) (1)–(8).)

Fee Factors

- ◆ **Preclusion of other employment**
- ◆ **Customary fee charged**
- ◆ **Time involved**
- ◆ **Results obtained**
- ◆ **Time exigencies**
- ◆ **Employment history with client**
- ◆ **Skill and talent of lawyer**

There are special requirements in Rule 1.5(c) and (d) for contingent fee agreements. First, contingent fee agreements are prohibited for policy reasons in both domestic relations and criminal cases. In those circumstances, the public policy requires the ability to compromise, which might be adversely altered by a contingent fee agreement. Further, the agreement must be in writing and clearly set out the particulars of what the contingent fee is based on, the amount of the fee in percentage terms, and what representation the fee covers. For example, it is not unusual that the contingent fee percentage be different for settlement as opposed to trial resolution. The rule also provides for a written statement of the outcome of any contingent fee matter showing the disbursal of funds.

Finally, Rule 1.5(e) deals with referral fees and generally provides that unless the referring lawyer is paid only in proportion to services performed, or the referring lawyer assumes joint responsibility for the matter, such fees are illegitimate. Some jurisdictions have departed from this rule and allow referral fees so long as the total fee is reasonable and the client consents to the distribution of the fee. (See PARPC Rule 1.5(e)). Pennsylvania and other jurisdictions allowing referral fees reason first that even when proscribed, such fees are commonly paid; and second, that the allowing of referral fees

encourages that cases be handled by those lawyers best qualified to do so.)

Although not required, we suggest that all fee agreements
and the basis for those agreements be put in writing. This gives
the clients clear evidence of their agreement, and fee disputes
can be more easily resolved.

2.5.7 Diligence and Communication

The most frequent complaints against lawyers are twofold:

(1) That lawyers do not handle their client's matters in a
timely way; and

(2) That lawyers do not regularly communicate with their
clients, even to the point of not returning phone calls.

These two frequent complaints are oftentimes related. While it
is true that some lawyers do not handle their client's matters in
a timely way, it is also true that other factors like court
backlogs, reasonable continuances, illness of witnesses, etc., also
serve to drag out the process of dispute resolution. When that
happens there is really nothing to report, so lawyers may go
months without communicating with their clients.

MRPC Rule 1.3, Diligence, relates to the first complaint
and MRPC Rule 1.4, Communication, to the second. The legitimate complaints of clients can be avoided or at least lessened if
at the time of the initial interview two things happen. First, the
lawyer should give the client a reasonable timetable as to the
progress of the client's matter, and explain why and how delays
might occur. Second, as we mentioned before, the lawyer can
set up a regular system of communication with the client, either by phone or in writing, whereby the client is informed of
the case progress. These two simple steps, with appropriate
follow-through by the lawyer or the lawyer's staff, can prevent
the problems from occurring or at least give the client notice
that they might occur.

2.5.8 Professionalism Concerns: What If the Client Lies?

One of the most frustrating feelings a lawyer can have that
can sour the relationship with a client is to feel lied to, so it is
important to understand the distinctions between lying and
being mistaken or confused, and understand the pressures on
the client to guess or hope something happened that may not
have happened.

The client may be unsure of the facts or be in a panic about what to do, and intentionally or unintentionally misrepresent facts. The undiscovered bad facts most often don't go away and the conflict between lawyer and client lies dormant until it is too late. Where the client flat-out lies, spotting the lie early is crucial to setting the correct tone and rules for the relation.

First of all, when a client lies he does not understand that the lawyer's professional role requires that he put the client's needs and confidences ahead of society's and his own. Where a client lies to his lawyer, the client doesn't understand that the lawyer is the client's partner in advocacy. The client understands that each choice he makes in litigation is something that involves risks and consequences that he must bear. The lawyer has better information about the risks and consequences of these choices, and before the client chooses to lie, the client should enlist the lawyer's analysis of the risks.

Of course, this is naive where the client has evaluated the risks in the situation and believes that it is better to have a lawyer who believes in him. The client may also believe, rightly, that there are limits to the lawyer's advocacy. As we have seen earlier, the lawyer must not assist a client in actions that merely harass, annoy, or injure another, or where fraud is perpetrated on another. The lawyer would be forced to withdraw in these situations. Yet, the client may not be consciously evil, but may want to win so badly that he commits himself to positions and facts that cause much more harm than good. If the client sees the lawyer as counselor rather than as judge, the client will have less incentive to commit himself to unsupportable positions without thinking.

The lawyer must be aware of the ways that a client might commit himself to false positions and the reasons why this occurs. Sensitivity to the client's position and empathy for the client are key to recognizing why a client might be less than forthcoming. As we will discuss regarding all witnesses, there are a number of inhibitors to good communication. They are ego threat, case threat, concern over social norms, bias, competing time demands, environment, perceived irrelevance and greater need, trauma, and memory failure. Each of these psychosocial influences can skew the client's delivery of information to the lawyer.

In addition to being aware of the psychosocial influences, the lawyer must be aware of how he may be encouraging the client to take unsupportable positions. For example, if Byrd admits to his lawyer that he had alcohol at lunch and the lawyer indicates through leading questions that the fact needs to go away—"Of course, you only had one, right? . . . because if you had two martinis, we are in big trouble"—then the lawyer is asking the client to lie. Or the client may run to the excuse that he doesn't remember. And these pressures can be inadvertently applied by the lawyer whether or not the lawyer explains that it is the opponent's burden to prove certain facts. And so, the client may come to believe he can say anything as long as the state or opponent cannot prove otherwise.

When the client suddenly doesn't remember, lawyers must ask how reliable this information is, especially when the lawyer has discussed the issue, given a negative consequence, and then asked a leading question in hopes that the client will be led away from bad information. The chances are very slim that a client will stand up and admit that there was some illegal activity. The lawyer's questioning technique sends a message that the client would be better off not admitting the bad facts.

Further open-ended questions that hold back judgment or evaluation of the client are more likely to produce reliable information. For instance, the lawyer should have asked, "How many drinks did you have? What effects did the alcohol have on you? What did you say to the opposing party, or police officer, about it?" Nonverbal delivery is also crucial. The tone must be curious and neutral; otherwise the evaluative aspect of the lawyer's role will inhibit the accuracy of the information. Again, the moral judgment is obvious, and the message that the client better not disagree with the lawyer's version of the facts restricts the flow of information.

Where the lawyer believes the client is lying, the relationship between the lawyer and the client is fundamentally affected. The lawyer is likely to feel uncomfortable with the client and assume that the client wants him to take a cover-up position regarding the "bad facts." But whether the client wants the lawyer to do this has never been discussed, and the client has not been counseled about the risks of taking differing positions. Instead, an adversarial tone starts to affect the relationship that leads both client and lawyer to distrust each other. The client feels that the lawyer doesn't really want to know what happened, and the lawyer feels that the client wants to win at all costs. Neither perception may be accurate.

Competent counseling will prevent the adversarial distrustful relationship from developing, yet the relationship is often formed and perverted before the lawyer explicitly engages in counseling. Open-ended fact-gathering and nonjudgmental information-gathering skills are essential before a counseling session can be effectively structured. A clear understanding of the lawyer's client-centered role, nonjudgmental information gathering, open-ended questions, and three-stage interviewing will greatly aid the lawyer's development of the proper relationship and help avoid the situation in which the lawyer's attitude toward the client affects the advice he gives and the willingness to work hard for the client that can occur in the early stages of the relationship.

Ways to keep misinformation from going too far:

- Know your case cold.
- Don't lead.
- Save judgment until you know all the facts.
- Consider why the client might unconsciously mislead you.
  - Ego threat. (Does the client need your approval?)
  - Case threat and bias. (Does the client believe the case rises or falls on his memory of crucial facts, or is the case of overwhelming importance to the very identity of the client and the existence of his important relationships?)
  - Social status concerns. (Would the client be embarrassed to admit to you the truth?)
  - Time constraints, perceived irrelevance, and greater need. (Is the client concerned about your fee? or believes that he isn't understood? or that you are focusing on irrelevant details? Is the client agreeing just to get you to move on to the more important stuff?)
- Stay curious and flexible.
- Save the counseling session until after you have had a chance to reflect and research both facts and law. (Resist the temptation to reassure the client too early.)

Ways to spot lies:

- Know your case cold.
- Look for changes in pace, pitch, tone, and volume of client delivery.
- Look for changes in physical positioning:
  - Changes in eye contact
  - Sitting back suddenly, sitting forward suddenly, crossing arms, rocking in the chair, wringing hands, rubbing feet together, pulling up socks, scratching ankles
- Consider the appropriateness of the information given in response to your questions.
  - Does the amount of detail in the answers change?
  - Does the client suddenly answer your questions with questions or suggestions of his own like, why is that important? or why do we need to talk about that? or can we talk first more about x or y?

Perhaps there is another reason to take time at the start of the relationship to listen not only to what the client says but to why he says it. As Will Rogers liked to say, "I never met a man that after I got to know him I didn't like." What is often taken as a value conflict is more often a misunderstanding between the attorney and client about the client's true feelings and values. For instance, are the client's anger and intransigence due to his values and beliefs, or are they evidence of the client's fear and confusion about the future? Are they instead a "fight" position that is brought about without reflection from the fact that the client has been attacked?

The legal interviewer must find out what is behind the client's positions. To do this the lawyer needs to be a good and active listener, and the lawyer needs to be interested in the client. The lawyer needs to use all the nonverbal probes at his disposal to prompt full and complete responses to his questions. The lawyer needs to ask open-ended questions that are clear and understandable. To do this takes some skill, and the three-stage model of interviewing is a helpful place to start to be open and ethical in interviewing.

ENDNOTES

1.   Most of what follows concerning goals and needs of lawyers and clients is borrowed loosely and adapted from David A. Binder, Paul Bergman, and Susan C. Price, *Lawyers as Counselors, A Client Centered Approach* (St. Paul: West Publishing Company, 1991): 32–45. We have added our own definitions from our experience.

2.   *Id.*

3.   *Id.*

4.   More will be said about these and related nonverbal probes in the chapter on interviewing.

5.   See *supra* note 1, at 171–179.

6.   See Tom Rusk's *Seven Steps to Understanding*.

7.   *Togstadt v. Vesely, Otto, Miller & Keefe*, 291 N.W. 2d 686 (Minn. 1980).

Chapter 3

Developing Case Theory for Fact Investigation

3.1 Introduction

The process of informal fact investigation has gained increased importance at the millennium. As local rules of civil procedure are limiting the number of interrogatories, the number of depositions and the length of those depositions, it becomes increasingly important that informal fact investigation lay the groundwork for the effective use of the formal discovery processes.

A limited formal discovery process rings the death knell of scorched-earth litigation tactics where interrogatories number in the thousands and depositions begin with a question that seeks the deponent's moment of conception and traces his life completely to how he would like to be remembered after his demise. Out of all of this, there existed the information necessary to construct and execute an effective theory of the case, albeit not in the most efficient or accessible form. In modern litigation processes we cannot afford the luxury or largess of this sort of discovery. Not only are courts limiting such inquiry, clients are demanding greater efficiencies in the manner in which their causes are handled.

In order to best serve civil litigation clients in cases where discovery is limited, or in criminal cases, and/or cases where the lawyer wants to take a more proactive role, it is necessary to identify potential case theories before formal discovery processes begin and thereby create guideposts for the effective use of the limited discovery available. Although a necessity in cases with artificially limited formal discovery, the methods that follow are equally useful and recommended in all litigation as they make lawyers more efficient and effective in handling client matters.

What follows is a description of a number of methods that can be used individually or, in most cases, in tandem, whereby potential case theories can be identified and tested before going through the formal discovery process. For plaintiffs this can be accomplished prepleading. For defendants, it should certainly precede the answering and filing of interrogatories and the taking and defending of depositions. The methods described help to narrow issues and focus litigation on the issues that matter. They represent, in method form, a basis for much of what trial lawyers have learned to be modern effective persuasion.

3.2 Definitions

The process begins with identifying potential theories of the case. Case theory operates at three levels: legal, factual, and persuasive.

3.2.1 Legal Theory

Legal theory defines the case in terms that describe why, as a matter of law, your client should prevail. Put another way, once the jury renders a verdict in favor of your client, how is it that the law will allow the verdict to stand in the face of appeal? Because legal theory is for judicial consumption, it is possible to run two or more legal theories of the case at the same time, and they may be inconsistent. For that reason a plaintiff may base a lawsuit concerning the sale of land on the law of torts, contract, and/or property. All that must occur at trial is proving sufficient facts to sustain a favorable verdict.

At the fact investigation stage of litigation, legal theories should be kept open and fluid. All that is necessary are sufficient provable facts to support *any* legal theory on appeal. If they exist, then the theory is viable. Formal discovery need only confirm that the facts necessary for each legal theory exist at the level necessary to support a verdict. So, in *Brown v. Byrd*, all that the plaintiff need prove to uphold a guilty verdict is evidence, in the light most favorable to the plaintiff, that supports duty, breach of duty, and proximate cause and damages

3.2.2 Factual Theory

Factual theory defines what the facts of the case really are. The factual theory answers the question, "What really happened in the case and why?" There can be several factual theories that evolve out of the same fact pattern presented prediscovery. It is important at the informal fact investigation phase to remain open to the possibility that facts as related by the client later turn out to be different than initially recalled and/or related. As evidence is gathered by way of documents, physical evidence, and testimony, the view of what is provable and not and what really happened and why changes. It is important to note that in developing effective factual theory it is not only the facts themselves that are important, but the perception of facts, that will drive the theory. Often the reality of facts and the common perception of them will be at odds, and it is for the lawyer to bring reality and perception of reality in line for effective factual persuasion. It is usually unwise to decide finally (to the exclusion of all others) on a factual theory of the case until all the evidence is gathered through pretrial litigation. To narrow the factual theory invites a situation where the theory fails because key facts do not fall into place and one is left with dispositive motions and trial with no viable factual theory. It is important, then, to attempt to develop several factual theories for the case so that if one, perhaps the initial and apparently most promising theory, fails in the gathering of evidence, there exists an alternative.

As facts are developed the potential factual theories should be tested. Do the facts as currently developed still meet the working hypotheses of what really happened and why? If not, then another factual theory must be sought. If factual theory is thought of as describing what is true, factual inquiry can follow along the lines of, "what else must be true?" If those facts do not develop, then the theory is faulty. For example, one way to explain away a witness's statement about an important fact in a case is to assume that the witness is lying. That same witness can be described as mistaken. The two potential theories of why the witness got the fact wrong can be tested by looking at what the witness has to say about the totality of the events, not just the important fact. A liar will oftentimes lie about a number of things and *consistently* for one party. A mistaken witness will usually only be mistaken occasionally and then is likely to have something good and bad to say for both parties.

By the time of trial, of course, it is usually the case that one factual theory will be identified and brought to the jury for its consideration. While it is possible to have alternative factual theories of the case, so long as they are factually consistent, normally one strong theory is better than two alternatives. It is the usual case that lawyers who attempt to ride two theory horses at the same time sustain substantial injury to their clients' causes. Alternative theories communicate lack of certainty in the facts of the case. If faced with one party that says that the facts happened in one way, and another party that says that the facts happened in one of several ways, it is easier to side with the party that is certain about what happened and why. The common sense of this proposition is illuminated by the classic argument made by plaintiff's lawyers when faced with a defendant that claims multiple, and factually inconsistent, theories of the case. In such a circumstance the plaintiff's lawyer tells the story of the cabbage and the goat.

> Members of the jury, the defendant here has given you all sorts of reasons why he thinks that he should win, while we've only given you one reason why the plaintiff is entitled to prevail in this case. A story about another case in another court might help you to decide which theory should persuade you. A while ago there was a lawsuit where one neighbor claimed that his neighbor's goat had come onto his property and eaten the cabbage that was growing in his garden. Rather than paying for the cabbage the neighbor had these excuses, much like the many excuses you've heard from the defendant here today. What he said was this. First, my client doesn't have a goat. But if he does, that goat never left his yard. But if that goat left his yard, he never went into the plaintiff's yard. But if that goat went into the neighbor's yard, he never went into that garden. But if that goat went into the neighbor's yard and into that garden he never ate any cabbage. But if that goat did go into that yard and into that garden and ate that cabbage, then he got sick and the plaintiff owes my client some money. Well, the jury in that case found against the neighbor with the goat, and you should find against the defendant today. He's got so many excuses, he must have done something wrong.

3.2.3 Persuasive Theory

Persuasive theory is defined as why, in equity, your client should prevail. Persuasive theory, sometimes described as a theme for the case, explains why it is that the jury should feel right about their decision in the case. Persuasive theory is grounded in the common human experience and is usually presented in common-sense terms that come from some authoritative source. Effective persuasive theory can come from the Bible (either Testament) in describing one of the parties as the "prodigal son," or from great literature, where a complaining witness is described as "protesting too much," or from fables, where the defendant is "the little boy who cried wolf," or from your parents, where a witness's credibility is denounced because the witness wouldn't "look the jury in the eye" when testifying.

Persuasive theory will usually strike at the core psychological values that most jurors share which motivates much of decision making. As such, an effective persuasive theory will resonate in fairness, redressing a wrong, doing the right thing, and in egregious circumstances, providing for a need to punish. To the extent that persuasive theory or themes can be identified at the fact investigation stage, they should be kept in mind in attempting to develop the evidence in formal discovery. As facts are developed, they should be looked at through a prism to determine the viability of the potential persuasive theory. It is not unusual for lawyers to change a persuasive theory several times before settling on a final persuasive theory for dispute resolution at trial or otherwise.

3.3 Theory Identification Process

With that introduction we now turn to the process of identifying case theory. It is important to note that case theory identification, testing, and selection is an ongoing process and that the techniques described below can and should be replicated as the story of the case unfolds. In that way, theory will be molded to the facts as developed and will continue to inform and provide guideposts for factual investigation as it proceeds through the litigation.

3.3.1 Legal Theory

The first level of theory we will discuss is legal theory. The potential legal theories of the case evolve as do factual theories. But after the initial client interview, through classic legal research techniques, potential legal theories of the case will suggest themselves based on the facts as communicated by the client. Other sources for potential legal theory are partners in the firm or other associates, "how to" reference books organized by substantive law categories, or perhaps a former professor or law school classmate known to have knowledge of the area of the law involved. An obvious source for potential legal theory for defendants is the plaintiff's complaint. That pleading will at least set out the plaintiff's view of the legal setting in which the case will be decided. Defendants must certainly answer the plaintiff's claims on the law, but of course are free to assert their own legal positions by way of affirmative defenses, cross-claims, and counterclaims.

From the above basic sources, at least a tentative legal theory can be identified. For many lawyers, it is critical that the legal theory of the case be identified before discovery occurs. For these lawyers, the legal theory of the case will drive all of the discovery and litigation of the case, and as such must be identified first. This view of a litigation is one in which the endgame is usually anticipated as a case-dispositive motion wherein the judge will decide the case as a matter of law, and failing that, the case will be negotiated to settlement.

In this setting, both formal and informal fact investigation is conducted against the backdrop of a clear, oftentimes written legal position on the case. It is especially appropriate in those cases that are based on previous litigation where a firm may have taken a successful legal position in an earlier matter based on essentially the same facts. For example, if a firm has successfully defended a products liability action brought by one plaintiff on the basis of a legal defense of product misuse, it is appropriate to let that legal defense guide the fact investigation in another lawsuit based on the same or similar accusations.

For other lawyers, the legal theory of the case is less important at the earliest stages of a litigation. For these lawyers the factual development of the case is more important as the facts will ultimately determine the appropriate law to be applied to the matter. As the facts are refined and clarified, so too are legal theories of the case. Lawyers with this point of view normally see the end result of litigation to be trial, or at least some fact-based form of alternative dispute resolution like arbitration and mediation.

The authors of this book believe that while legal research, both formal and informal as described above, is an important beginning point for a litigation, the facts and not the law should drive the determination of the matter. Once tentative legal theories are identified, the facts should be developed unfettered by any sort artificial restraint imposed by strict compliance with a particular legal theory. This avoids attempts to force "square peg" facts into a "round hole" theory. In addition, to limit factual development by whether it fits a particular legal theory misses the point of having each legal matter decided on its own *factual* as well as legal merits.

That being said, in some cases, some legal decisions *must* be made before proceeding to formal discovery. For example, if defending a corporation, does in-house counsel want to first conduct an internal investigation? Will the results of such an investigation be discoverable by the plaintiff or protected as privileged or within the scope of protected work product? Does the corporation want counsel to promise confidentiality or job security before conducting interviews of key employees? Is there is a possibility that certain employees will have personal liability within the context of the lawsuit that might cause conflicts of interests problems? If so, is the corporation willing to waive the potential conflict and allow counsel to represent the employee individually together with the corporation? In this and many other circumstances, the law will necessarily limit, or at least style, both informal and formal fact investigation, and as a result at least some legal issues must be determined before the fact investigation process continues.

At the end of the day, there must be well-developed factual theories of the case. In the optimal case the legal, factual, and persuasive theory of the case will be unitary. In a personal injury case arising out of a car accident a plaintiff can seek recovery for injuries because the defendant failed to stop, look, and listen before entering onto a highway from a parking lot. The failure to stop, look, and listen describes fault (legal theory), what really happened and why (factual theory), and a commonly known truism learned from our parents on being careful (persuasive theory).

As noted above, legal theories may be inconsistent, so long as that inconsistency does not get presented to a jury. All that is necessary for a successful legal theory is that at the conclusion of a trial resulting in a favorable verdict for your client there exists a legal basis for upholding the verdict. For that reason, in some cases the legal theory of the case will hardly be mentioned in the lawsuit. For example, in many contract cases based in law on offer and acceptance, jury argument and decision making are made on the grounds of which party is at fault in the failure of the contract, or which party, in fairness, should be held responsible in the situation. The likelihood that the jury can comprehend the law of offer and acceptance and apply it after a hurried thirty-minute instruction from a judge, delivered in language previously unheard by the jury, is slim. In those circumstances, the jury does what it does best—the "right thing"—usually based on findings in terms of "fault" and most importantly, "fairness."

3.3.2 Factual Theory

Armed with at least tentative legal theories of the case, factual investigation can be enhanced by the development of potential factual theories of the case. As noted above, factual theory answers the questions of what really happened and why it matters. Identifying potential factual theories after the initial client interview and review of the pleadings has the same potential benefits and vices. If bound by a predetermined factual theory, both formal and informal discovery will consist of nothing more than looking for theory verification. If at the end of litigation the factual theory fails, then so does the client's claim or defense. Just as important, a factual theory that initially appeared to be of lesser promise might gain life when informed by new facts.

At the same time, the failure to identify potential factual theories before entering into the fact investigation of the case wastes time and makes the process nothing more than a fishing expedition without a guide. Potential factual case theory has the benefit of providing organization for factual investigation and the ability to test potential theories against the facts available to prove them. The factual theories of both your client and your opponent should be identified preliminarily to make the most efficient use of the potentially limited formal discovery process. Even if discovery is not artificially limited (number of interrogatories, number and time of depositions, time, etc.), the identification of potential factual theories of the case will make investigation of the case easier and more efficient.

There exist a number of devices for identifying potential factual theories of the case, none of which are exclusive of the other. Used in tandem, these devices make for identification of coherent factual theories that can be tested in the litigation process.

3.3.2.1 Time Lines

Early in a lawsuit, perhaps as early as the initial interview with the client, the creation of a time line can be a great assistance in understanding the facts of the case. During the client interview the time line can assist in making sure the chronology of events is understood and, further, in asking questions about what occurred during any particular time frame as it related to the lawsuit.

For example, in our case of *Quinlan v. Kane Electronics* the time line might look like this.

Time Line

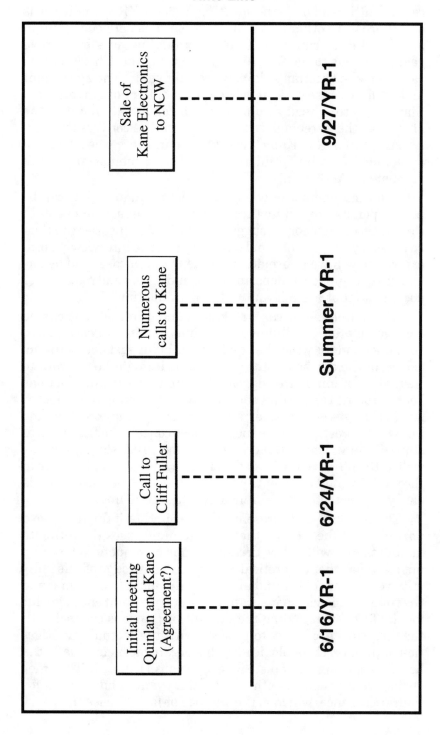

Look at the time line and start asking questions. Is the first real event in the case the meeting of 6/16/-YR-1? As it turns out, there were other relevant conversations between Quinlan and Kane concerning the sale of Kane's business in the five years previous to the first item on the time line. These conversations make Quinlan's claim more believable. The agreement makes more sense when it is based on a history of conversation that comes to a head as opposed to a conversation out of the blue. Was the agreement based solely on the conversation between Quinlan and Kane? As it turns out, there was a letter of agreement sent by Quinlan to Kane that memorialized the agreement. And so on.

The time line not only suggests factual inquiry, but can be used to persuasively state the case for and against your client. In so doing, factual theory is suggested. Suggested theories can then be tested by further informal discovery such as interviewing others who may have information (in the *Quinlan* case) and by formal discovery (such as deposing Kane and others and requests for documents that are relevant to filling in the time line).

A time line in our car wreck case and criminal case can be equally helpful. In filling out the time line in *Brown v. Byrd*, such questions as what the parties were doing just before the accident, or the day before the accident, as it might be relevant to their state of mind, are suggested. Were there any distractions because of the time of day, such as children leaving the school or sun in the eyes of the driver, etc.? In *State v. Lawrence,* the time line will suggest questions such as those concerning the physical state of the victim of the crime (was she tired, sleepy, etc?) as well as the physical layout of the crime scene as it might relate to the victim's ability to identify her assailant. All of this inquiry is easily suggested by the chronology of the time line.

The time line does present a danger in that it might cause a narrowing of the focus of the case. In many cases the ultimate factual theory will not be driven by time or sequence of events, but by some other theoretical construct. Knowledge of this infirmity reduces its effect and allows for the main benefit in using the time line. Because it stimulates a starting and ending point for the facts surrounding the lawsuit, it provides counsel with the structure necessary to proceed with the factual investigation of the case chronologically. This organization is usually the best for ensuring a complete investigation of a matter. The order of the events suggests other potential events and reasons for their occurrence, which is the essence of factual case theory.

Moving forward on the time line, a number of questions are immediately raised. While events are portrayed on the time line, the need for inquiry regarding the motivations of the actors will be suggested by those facts, listed in that order. When the case involves a business transaction or the activity of an organization, the time line will suggest the need for inquiry as to organization policies and procedures that govern that activity. The time line will likewise suggest inquiry into records that may make the events on the time line favorable to your client and more believable.

Finally, the time line will suggest things that were not done that could have been done. In the *Quinlan* case, for example, why didn't she send further correspondence or contact any of the parties personally? Sometimes it is the case that the failure to act is not only the predicate to liability in a tort case, but also an indicator of the true state of affairs in any case. For example, the failure of Fitzgerald in the *Lawrence* case to give anything more than a very general description speaks loudly to the factual theory that for whatever reason (lighting, fear, focus, etc.) she was unable to get a good look at her assailant.

3.3.2.2 Relationship Charts

Another classic method for determining appropriate factual theory is through the study of the relationships involved in any case. An easy method for understanding those relationships is through the creation of a relationship chart. The chart, as a visual presentation of the interactions and possible interactions between the parties and other important actors and institutions in a case, will often help to explain what really happened and why. The chart can be used by itself to help understand a case or in conjunction with other devices such as a time line.

The relationship chart is particularly helpful in cases where there are multiple parties with varying motives. If it takes longer than ten minutes to explain who the parties and ancillary important actors are, why they are important, how they impact each other in the context of the case and otherwise, and what they all hope to gain or avoid losing, then the relationship chart is likely to provide insight into the matter. The chart is not only a good beginning point in understanding such a case, but will suggest potential areas of inquiry for the fact investigation process. As the facts of the matter are more fully developed, the relationship chart will be too, as more intricate relationships are identified. And the chart is dynamic in that it will often change not only in content, but in form, as relationships once thought important are discarded, apparent insignificant relationships gain significance, and new relationships are ferreted out.

The creation of the chart begins by identifying all the parties and ancillary actors in the matter. When making this identification, errors should be made in terms of inclusion on the chart as opposed to exclusion. Apparently minor players may prove to be exactly that, or gain importance by helping to explain major events under consideration in the litigation. Lines of relationship between the parties and the other actors should be labeled with significant interactive facts.

Once completed, the chart will usually suggest other relationships and other actors. It will also suggest other interactions that may or may not have occurred. This is important in that the absence of a relationship or interaction can be as critical as their existence. As a result, the chart will suggest a number of explanations of what really happened and why—potential factual theories of the case. In turn, areas of inquiry for the informal and formal discovery process will be suggested in terms of witnesses to be interviewed, potential exhibits to be sought, and testimony to be memorialized.

On the following page is a relationship chart for the case of *Quinlan v. Kane Electronics*. This relationship chart shows the parties and their known interactions, together with other significant or potentially significant relationships in the *Quinlan* case. Also shown in the chart are potential areas of inquiry that will either assist or detract from the viability of Quinlan's claim for a brokerage fee for the sale of Kane Electronics to NCW.

From the chart we know that there was relatively little interaction between Quinlan and Kane and Quinlan and NCW. That in and of itself is significant. Because the interaction seems, at first blush, to be less than what one might intuitively expect in a brokering relationship, it is necessary to consider other relationships. For example, on this chart we would look into Quinlan's common business practice. Did she often work in the way she did here? Is it normal to form a brokerage agreement based on an afternoon's conversation followed by a letter? Does her activity in the sale typically amount to nothing more than suggesting the seller to the buyer? Had she ever provided purchase targets to NCW or any other of her husband's clients?

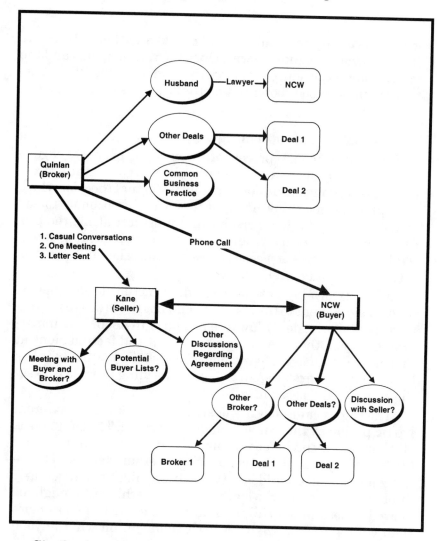

Similar inquiry is suggested regarding Kane and his activity. Had he ever had a meeting with any other brokers or buyers? Had he inquired about or received potential buyers lists himself or through others? Did he have other discussions with Quinlan about the deal? Did he know of NCW as a potential buyer from any other source?

And what about NCW? Had they ever dealt with Quinlan before? Do they normally work with brokers? If so, to what extent? Do they have other brokers who did what Quinlan did here, and as a result have received a brokerage fee? Have they paid such a fee themselves?

As these and other questions are answered and as more information is obtained, the chart will expand. In all likelihood it will be necessary to create several charts and then interrelate them in some explanatory way. Once the relationships and the motives and experience of the parties and other significant actors are understood, potential factual theories of the case can be stated.

3.3.2.3 Brainstorming[1]

Brainstorming is a process of encouraging people to engage in free thinking about a particular topic. The goal of the process is a wide-ranging discussion of potential factual theories which is helpful to focus thinking at any stage of litigation up to and including trial. While a person can brainstorm alone, the process is far better with a group. Brainstorming regarding potential factual theories of a case is best accomplished in a group of between five and fifteen people.

A brainstorming session regarding factual theory begins with an agreement to discuss facts and not the law. This agreement is easily made by lawyers but hard to keep. It is important, however, that the inquiry be factual and factual alone at this juncture. Once an agreement to leave the law out of it has been made, the first step in the brainstorming process is to set the rules for the session.

The rules that follow are designed to encourage maximum participation by those involved in the session. The first rule is (1) there are no bad ideas. From this rule follow three others: (2) do not self-censor; (3) do not critique other ideas; and (4) do not comment on other ideas. These three rules are particularly difficult for lawyers, who loathe to say something that might be viewed as less than brilliant and, at the same time, are more than willing to criticize or at least comment on what anyone else might say.

For brainstorming to be effective, these rules are critical. The worth of the technique depends on a volume of thoughts or partial thoughts that can be put together or taken apart to get at the essence of the case. If a participant is self-censoring, two bad things are happening: the process is deprived of the raw thoughts of that participant, and through the process of self-censoring the participant is attempting to refine his thoughts to the point that he fails to listen to others in the group. One corollary to Rules 1–4 that can ensure wide participation from everyone in the group is to insist that no one speak twice until everyone has spoken once, no one speak three times until everyone has spoken twice, and so on. Particularly where the leader determines that there is a need for a fresh look and diversity is most important, hearing from everyone may be worth the restrictions on who can speak and when.

A participant who criticizes or comments on the thoughts of the other session participants renders a similar result. If participants are keen to criticize and comment, they are focusing on others' thoughts and not providing their own. Additional comment and criticism will likely cause other group members to self-censor for the very same reasons and effects as outlined above.

The next rule is only for lawyers. One form of self-censoring or critiquing or commentary about another's facts concerns the admissibility of the fact in a court of law. The rule is: (5) the rules of evidence are irrelevant. It is much too early in the process to be making a determination of the application of the rules of evidence to the facts. First, evidentiary considerations or discussions interfere with the free flow of the session. Perhaps more to the point of the exercise, the application of the law of evidence is virtually impossible until we know the theory of the case. Case theory, and therefore relevance of evidence, will often impact the application of the other rules of evidence. Thus, to consider potential evidentiary rules outside the context of an articulated case theory is putting the cart before the horse.

The next rule of brainstorming regarding facts is: (6) only facts and not conclusions or inferences may be stated. It is important for this process that facts and not their spin be stated for the obvious reason that facts can be taken in more than one way. By spinning the fact, the other inferences are precluded, thereby limiting the scope and value of the brainstorming.

To obtain maximum value the facts elicited in brainstorming have to be remembered, so the next rule is: (7) all facts must be recorded. This rule really helps to implement the others. The recording of facts, and visibly so to the group, ensures that thoughts aren't lost. The recording also stimulates other facts from other participants. Often the order and flow of facts among the group can develop discernible patterns leading to important insights as to potential factual theory.

The final rule of brainstorming is: (8) the brainstorming session is time limited. By limiting the time for the session, interest is usually maintained (because there is an end in sight), while at the same time creating a sense of urgency that also encourages focus. When time runs out, an extension of time can be negotiated among the group, but it must always be definite in duration.

Rules for Brainstorming

- ◆ **There are no bad ideas**
- ◆ **Do not self-censor**
- ◆ **Do not critique other ideas**
- ◆ **Do not comment on other ideas**
- ◆ **The rules of evidence are irrelevant**
- ◆ **Only facts may be stated**
- ◆ **All facts must be recorded**
- ◆ **The session is time limited**

The rules of brainstorming are enforced by a group facilitator. The facilitator's enforcement authority is absolute. In the ideal situation the facilitator will be someone with experience in the role and no particular stake in the outcome of the session. For example, it would be inappropriate for the facilitator to have tentatively determined a factual theory for the case as it might cause leadership of the group in that direction. The only other personnel necessary for the session are people to record the facts as stated.

The goals and rules of brainstorming are advanced by the physical setup of the room. In the ideal circumstance, participants will sit facing the facilitator and a flip chart (or two) for recording. Sitting face to face encourages both self-censoring and comment or critique. There also has to be room on the walls to tape filled flip chart pages for later reference.

With knowledge of the rules, a proper room setup, and a facilitator and recorder, the session can begin. The first goal of the session is to identify the "good" facts and the "bad" facts of the case from the perspective of your client. The participants are encouraged to just call out the fact by stating good fact (state the fact) or bad fact (state the fact). The recorder should then record the fact under the good or bad fact column. Two flip charts and two recorders are helpful but not necessary.

There will be disagreement as to whether the fact is good or bad, but because no comment or critique is allowed, the way to register disagreement is by listing the fact in both the good and the bad column. It is common that many of the facts in the case will be double listed. In most litigations, most of the facts are not in dispute. What is in issue is the meaning of those facts in the explanation of what really happened and why. Because what happened is often agreed upon by the parties, it is the "why" of factual theory that decides the case. The facilitator will have the final word as to what goes on the flip chart, but should err on the side of inclusion. For example, a conclusion masquerading as a fact can always be deleted from the chart at a later time.

Once the list of good and bad facts has been exhausted, participants are encouraged to list the three best facts of the case and to state why. This exercise begins the first articulation of factual theories. That is, as the participants state the three best facts of the case and explain why, they are necessarily putting the facts of the matter in a theoretical context that will articulate potential case theory. All participants should be encouraged to participate in the process even if they believe a previous listing of the best facts of the case. This is important as their reasons for selecting the best facts may differ in tone or tenor such that a slightly different case theory is articulated.

The process of the best-facts analysis is completed by voting on the best facts of the case as currently known. It will often be the case that in so voting, the participants show their preference for one theory of the case over another. Potential case theories should then be listed, together with the facts that support them.

The same process should then be repeated for the "worst" facts in the case. By listing the three worst facts and hearing the reasons for their being so denominated, the process of identifying the factual theory for the opposing party has begun. The results of this process together with other theory identification processes and the opponent's pleadings in the case will provide good insight as to the opponent's view of what really happened and why; in other words, his factual theory of the case.

A review of the best and worst facts lists may also be helpful in identifying preliminary persuasive case theory or themes for the case. The facts as they amalgamate and are explained may often be described in thematic terms. For example, *Quinlan v. Kane Electronics* may begin to look like

David and Goliath, and if it does, facts to support that theme must be found and preserved.

In some cases the brainstorming session will be the last act in preliminary theory identification. If so, counsel can move on to the process of developing a fact investigation plan that will flesh out the potential legal, factual, and persuasive theories of the case. There exists, however, a powerful tool that can test the result of brainstorming and at the same time suggest other potential theories of the case for exploration— the device of using focus groups.

3.3.2.4 Focus Groups

The use of focus groups to pretry cases has become commonplace. In virtually every case that will support it economically, lawyers are enlisting the services of social scientist consultants to test-drive their cases with mock juries. Some lawyers are so familiar with the process that they can conduct their own mock trials to help predict what the jury will do in a given matter and which jurors, in demographic and attitudinal terms, are most likely to be receptive to the point of view of the lawyer's client. This science, which might be more aptly described as an art form, is also available at the pretrial stage, and we suggest that in the appropriate matter a social scientist be enlisted to assist in developing preliminary case theory in order to make both informal and formal discovery more effective and efficient. This is especially so in cases where discovery is artificially limited by judicial rule.

The authors of this book have had the privilege of working with two social scientists who have raised their craft to an art form. Dr. Amy Singer of Trial Consultants in Ft. Lauderdale, Florida, and David Ball of Jury Watch in Durham, North Carolina, have distinguished careers in assisting trial lawyers and litigators in getting the most out of their efforts for their clients and are responsible for all that is helpful that follows in this section.

The goal of the focus group techniques described below is to identify the areas of factual inquiry that will be of greatest interest to a jury should the case go to trial. In addition, the process can alert lawyers to facts and witnesses that a jury is likely to want to hear in making a determination in the case. Finally, the focus group process can identify psychological hot issues that the jury will have to decide by operation of the judge's charge on the law and verdict forms that must be answered at trial.

Goals of Focus Groups

- ◆ **Identify areas of factual inquiry**
- ◆ **Alert lawyers to facts and witnesses a jury will want to hear from**
- ◆ **Identify psychological hot issues**

There are several focus group techniques that are designed to meet the above-stated goals. All require selecting ten people from a fair cross-section of the community or a similar community from which the eventual jury will be selected. In optimal circumstances the group will be led by a trained social science researcher, but over time lawyers can learn to perform that function in cases that will not support the hiring of a professional focus group leader. The members of the focus group should be paid for their time so that they remain committed to the process, and they should also be made to sign a confidentiality agreement. Arrangements should also be made to contact the members of the group within some time certain after the process, usually within two weeks. The party to the controversy that commissioned the focus group should not be identified to avoid the group's responding in the way they think that party would want them to respond.

The leader should gather basic demographic information from each of the members of the group, as well as have them fill out a survey that tests basic values of the group members. One of the most important values to test is how group members feel about their control over events. People generally fall into one of two categories: they believe that events are either within their control or outside their control, and this belief will impact virtually every decision they make about the meaning and conclusions to be drawn from facts. Once this and other relevant core values are identified, each member of the group is then assigned a number, and whenever a group member speaks he should identify himself by that number. Finally, the entire session should be recorded, preferably by videotape or some other method that does not interfere with the communication between the leader and the group and among the group, in addition to a court-type transcription of the session. These ground rules apply to all of the focus group methods that follow.

In the first method, the session begins with the leader describing what he knows about the case in as neutral terms as possible. This statement should include both the best facts and the three worst facts as gleaned from the brainstorming session. For example, in *Quinlan v. Kane Electronics* the fact statement made for the plaintiff might be:

> The plaintiff is a business broker whose job it is to put buyers and sellers of businesses together. The defendant is an acquaintance of the plaintiff. He owned a business, and over a period of years mentioned several times that he was interested in selling his business. The plaintiff offered her services when he was ready to sell. Last year the defendant told the plaintiff at a social event that he was ready to sell his business and wanted to talk to the plaintiff about it. The two of them met the next day, which was a Sunday, at the defendant's home and discussed the sale of the business. At the end of the meeting, the plaintiff believed that the defendant wanted her to broker the deal. In fact, she wrote and mailed a letter to him to that effect. The plaintiff then called a lawyer for a company that she thought might be interested in purchasing the defendant's business. After the phone call, the lawyer contacted the defendant on behalf of his client and within several weeks they had signed an agreement of sale for the defendant's business. The plaintiff is seeking to receive her fee of 5 percent of the net closing value of the sale of the business because she found the buyer for the defendant's company. The defendant says that she did nothing to earn a fee which would amount to hundreds of thousands of dollars. The defendant denies that there was any agreement between the two and says that he never got the plaintiff's letter.

With this brief statement of the case the leader now asks questions of the group. The questions first seek the visceral reaction of the group such as, "Is the plaintiff right? Is the defendant right? Is the plaintiff crazy?, etc." All members of the group should answer these questions either by raising hands or otherwise and then be asked to explain their feelings.

The session continues by asking the group members for any assumptions they have made after hearing the basic facts of the matter. The assumptions can be about the facts of the case, the people involved, or anything else that occurs to them. In essence, the group is being asked the question, "If what I tell you is true, what else must be true?" Specific inquiry should then be made by the leader as to what information the group would like to find out and people it would like to hear from and about in making a decision in the case. If the group asks questions that can be answered, they should be answered. If the answer to the questions is that the leader doesn't know, that should be communicated as well, as should an honest response that the information requested does not exist, and if it does not, why that is so if the reason is known (e.g., the plaintiff destroyed those papers). At the end of the session the group should be asked to vote for the party it believes, should win the case.

Focus Group Question Format

1. **Is the plaintiff right? Vote**
2. **Is the defendant right? Vote**
3. **Explain your vote, reasons, and feelings**
4. **Assumptions made which support their vote**
5. **If it is true, what else must be true?**
6. **What would you like to find out and who would you like to hear from? (asked of each member)**
7. **Final vote**

The second method is commonly known as unpacking your case. It begins with the statement of several facts. For example, for the plaintiff in *Brown v. Byrd*, the leader might begin with the facts—"car, intersection, school"—and then ask the group what happened. After getting an initial response, more facts are added—for example, "second car, 2:30 P.M., sunny day"—and reactions are then sought. The process continues with the leader unpacking the facts of the plaintiff's case and getting reaction to them as to assumptions made from the facts. Periodically in the unpacking process the group should be allowed to ask questions with the leader providing accurate responses. By the end of the session the leader should have unpacked all of the good and bad facts uncovered by the brainstorming session, and through the process of questioning from the group determined other potential areas of inquiry. Again, at the end of the session, the group members should vote on who wins based on the information available to them.

The third method works in any case, but is particularly helpful in a matter where the jury will ultimately be required to apply the law and interpret facts that are outside the normal range of experience. In these cases, the law as contained in jury instructions and as interpreted by the jury in a Special Verdict, where they answer interrogatories to state their findings in the matter, is critical to the outcome of the case because the jurors are acting and reacting to matters not within their comfort zone. For that reason, unlike in a negligence case based on fault, the judge's instructions gain greater importance in that they are more likely to be listened to carefully and applied with greater precision.

Not surprisingly then, this form of focus group begins with a listing for the group of the elements of claim or defense that must be proved at trial as would be contained in the judge's instruction. Group members are then asked to react to the judge's charge by stating which of the elements is most important and why. That process is followed by a neutral statement of the facts of the case, again containing the three best and worst facts as elicited in brainstorming. With this background, the group should be asked to respond to whether there has been sufficient evidence to prove the things that are required in the judge's instruction. From this point on, the session is much like that described in the first focus group method example, whereby the group asks questions of the leader, identifies information that it would like to have and the people that it would like to hear from to make the decisions required of it in the judge's instruction. The session concludes with group decision making and individually stated rationale for the decision.

By using any of the three methods, or others that are similar, the lawyer uncovers those areas of inquiry that need to be made in other informal discovery and then formal discovery. Because the hot points for the jury are better known, discern can be efficient in that it can be directed at the information likely to be persuasive for a fact finder in the case. The process also identifies witnesses that the fact finder would like to hear from in the litigation. In a rare case the focus group might even advise against bringing a lawsuit, or at least on a particular theory. It should be noted that for court trials there exist organizations that can provide experienced retired judges with similar judicial records to that of the trial judge in question to participate in a focus group designed to identify facts and witnesses that the judge is likely to want to hear in the case.

Armed with the above information, lawyers are better able to identify relatively sophisticated factual theories of the case as to what really happened and why at an early stage in a litigation. It may never be possible to reject potential theories because of the lack of positive response in focus group testing. In addition, the process may suggest legal theories of recovery and defense that are problematic, so much so that they might be dropped out of the lawsuit. At any rate, the information gathered from all sources mentioned prepares counsel to take the next steps in the lawsuit that should be guided by a well-informed fact investigation plan.

ENDNOTES

1. Sandra L. Johnson, Johnson and Johnson, Raleigh, North Carolina, first suggested these rules to us.

Chapter 4

Fact Investigation Plan

4.1 Introduction

The fact investigation plan represents the culmination of the determination of potential legal and factual theories of the case. Each potential theory will have to be developed factually to see if the theory is ultimately provable at trial or other dispute resolution mechanism. Even if a case will not go to trial there will come a time when the legal and factual theory of the case must be articulated. And whether that articulation occurs in the form of a case-dispositive motion, a mediation, an arbitration, or in a negotiation, unless and until a clear legal and factual case theory, supported by admissible facts, can be stated, the matter may not be ready for successful conclusion.

The fact investigation plan provides a system whereby a lawyer can be assured that whatever the ultimate dispute resolution mechanism, the factual predicate for the client's position will exist. There is a word of caution—although the various methods of dispute resolution are beyond the scope of this book, we feel the need to say at least this: Except in unusual circumstances where parties to a contract or other agreement have provided for dispute resolution of a certain sort that is binding, the ultimate dispute resolution mechanism is trial. If all else fails, the trial is always available to decide the matter. As a result, we suggest that no matter what dispute resolution mechanism is likely to dispose of the case, a lawyer is not ready for that mechanism until the closing argument for trial, should there be one, can be at least outlined.

We say so because the closing argument is the time when the legal and factual theories of the case are finally articulated, styled by a persuasive theory or theme. And this articulation will have to be supported by admissible evidence. Because the closing argument provides the basis in law and equity for a successful resolution of the case, its creation will necessitate the final analysis of any case that determines, in civil litigation, the value of the case, and in criminal litigation, the likely outcome in terms of guilty or not guilty verdicts on the full range of chargeable offenses. No matter what resolution device is used, unless an evaluation of the "worth" of a case at trial has been made, no evaluation by any other device can be realistically made.

What we suggest is that without such an evaluation, no informed decision as to whether to settle or plea bargain can be made; no mediator's resolution can be accepted; no arbitration award can be accepted without appeal; no judge's ruling on a dispositive motion can go unappealed; and no settlement value in negotiation can be accepted. Most important, until a trial evaluation has been made, it is virtually impossible to effectively and competently counsel a client on any other resolution of the dispute.

The basis for all of this is the development of facts that support the closing argument that is the ultimate device necessary for the evaluation of a case. Facts can be developed from clients and friendly lay witnesses, adverse parties and unfriendly lay witnesses, neutral lay witnesses, documents, physical evidence, and expert witnesses. They include facts that are substantive in that they are necessary to support the particular claims and defenses in a matter or can be facts that support or attack the credibility of witnesses. Once the facts are developed, their presentation can be enhanced through the use of visual aids or illustrative exhibits that assist in explaining the testimony of witnesses, both lay and expert, documents, and physical evidence.

4.2 Fact Investigation Devices

There are numerous devices that can be used by the litigator to develop and learn the testimony of witnesses and to discover and preserve documentary evidence and physical evidence. They range from informal interviews of witnesses to requests for judicial notice of facts. And all of the devices available should be considered as part of the fact investigation plan. Of course, the plan is dynamic and as the facts of the case unfold, the appropriate device for discovery or preservation of a fact may change. It is helpful at the outset to identify the potential investigation devices available in first civil and then criminal litigation.

4.2.1 Devices Available in Both Civil and Criminal Litigation

Some of the devices available in both civil and criminal litigation include:

- client interviews;
- witness interviews;
- obtaining relevant documents from the client or for the government in a criminal case, the complaining witness;
- obtaining relevant physical evidence from the client or for the government in a criminal case, the complaining witness;
- professional investigators (public and private);
- public records; and
- consulting expert witnesses.

4.2.2 Devices Available in Civil Litigation

In civil litigation the following discovery devices are also typically available:

- mandatory reciprocal discovery (FRCP 26);
- interrogatories (FRCP 33);
- depositions (FRCP 30–31);
- document production (FRCP 34);
- physical evidence production (FRCP 34);
- requests for physical examinations (FRCP 35);
- requests for admission (FRCP 36); and
- judicial notice (FRE 201).

As a corollary, devices that limit the discovery of information including protective orders, the law of privilege, and the rules protecting attorney work product from discovery exist in civil litigation. Information may also be precluded from discovery—at least from opposing counsel—due to the rules of professional responsibility regarding protection of confidential client information from disclosure by an attorney. (See MRPC Rule 1.6.)

4.2.3 Devices Available in Criminal Litigation

- preliminary hearings;
- grand jury proceedings;
- subpoena for witnesses and/or physical or documentary evidence;
- witness statements; and
- notice of affirmative defenses.

In criminal litigation, obviously, inquiry by the government regarding the defendant's case is severely limited by the defendant's privilege against self-incrimination. In a limited number of jurisdictions, depositions of nondefendant witnesses are available as a discovery device. In addition, the government is required to disclose to the criminal defendant all exculpatory material, no matter what its form.

Armed with the above potential discovery devices, counsel is ready to devise the fact investigation plan. The only real limitations of the plan are the creativity of counsel and the discovery budget that is available for the case.

Not every case will support the full range of fact investigation devices. For example, although the use of focus groups as mentioned in chapter 3 is helpful in identifying case theory and thereby suggesting factual inquiry, their use may not be financially available in every case. Likewise, the use of consulting experts to assist in case theory development is helpful, but not economically viable in every case.

4.3 Plan Structure and Fact Investigation Chart

The fact investigation plan will usually take the form of a chart that lists the information sought down the length of a chart and the sources of information across the top. The plan is filled in by noting the availability of information sought after through the various devices available. The real question is what will control the vertical axis of the chart: legal or factual theory? The answer, of course, is that neither type of theory should control because to do so might limit the scope of the factual investigation. The vertical axis then should list not only the factual elements of the potential legal claims or defenses, but the factual elements of the potential factual theories of the case.

Elements of Negligence	Facts 1. True Facts 2. Believed true 3. Hoped true	Source	Discovery Method	Assessment
Duty				
Breach				
Proximate Cause				
Damages				

The idea of the above chart is to help the lawyer to start thinking strategically about fact investigation planning. It is a way to start integrating the facts and the law. It focuses at the start by listing the elements of the cause of action and/or defenses. And it then makes a planner distinguish between conclusions (the defendant was negligent) and facts (the defendant was driving above the speed limit).

Charting also requires the lawyer to pinpoint who or what might be evidence of a particular fact. In some ways, then, the source column may be the most important column. If the lawyer can get more than one kind of information from one source, then it may mean he would go to that source first. Also, the discovery method column makes the lawyer think about the advantages and disadvantages of informal discovery, of interrogatories, of request for admissions, of document subpoenas, and of depositions, and requires him to list the possible methods to see whether more than one source and more than one method might produce evidence of a fact. The assessment column asks the lawyer to think not only about cost and efficiency, but also about professional ethical issues, like conflicts, or the unrepresented witness, or the represented witness who may not be contacted until after the lawyer calls that lawyer.

For even the most simple of cases, the fact investigation plan as represented in chart form can become complicated and thereby lose the clarifying benefit of making a chart. For that reason, it is usually best to create a separate chart for each of the potential legal theories as well as for each of the potential factual theories. All the charts, taken together, will result in the fact investigation plan.

Although the charts for each legal and factual theory are distinct, the execution of the plan will run along all theories simultaneously. That is, if witness A has information that is necessary for Legal Theory I and Legal Theory II, that information can be obtained in the same interview. The same, of course, will be true for different potential factual theories. And it is also true that the facts that support one theory, either legal or factual, will simultaneously support alternate legal or factual theories. This is true, as the core facts of any case will be the same for virtually any legal or factual theory for a given case. It is the facts around the margins that will distinguish one theory from the other.

The following are some examples of fact investigation charts from the *Brown v. Byrd* case.

Fact Investigation Plan

Legal Negligence	Facts	Potential Source	Discovery Method	Assessment
I. Duty	A. Control car B. Safe speed C. Obey traffic signals	1. Brown 2. Byrd 3. Crossing guard 4. Schoolchildren 5. Ice cream truck operator 6. Police report	1. Interview 2. Interview/ Interrogatories/ Deposition 3. Interview/Deposition 4. Interview/Deposition 5. Interview/Deposition 6. Subpoena/copy of public record	1. OK 2. Interrogatories first; deposition; no interview represented party 3. Interview 4. Hold on interview; no deposition 5. Interview; hold on deposition 6. Subpoena
II. Breach of Duty	A. Too fast B. Not looking	Same as Element I	Same	Same
III. Proximate Cause	A. Speed B. Distracted C. Tired D. Sun in eyes	Same as Element I plus expert witness for D. from National Weather Service	Same	Same but no expert needed with rear-ender
IV. Damages	A. Back injury B. Unable to play tennis C. Unable to consume alcohol D. Time off work	**For A.** 1. Brown 2. Tennis friends 3. Coworkers 4. Spouse 5. Children 6. Medical records 7. Experts **For B.** Same but exclude coworkers **For C.** Same but exclude coworkers and children **For D.** Same as C. Employment records	Same	1. OK 2. Interview; hold on deposition 3. Interview; hold on deposition 4. Interview; no deposition 5. Interview; no deposition 6. OK 7. OK; try for treating Dr. B. OK C. OK D7. OK

79

The preceding chart will likely be the most complicated of all those in the case as it encompasses most of the facts and witnesses available in the case. As the fact investigation process proceeds, the chart should be updated to reflect what has been accomplished and what still needs to be done. Should the preferred way of accomplishing a task fall through (e.g., the crossing guard refuses to be interviewed), a future assessment needs to be made as to whether her deposition should be taken, given the attendant risk that you don't know what she will say. In addition, the execution of the plan as reflected in the chart will suggest additional witnesses and sources of information that should be added to a revised chart. As facts are confirmed and Category Three Facts (facts hoped to be true) become Category Two Facts (facts believed to be true) or Category One Facts (facts known to be true), that change in status should be noted and kept in a separate list that lists the fact, its category, and the source for the category designation (interview of crossing guard, Byrd interrogatories, etc.).

What follows next is a fact investigation chart for a factual theory of the case that the plaintiff believes might be a theory that the defendant will advance at trial. The theory could have been the result of brainstorming or a focus group and is a potential explanation for what really happened and why. The potential defense theory is that Brown was distracted from the road and the traffic light by the schoolchildren on the corner, then looked up, saw the light change, and in panic stopped, causing the accident. This chart, because it deals with a fairly narrow factual issue, is more limited than what we have seen previously.

Elements	Facts	Potential Source	Discovery Method	Assessment
Contributory Negligence	A. Presence of schoolchildren B. Location of children C. Location of the traffic light D. Timing of the traffic light E. Speed of the car F. Skid marks	1. Brown 2. Byrd 3. Crossing guard 4. Schoolchildren 5. Ice cream truck operator Fact D same as A–C and E plus 6. Police officer who works area 7. Parents of school-children who pick up kids 8. Investigating officer 9. Police report	1. Interview 2. Interview/ Interrogatory/ Deposition 3. Interview/Deposition 4. Interview/Deposition 5. Interview/Deposition 6. Interview/Deposition 7. Interview/Deposition 8. Interview/Deposition 9. Subpoena	1. OK 2. Interview—no (represented party) Contention interrogatory—OK Deposition—OK 3. Interview/ hold deposition 4. Interview/ hold deposition 5. Interview/ hold deposition 6. Interview/ no deposition 7. Hold interview/ no deposition 8. Interview/ hold deposition 9. OK

4.4 Executing the Plan

The execution of the plan will typically begin with a second interview of the client both to gather further information that was sought after the first interview and to verify other sources of information in the case. For example, in many cases after the first interview, the client will be asked to gather up and deliver to the lawyer all of the documents and physical evidence relevant to the case. Often those potential exhibits will be so voluminous that it requires a lawyer's staff members to go to the client's place of business to identify, copy, and preserve them. In addition, many of the relevant potential exhibits will be in the hands of opposing parties who may not have been sued as of yet.

After or during the document identification and gathering stage of fact investigation, the most likely next step will be the interviewing of witnesses in the case who are denominated as friendly to your client. It is anticipated that these witnesses will be corroborative of what the client has to say about the case. If they do differ, and if the differences are regarding significant matters, those differences should be immediately re-explored with the client. That is, it is unlikely that friendly witnesses will contradict the client about important matters. If they do, one of two things must happen: (1) the witness should no longer be denominated friendly as the witness provides information contrary to the client's position; or (2) (and more likely) the client's position about a particular fact should be re-examined as to both its occurrence *and* its importance to case theory. Put another way, when friendly witnesses do not corroborate facts necessary to a particular case theory, it is likely that the theory will fail and should be abandoned.

Once potential exhibits have been identified and friendly witnesses interviewed, the case is usually ready for significant decision making. For plaintiffs, some legal or factual theories can be eliminated, others will suggest themselves, and the case will likely be ready for formal filing. At this juncture the best decision for a client might be to drop the matter. Before a lawsuit is formally filed, it is always appropriate to seek informal resolution of the matter. Potential plaintiffs, having already engaged in significant investigation, may be ready to do so efficiently and effectively. Of course, potential defendants faced with such a request should take the time to engage in their own informal fact investigation before responding to resolution requests from their potential adversaries.

Once a decision is made to seek relief in the form of a law-suit, the course of the fact investigation will be governed by the nature of the case. For example, a consulting expert witness might very well have assisted in guiding the pre-suit investiga-tion of the case. In some cases testifying experts may also have been retained. This is especially so in cases where a particular expert is thought to be the best qualified. For this reason, fo-rensic economists will not typically limit their retainers to cases involving either plaintiffs or defendants in order to main-tain objectivity. If a particular forensic economist is thought to be the "best" for the contemplated case, that retainer should be sought before the lawsuit is even filed. In other cases, testify-ing experts can be retained at a later time with no significant impact on the case.

As mentioned earlier, the economics of the case frequently will dictate and will always impact on how a matter is litigated. The timing and extent of formal discovery, the hiring of ex-perts, the use of trial consultants, and virtually every other de-cision that costs the client will be impacted by the available budget.

However fact investigation proceeds, the fact investigation charts for each legal and factual theory should be periodically updated. In so doing, theories can be expanded, modified, changed, or dropped entirely. By necessity, as the facts develop, case theory at both the legal and factual level will change, if not radically at least in nuance in most cases. By accurately filling in the fact investigation charts, those changes can be antici-pated and identified as early as possible to avoid traveling down unfruitful avenues of factual investigation. The charts, as followed and completed, will allow for evaluation of the qual-ity of the facts as they are developed.

One helpful technique to keep track of the changing nature of the case is to denote the nature of facts. This technique is particularly helpful in determining whether to propound re-quests for admission in a given case.

The facts of any case fall within three categories:

1. facts that are true;
2. facts that are believed to be true; and
3. facts that are hoped to be true.

At the outset of any fact investigation plan, few facts will fall within the first category. Because the plan is normally formulated after the initial client interview, and because clients are fallible in their perception and recollection, there are very few facts that are *known* to be true. And truth here is not defined in the normal sense. A fact to be *true* for litigation purposes need not be *true* in an ultimate sense; it need only be a fact that is agreed to by your opponent. If there is agreement between or among the parties as to the veracity of a fact, then for litigation purposes it is a *true* fact. For example, in *Brown v. Byrd* if both Brown and Byrd stated to the investigating officer and agree in deposition that the traffic light changed from green to yellow for two seconds and then to red, it makes no difference that further investigation would have divulged that the light was actually yellow for three seconds. For the purpose of that case it is *true* that the light was yellow for two seconds, because that is the fact about which the parties agree.

An example of a *true fact* at the end of the client interview is a fact that the plaintiff has pled as true in the complaint and during the initial interview, with which the defendant agrees. For example, in *Brown v. Byrd*, if in his complaint Mr. Brown alleges that he was driving a Volvo, and in his interview Mr. Byrd says that Brown was driving a Volvo, then it is *true* that Mr. Brown was driving a Volvo. If, however, in his complaint Mr. Brown alleges that he was driving a Volvo, and in his initial interview Mr. Byrd says that Mr. Brown was driving a Saab, then the type of car that Mr. Brown was driving is not *true* as of yet for litigation purposes. Now it is unlikely that Mr. Brown was wrong about what kind of car he was driving, but until the parties agree, it is not a *true* fact for litigation purposes and it must be verified by the fact investigation of the case.

Category One facts, then, are facts about which the parties affirmatively agree. There is no controversy as to the existence of these facts, and they may be relied on for proof of any legal or factual theory of the case. A lawyer would like to have as many of the critical facts of case theory as possible fall within this category.

Category Two facts are facts that are believed to be true. In our earlier example, there is no reason to believe, as a general matter, that Brown would be either mistaken or have a reason to fabricate as to the make of the car he was driving. A wild theory of the case could be constructed whereby Brown was driving a car other than what he stated in his pleadings, but it is unlikely that was the case. That Brown was driving a Volvo on the day of the accident, despite Byrd's recollection to the contrary, is a Category Two fact, one that is believed to be true. It can easily be moved to Category One once it is verified that Brown was driving the car he said he was driving by some other source like a police report concerning the incident, and Byrd agrees that he might have been mistaken about the make of Brown's car.

It is likely that most of the important facts in a case as identified in potential legal or factual theory will begin as Category Two facts. The plan will be designed to verify those facts by its execution. Once a fact is corroborated by some other likely accurate source, it does not become a Category One fact merely by that process. Another example from *Brown v. Byrd* illustrates the point. Assume that Brown claims that as a result of the accident he received a back injury that precludes him from engaging in any strenuous physical activity. In his deposition Brown testified that before the accident he played tennis at least twice a week and that since the accident he has been unable to do so. Assume further that Brown's testifying expert physician says that he has examined Brown, and that in the expert's opinion Brown cannot play tennis without considerable pain. And finally, assume that interviews of Brown's former tennis partners corroborate that he no longer plays tennis with them.

All of the above might suggest that Brown's inability to play tennis is a Category One fact—that is, a *true* fact. But unless and until the fact is conceded as true by Byrd, it remains for Brown a Category Two fact. Byrd may still contest Brown's allegation by resort to testimony of an expert witness who will examine Brown and opine that Brown is a malingerer, or hire an investigator to follow Brown to photograph him playing tennis or engaging in some other equally strenuous physical activity.

For Brown at this juncture it is a Category Two fact that his back is injured such that he can no longer play tennis—a fact that is believed to be true. Simultaneously, it is a Category Three fact for the defendant Byrd that Brown has no back injury at all. That is, Byrd hopes that it is true that Brown is faking his injury only to return to the tennis courts when the case against Byrd is over. For the defendant, the fact investigation plan must be further executed to test its hoped-for fact. He must go forward with further investigation to test the viability of his Category Three fact, that Brown's injury is illusion, and hire an investigator to follow Brown or demand a defense medical exam.

For Brown, then, at this juncture the condition of his back is a Category Two fact, one that is believed to be true. And this belief not only is based on the testimony of the plaintiff, but is corroborated by the expert medical witness and the former tennis partners of the plaintiff. For the plaintiff to move this fact to Category One, something further must happen. For example, the defendant's only medical expert can examine the plaintiff and agree with the plaintiff's expert that Brown has a back injury. At this point it would be a *true* fact, a Category One fact, that the plaintiff has a legitimate back injury. That, of course, does not end the matter for litigation of this matter, because according to the fact investigation plan for the plaintiff in *Brown v. Byrd* based on the legal theory of negligence, not only must Brown have been injured, but that injury must have been caused by the accident.

The defendant may still claim that Brown's injury to his back was preexisting, or caused by some event after the accident in question. Until the plaintiff verifies by way of defense agreement that the injury to Brown's back, in addition to being real, was caused by the accident, that fact remains in Category Two. The plaintiff must either get agreement from the defense medical expert as to the cause of the injury, or use some other device, such as a Request for Admission, to get defense agreement on causation, thereby moving the fact of causation to Category One.

At the time of trial the physical condition of Brown's back might be described in the following ways:

> 1. For Brown, it is a Category Two fact that the condition of Brown's back is such that he can no longer engage in strenuous physical activity such as tennis; and

> 2. For Byrd, it is a Category Two fact that there is nothing wrong with Brown's back, that he can engage in strenuous physical activity.

When the *truth* about any fact is contradicted and thereby listed by the opposing parties as opposing Category Two facts, these are merely facts that will have to be ultimately decided by the fact finder. The *truth* about Brown's back condition will be the subject of a good deal of testimony at trial and will be critical to the outcome of the case. And this can be said any time opposing parties have Category Two facts that oppose each other. In the typical case, when this occurs, the topics of the opposing Category Two facts will likely be central to the case, for it is here that the parties disagree. In evaluating the case for resolution, the relative strength of the remaining Category Two facts for each party will often determine the likelihood of prevailing.

The evaluation of the facts of the case as Category One, Two, or Three facts will help to evaluate the potential case theories that they support. A legal or factual theory supported by Category One facts is strong. A legal or factual theory supported only by Category Three facts can fairly be said to be no theory at all, but a wish. In reality, most theories will be supported by a combination of facts from all three categories. It is true, however, that the more certain the facts that support the theory, the more certain the theory. And the more certain the theory, the more likely it is that the theory will ultimately prevail.

Chapter 5

Witness Interviewing

5.1 Introduction

Once the client has been interviewed and collecting and preserving potential exhibits has begun, the process of witness interviewing can occur. At the outset it is important to note that the tactics and skill of witness interviewing are actually an amalgamation of various tactics and skills. No one tactic will work with every witness. This is so because potential witnesses can be friendly, neutral, or hostile. The tactics and skill required to accomplish the task of interviewing each sort of witness will be different. First, some definition.

Friendly witnesses are those who know something about the facts that underlie the matter and have a favorable disposition toward the client. These witnesses will typically have some relationship with the client in addition to the fact that they were involved in the matter now under scrutiny. This, of course, is a matter of common sense in that people are normally surrounded by others with whom they have some sort of relationship. If the case involves a car accident, such as *Brown v. Byrd*, and the potential witness was in the car with Mr. Brown, it is likely that Brown and the potential witness have a relationship that preexists the accident. The two people are likely friends, neighbors, relatives, or work colleagues. Otherwise, why would they be in the car together? If the matter involves a business transaction, the relationship between client and witness is likely to be employer, employee, coworker, etc.

It is possible, however, that a potential witness has a favorable disposition toward the client solely because of the matter involved in the lawsuit. In this circumstance, the favorable disposition toward the client usually arises from the fact that the client and the potential witness have a similar stake in the matter. That is, their interest in the resolution of the matter is the same or similar. This will always be the case in describing the relationship between the government in a criminal matter and the police and complaining witness. The favorable disposition toward the government on the part of the police and complaining witnesses comes from the fact that all the parties have the same goal—the conviction of people responsible for criminality.

On the other end of the spectrum, hostile witnesses are those witnesses who have a favorable disposition toward the opposing party. Again, this favorable disposition toward the adverse party usually arises from some relationship that pre-existed the facts that underlie the lawsuit. For this reason, it can be expected that these witnesses are not likely to be helpful, in a voluntary way, to the client. For that reason, Brown's passenger is likely to be hostile to Byrd.

The third category of witnesses consists of those who are neutral. These witnesses have no apparent favorable disposition toward either party. They will typically have no preexisting relationship with either party, and therefore no apparent reason to side with one party or the other. Examples of these sorts of witnesses are the people present at the scene where the Brown and Byrd accident occurred, like the ice cream vendor or the crossing guard.

Witness Types

Friendly ➤ **Favorable disposition toward client**

Hostile ➤ **Favorable disposition toward opposing party**

Neutral ➤ **No favorable disposition toward either party**

The denomination of friendly, hostile, or neutral is *not* descriptive of the evidence that these witnesses possess. That is, a friendly witness may possess very damaging evidence to the client's cause, and the hostile witness may have the very evidence that makes the client's case. The denomination merely describes the preconceived tendencies toward providing information to the lawyer. It is the predisposition of the witness that will dictate the tactics used in conducting the interview of the witness, not the ultimate facts that can be obtained. A witness who wants to help presents different interviewing problems than a witness who wants to do damage to the client's cause. With that introduction, we can proceed to a discussion of witness interviewing.

90

5.2 Lawyer Roles

Witness interviewing occurs after there is some tentative identification of the legal and factual theories of the case. In fact investigation charts, the lawyer has already set out the potential use a witness might have in the proof of a particular theory of the case. It is for that reason that there arises a potential conflict in the roles of the lawyer.

As we have discussed earlier, in every representation a lawyer has a dual role as a researcher and a storyteller. There is nothing more important to the lawyer's dual role of researcher and storyteller than witness interviewing. It is in witness interviewing that the beginning lawyer often faces the adversarial nature of the practice of law for the first time. It is in the context of witness interviewing that one of the first lessons regarding the fallibility of eyewitnesses is taught by demonstrating how different witnesses to the same event can see things so completely differently. This fallibility by witnesses is often misinterpreted as "lying" by those witnesses that disagree with the client, when actually all that is happening is "truth" telling by fallible witnesses. And the dual lawyer roles of researcher and storyteller add yet another level of complexity to the process.

Because tentative legal and factual theories have been identified at the time of witness interviewing, it is easy for the lawyer to allow the role of storyteller to overpower the role of researcher. Because of theory identification, the lawyer has made some tentative decisions on the story of the case that will be told to the fact finder. Those tentative decisions can drive the entire process of witness interviewing. When this occurs, witnesses become nothing more than devices for theory verification as the lawyer uses them to check the "story" of the potential legal and factual theories.

In reality, the role of researcher should still predominate in witness interviews. Witnesses may provide facts and insights that lead to new case theories, or at least modification of existing case theory. Lawyers who allow the storytelling role to predominate at the time of witness interviews miss the major point of conducting them. Friendly witnesses can become contradictory of the client, hostile witnesses can make the case, and neutral witnesses can provide information that is anything but neutral.

A story from a recent case illustrates the importance of not allowing the lawyer's role as storyteller to overcome the research function of witness interviewing. The case involved a claim of an exploding rear-end pickup gas tank that resulted in the death of the driver of the truck. The defense trial lawyer and his firm were called into the case late after much of the discovery had been completed. In brainstorming about the case they came to focus on a factual theory that the plaintiff would have died anyway. In other words, the plaintiff was killed from the initial collision with the other car and not from the defendant's design choice in the placement of the gas tank in the rear end of the plaintiff's pickup. When witness statements, both informal and in deposition, were checked, the theory appeared viable, at least to the extent that there appeared no contradictory statements. The lead defense lawyer became so attached to the theory that he featured it prominently in his opening statement, saying that while he was sorry for the plaintiff's death, the design of the truck had nothing to do with it.

The first witness called by the plaintiff's counsel was a nearby witness to the accident. When this witness was interviewed by former defense counsel, the theory of the driver dying from the impact of the accident was nonexistent. And because those lawyers did not explore other potential theories with the witness, his testimony regarding such a theory was unknown to the current defense counsel. The current defense counsel had a theory he liked and found nothing regarding the interviews or depositions of witnesses that precluded such a theory. After describing the events leading up to impact, the plaintiff's lawyer asked the witness, "Then what happened immediately after impact?" Answer: "I saw the truck become engulfed in flames, which spread almost immediately into the driver's compartment. Then I saw the plaintiff struggling to control the vehicle, *and steer it over to the side of the road.* He first sat up straight, and then slumped over the wheel."

Of course, at this point the defendant's factual theory was not worth much. The defendant's credibility would never recover, resulting in one of the largest products liability jury verdicts in Atlanta's history. The problem, of course, is that the defendant had a factual theory that had not been tested in the investigation stage of the case and turned out to be negated by one of the key eyewitnesses. The defendant's advocacy storytelling role had become too prominent, to the exclusion of the researcher role. At a minimum, witnesses in the position to contradict the defense theory should have been reinterviewed to avoid precisely what happened at trial.

It is essential that the lawyer understand the dual role of researcher and storyteller and how his role will change depending upon the witness he is interviewing and the stage of the interview. While the goals of the interview of any sort of witness whether friendly, neutral, or hostile, will remain the same, to obtain new information and test potential case theories the tactics that are necessary to advance those goals may very well be different.

5.3 Interviewing the Friendly Witness

5.3.1 Timing

The initial interview of the friendly witness should occur as close in time to the client interview and the gathering of easily obtainable potential exhibits as possible. Because the assumption usually is that the friendly witness will have information favorable to the client, information about the events in question should be obtained while they are fresh in the witness's mind.

5.3.2 Preparation

Tentative legal and factual theories of the case will already have been determined as of the time of the typical interview of the friendly witness. Counsel should bring to the interview other information in the form of potential exhibits that the witness either knows or should know about the case.

If the case involves a physical scene such as a car accident, the lawyer should visit the scene to obtain whatever information is available. If the accident took place at 3:00 P.M. on a warm sunny day, counsel should visit on such a day. If the client was in a car and the opposing party in a truck, the lawyer should obtain those views in the site visit. If the position of the witness to be interviewed is known, the lawyer should be sure to take up that position at the site visit to see from that point of view.

If a matter involves a business transaction, the lawyer should try to learn from the client everything about the business that has anything to do with the transaction. Such matters would include the people typically involved in such a transaction, their positions in the business entity, how such a transaction is typically accomplished, and whether the transaction at issue was handled in a typical way.

Finally, by way of preparation, the lawyer might want to create an outline of things to be covered in the interview. It is important that the outline be fluid to allow the lawyer to follow any information that the witness presents. The outline is intended to prevent missing information; it is not intended to exclude the seeking of any information. In addition to the outline, a visual device that will be helpful in understanding the witness's information should be considered. The car accident witness, such as in *Brown v. Byrd,* should be interviewed with the aid of a diagram of the scene. A witness in a business transaction such as that in *Quinlan v. Kane Electronics* might find a time line or relationship chart helpful in providing information (see chapter 3, Case Theory). Because the witness interview is against the backdrop of the client's version of the matter, such devices can be anticipated as being helpful to eliciting information and should become part of the interview preparation.

5.3.3 Conducting the Interview

When interviewing the friendly witness, the lawyer's first goal is to establish rapport with the witness. This rapport not only helps the lawyer get information, but it can enlist partisan support that can engender a number of side benefits, including moral support for the client, as well as a certain unapologetic enthusiasm for the lawyer and the case.

Once rapport has been established, the overall second goal is to obtain all the relevant information the witness has. Third, favorable facts must be preserved. Fourth, unfavorable information should be understood and circumscribed or subordinated (not suppressed). Fifth, leads to other facts, evidence, and witnesses must be obtained. And finally, the information received must be preserved and memorialized.

Interviewing the Friendly Witness

- ◆ **Establish rapport with the witness**
- ◆ **Obtain relevant information**
- ◆ **Preserve favorable facts**
- ◆ **Do not suppress unfavorable facts**
- ◆ **Obtain leads to other facts, evidence, and witnesses**
- ◆ **Preserve and memorialize information**

With most friendly witnesses the interview should proceed in much the same manner as the client interview. At least at the outset, information should be obtained through open, non-value-laden questions, to ensure that the information received is information that the witness actually has, as opposed to information provided because the lawyer suggests it would be helpful through the use of leading questions. All of the devices for facilitating information gathering available in client interviews are available here. Likewise, inhibitors to information that exist for clients will also likely exist for the friendly witness. In a later section of this chapter we will explore some additional facilitators and inhibitors that are also present with most witnesses.

Information received in the interview can be memorialized through the vehicle of a signed witness statement that will provide some assurances against memory failure as the signed document could be admissible as a recorded recollection at a later time. The friendly witness should be encouraged to think further about the case and bring to the lawyer any further information in the form of testimony, other witnesses, or potential exhibits as the information is discovered. Finally, counsel should inform the witness of the next likely steps in the matter and of his potential role in future activities regarding the case. This should be done at the time of the interview and followed up on as the matter progresses.

5.4 Interviewing the Neutral Witness

5.4.1 Timing

The neutral witness is neutral because the witness has no predisposition toward any of the parties to the matter. For that reason, many suggest that the testimony of the neutral witness is the most valuable, in credibility terms, of any witness in the case. Because neutral witnesses have no relationship with any of the parties in interest, they have the potential to have great impact on the fact finder in the case.

Because of their potential value and because their neutrality makes it less likely that the events to which they are witness will have any lasting impact, an early interview of the neutral witnesses is usually advisable. Some lawyers suggest they should be the first witnesses to be interviewed. Others would counsel to first interview the friendly witnesses so that potential case theory can be fairly well developed before speaking with the neutral witnesses. At any rate, the common advice is "sooner rather than later" in the timing of these interviews.

It is possible, of course, that the presumed neutral witness will turn out to be either friendly or hostile because of some unanticipated attachment to the case or one of the parties. For example, the crossing guard in *Brown v. Byrd* may turn into a friendly witness for the plaintiff because she believes that cars should never go through a school intersection on a yellow light. If the witness turns out to be friendly, then the tactics for interviewing friendly witnesses described above should be utilized. If hostility proves the more accurate predisposition of the witness, then the tactics discussed later in this chapter will be more appropriate.

5.4.2. Interview Planning

An effort should be made to obtain as much pre-interview information about the neutral witness as possible. This will go a long way to determine if the witness is actually neutral as opposed to a closet friend or enemy. Information gathered should initially be demographic in nature to get a sense of who the witness is and what he is about. Such information helps to predict potential problems of the witness in identifying with your client, a strong factor in influencing testimony. Assume, for example that in the *Brown v. Byrd* case Mr. Brown is in his seventies and a retired factory worker, and Mr. Byrd is a twenty-two-year-old recent college graduate who works in sales for a large company. If the potential witness is a college student majoring in business, it is much more likely, in the typical situation, he will identify with Byrd rather than with Brown.

Information should also be obtained as to how it is that the witness came to be a witness. Again, in the case of *Brown v. Byrd* the witness's name was obtained from a police report where it stated that he was a volunteer witness; therefore, he is likely to be eager to give his story, and the earlier a visit can be made, the better. You will want to be the first party to show interest in what he has to say.

The fact investigation plan will have identified the potential information available from the witness. As such, particular preparation to assist the witness in recalling information that might be obscure but important to a potential case theory, should be accomplished by reference to the facilitating devices noted in chapter 2 on client interviewing, as well as those that follow later in this chapter. An outline for the interview—again to assure, not limit, coverage of the interview—will be extremely helpful. Finally, some thought should be given as to where to conduct the interview. A neutral witness may be put off by a request to come to a lawyer's office. Additionally, if the goal is a forthcoming witness, most people are more comfortable speaking in familiar surroundings. At the bottom line, the location of the interview should be left to the witness, making it clear that the lawyer is willing to accommodate the witness's desires.

5.4.3 Conducting the Interview

To the extent possible, the interview of the neutral witness should closely model the form of the interview of the client or the friendly witness. The interview should begin with rapport building during which the lawyer can size up the witness's attitude toward the case and the giving of information, which will provide significant information on how to proceed with the interview. In addition, if in building rapport with the witness a rapport is also begun with the client's position, that too will be useful.

The goals of obtaining information, preserving favorable facts, subordinating unfavorable facts, obtaining leads on other facts, witnesses, and evidence, and preserving and memorializing information are present with neutral witnesses as well as with the client and friendly witnesses. The interviewing tactics previously discussed for those witnesses are equally available here.

If, however, the neutral witness does not respond to open questions and neutral probes for information, the lawyer must be prepared to conduct the interview in a more direct way. A first step away from the completely open questions should be the who, what, where, why, when, and how questions discussed in chapter 2. These questions have the advantage of directing the witness to the type of information sought, but still require the witness to respond by more than a yes or no. In addition, as noted earlier, when the who, what, where, why, when, and how of any event are known, the information about that event is fairly complete.

As a last resort, counsel should be prepared to ask for the particular information identified in the fact investigation plan as helpful to legal or factual theory development. These questions should be clear, short, one-fact-at-a-time inquiries so that the answers are clear as to the sought-after information. If the questions at this stage of the interview are imprecise, rambling, or even compound, the purported information gathered will be of little assistance because it will be unreliable.

The memorializing of information from neutral witnesses is more problematic than for the friendly witness, who will usually be willing to sign a witness statement. Many neutral witnesses are unwilling to do so. Likewise, they may be unwilling to allow for the tape recording of the interview. These potential problems should be anticipated and provided for by bringing another person from the firm along for the interview who can listen to the interview and take notes. If the witness agrees to sign a statement, the notes can provide a basis for the statement. If he refuses, at least there is another person who can testify at a later time to the witness's statements during the interview should the witness's version of the facts change in some detrimental way.

5.5 Interviewing the Hostile Witness

5.5.1 Timing

By the very nature of the hostility of the witness, it is unlikely that the witness will agree to more than one interview by an opposing party, if at all. It may be that the witness's information can be obtained only through formal discovery like a deposition, and if that is the case, so be it. If, however, the opportunity to interview the hostile witness exists, such an interview is typically one of the last acts of informal fact investigation that occurs before resorting to more formal processes.

Before interviewing the hostile witness, the lawyer needs to have a good idea how the witness fits into the grand scheme of the case. For that reason, to the extent that legal and factual theory can be well developed before the interview occurs, it is desirable. As a result, the lawyer would like to have interviewed all of the friendly and neutral witnesses, plus obtained all relevant potential exhibits before such an interview occurs. At that point, the lawyer is prepared to ask the likely necessary questions to inform or disprove potential case theory. If the interview occurs too early in the process and the interview is, as is the norm, limited to one interview of a relatively short duration, potential case theories, both legal and factual, may go untested with potentially disastrous results, as our exploding gas tank episode pointed out.

There is, however, one strong factor militating in favor of an earlier, as opposed to later, interview of a hostile witness. If the witness is truly hostile, the further along the process the interview occurs the more likely it is that the witness will refuse the interview, or more typically, ask that the lawyer for the party toward whom he is favorably disposed be present at the proceeding. To the extent that the interview can take place before such a hardening of identity for the witness has occurred, it will be beneficial for obtaining accurate and complete information. Potential plaintiffs in lawsuits have, as a result, an enormous advantage as they can complete informal fact investigation before a claim is filed and opposing parties and potential hostile witnesses are put on guard.

But all of the above comes with a huge caveat. We have defined a hostile witness as a witness who has a friendly disposition to a party opposed to the interests of the client. Definitions aside, the "hostility" of a witness is not always easy to determine. A witness who is the employee of an opposing party would facially appear to be hostile, but the witness may dislike his employer. A witness traveling in Mr. Byrd's car in the *Brown v. Byrd* case would normally be one thought of as hostile in that only someone with a friendly disposition to Byrd would be thought to be riding around with him. The witness may, however, turn out to be a hitchhiker. So, if there is any question of the hostility of the witness, err on the side of treating the witness as neutral using all of the tactics listed in the previous section of this chapter.

5.5.2 Interview Preparation

The preparation level for the interview of a hostile witness follows from the above. Once the hostility of the witness is determined, and because the interview is far along in the process, the preparation for the interview can be quite detailed. Case theories and the witness's place in the those theories are usually well known. There is no reason that an extensive outline cannot be prepared as to the witness's likely place in the grand scheme of the lawsuit. The danger of that outline, of course, is that the more complete the outline, the more likely the lawyer will treat it as exclusive of the information to be sought. As long as the danger is acknowledged and guarded against, the detailed outline has the benefit of assuring complete coverage of known theories with the witness.

The same sort of background information regarding the neutral witness should be sought for the hostile witness. This is implicit in determining that the witness is hostile, as we have defined hostility (friendly disposition towards an opposing party) as being born of the relationship between the witness and an opposing party that most likely exists outside the bounds of the matter at issue.

The preparation for the interview of the hostile witness takes on an additional dynamic not present explicitly in the witness interviews previously discussed. The witness's hostility will form a basis for the impeachment of the witness should the matter come to trial. That hostility (relationship with an opposing party) should be explored, and to the extent possible, memorialized during this interview. In addition, care should be taken to explore other potential avenues of impeachment during the interview so as to get a leg up on trial preparation.

5.5.3 Conducting the Interview

The first step of this interview should be to confirm that the witness is indeed hostile. Perhaps the best way to do so is for the lawyer to identify who he is and who he represents and then attempt to establish some rapport with the witness. If the witness responds to small talk with suspicion and reticence, it can be assumed that the witness is in fact hostile. Nonetheless, open-ended questions should be attempted in order to get an overview of what the witness knows about the matter.

With a hostile witness, however, initial attempts at open-ended questions are not likely to be fruitful. It is for that reason that we suggest that rather than attempt a funnel approach as would be used with a client or a friendly witness, the funnel be inverted. The interview can begin with specific questions about the events involved in the lawsuit, seeking specific responses. Once the witness understands that the lawyer is truly interested in what the witness has to say, it is more likely that the witness will open up to the lawyer. At that juncture, open questions may prove more successful. The chart on the next page demonstrates the different approaches.

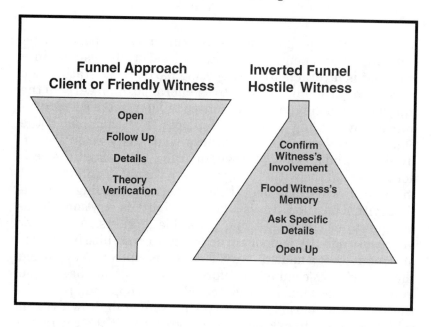

The goal of the interview, of course, is to answer as many of the key fact questions of the case as possible in what is likely to be a single meeting. The lawyer should seek, at a minimum, to have the witness answer questions about important facts where the witness is, or was, in a good position to answer. For example, if the witness was a passenger in Mr. Byrd's car in the *Brown v. Byrd* case, he would be in a unique position to know whether Byrd was looking straight ahead or was distracted immediately before the accident. The secretary to Mr. Kane in *Quinlan v. Kane Electronics* would be in the best position to know whether the letter from Quinlan was ever received by Kane, or whether he received Quinlan's voice message, or whether the voice mail system was working on the day in question when Quinlan says she called.

Important questions should also seek negative information. While every lawyer will agree that it is better to know about the bad news as early in the litigation as possible, many lawyers will not ask direct questions that seek that information. Bad information doesn't go away if not asked about; it just becomes more damaging for failure to acknowledge the information and to attempt to neutralize it. The passenger in Byrd's car should be asked whose fault the accident was and why. Only then will the true potential impact of the witness be known.

In many ways, with a hostile witness the inverted funnel is preferable to open-ended questions. Because the hostile witness has a favorable disposition toward the opposing party, in responding to an open question he will naturally respond in a way that is favorable to the opposing party. By so stating, the witness may commit himself to a general position early in the interview that can poison responses to later, more specific inquiries, by leading to false inferences. For example, if the plaintiff's lawyer asks the witness who was a passenger in Byrd's car and hostile to Brown, up front, whose fault the accident was, and the witness says Brown, then it is unlikely that the witness will "remember" that Brown was speeding. In addition, with a hostile witness a lawyer might also try some leading questions. By suggesting favorable answers, the lawyer may cause a faulty memory of an event to crystallize in a favorable, or at least a neutral, way. This is especially possible when the interview is conducted before formal litigation has begun and the witness has been contacted by the opposing party. In the above example of talking to the passenger in Brown's car it might be better to ask fairly early on, "You hit the car in the rear?" or "Now, the light had turned to yellow, I take it, or the car in front of you wouldn't have stopped?"

If you are able to get to the potentially hostile witness early enough, before he has been biased against you, you have to be very careful in your planning and approach in order not to scare the witness away. Essential to this planning is to again review the reasons why a witness might not want to talk to you at all. Binder and Price catalog the reasons why a witness might not want to talk to you as inhibitors,[1] and it is important to diagnose the likely inhibitors so that you can prepare a response should they arise. We will spend some time in the next section of this chapter going over what they are to assist in preparing appropriate strategies to overcome them, should they be encountered.

Once the maximum amount of information the witness is willing to provide is obtained, there must be some way to memorialize the interview. At the worst, the lawyer should bring another person from the office to be a witness to inconsistent statements should they occur at trial. That person can take notes and prepare a proposed statement for the witness. If the witness is truly hostile, however, it is unlikely that the witness will want to sign a statement. However, insurance investigators have known for years that while a witness may not sign a statement, he is more than willing, sometimes eager, to correct one. For that reason, professional investigators will prepare narratives of interviews and ask witnesses to review the narratives for mistakes. Mistakes about routine items such as names, addresses, occupations, times, etc., are intentionally made, at least one to a page. When the witness reads over the narrative and finds such an error, on request he will correct and initial the error on the narrative. In the end, even if he refuses to the sign the narrative, the corrections and initials will have the same effect—a reliable recording of what the witness said.

5.6 Inhibitors to Witness Testimony

While all of the inhibitors mentioned in the chapter on client interviewing are potentially present with witnesses as well, there remain several inhibitors that are most likely to occur in witnesses that require special responses.

5.6.1 Ego Threat

The witness may be inhibited to reveal information that threatens his self-esteem. For example, a witness might not want to reveal specific information in his employment history where he failed to live up to either his own or his employer's expectations. Other examples could include the facts that are more case-specific. The crossing guard in *Brown v. Byrd* might not want to admit that she didn't see the accident because she was distracted by a child who had gotten away from her. To admit that the child had not obeyed her command might threaten the guard's view of what makes a good crossing guard.

If the lawyer diagnoses that the client is afraid of personal embarrassment in the answers he gives, then the lawyer should offer reassurance about his role as advocate and friend, not judge. If confidentiality can be offered, then this can often alleviate the hesitation. Yet, where it can't be offered (see discussion below), the lawyer is left to using his skills at developing rapport. These skills include the use of nonverbal probes and active listening techniques in order to get the witness to feel complemented and safe enough to reveal what is really on his mind.

A quick review of these probes, then, is in order here. The first is to choose a place for the interview that is nonthreatening. Don't call the witnesses into your office, but go out where they are comfortable, where they feel safe. Pick a time when they are likely to be relaxed, such as early evening after they have eaten. Many nonprofessional witnesses don't like to be bothered at work or right before dinner when they are rushing around doing family chores. On the other hand, meeting someone for drink after work at a favorite watering hole can provide you with the atmosphere you are looking for.

The second thing is to again prepare an icebreaker. Pick a common friend or shared interest to talk about. Give each of you a chance to relax and get to know the other's habits of speech and manners of behavior.

Third, establish that your goal is to reach an understanding of the witness's knowledge and feeling for the subject. More will be said about this in the section on listening.

Use silence, eye contact, head nods, mm-hms, restatement, and reflection. Wait the witnesses out. They have the same needs for catharsis and meaning that we talked about with regard to client interviewing. Premature questioning or judgmental responses can kill a good narrative. Use head nods and silence to wait out the witnesses, giving them time to choose their own words and order their thoughts. Restate what you hear, and if this doesn't work, reflect the feelings you see on their faces in order to show that you care to reach a complete understanding and that their feelings as well as their thoughts are vital to this process. These probes often take time to work, and the best thing is to lend a sympathetic ear and exercise patience.

Active Listening Probes

- Silence
- Eye contact
- Head nod
- OK
- I see . . .
- Mm-hm
- Restatement
- Reflection

5.6.2 Job Threat

Witnesses' belief that certain information could threaten their continued employment (or own responsibility) makes them hesitate to answer the lawyer's questions. For example, if Kane's secretary in *Quinlan v. Kane Electronics* is being interviewed by Kane's lawyer and knows that Kane has taken the position that he never received Quinlan's letter, and further believes that she in fact opened such a letter, she might feel that such information could be a threat to her job. Similarly, the police officer in *State v. Lawrence* might have violated police procedure by showing the complaining witness Gale Fitzgerald only one picture of his suspect, as opposed to a photographic array or a lineup, and therefore may fear departmental sanctions.

If you anticipate a situation where an employee like the police officer in the *Lawrence* case is concerned he may be sanctioned for his activity, you might respond in a number of different ways. First, if there is some already existing evidence that he did make a mistake (e.g., the statement of Fitzgerald that she was only shown one photo), you might first go to the organization's in-house counsel (the police legal adviser) and ask how he or she wants to treat the employee. Perhaps counsel will waive the conflict and offer assurances to the employee that they are all in this together. It may then be possible for the lawyer to offer joint representation, if necessary, and promise confidentiality and immunity from firing in exchange for the witness's cooperation and truthful testimony.

Or the organization might take the position that it is unwilling to make such promises until it finds out more about what the witness did. If this is the case, the lawyer needs to guard against creating the reasonable impression in the witness that his statements are confidential. The lawyer needs to be careful to state who he represents and what is and is not confidential from the employer. In appropriate cases, the lawyer might suggest counsel to the employee if fairness dictates that the employee is under suspicion. In any event, the lawyer should seek advice from the client before interviewing employees who are fact witnesses as to how the potential conflicts will be handled.

Or the secretary might be unwilling to recall receiving the letter from Quinlan for fear that her boss will be angry with her. The lawyer should speak with Kane first to get his assurances that the secretary would not be disciplined in any way for telling what she knows. After all, assuming Kane is truthful in stating that he never saw the letter from Quinlan, it is of little further damage that the letter was received. The real push in the case concerns what Quinlan did, not whether she sent a letter that was never confirmed by Kane.

5.6.3 Role Expectations

The witness may be inhibited by his understanding of what behavior is appropriate within certain relationships. Just as you act a certain way toward your parents, your in-laws, your teachers, or new acquaintances, the witness might feel and say different things to you because of who you are, and vice versa. If an associate goes in to speak to a senior vice president of a major company when doing due diligence, it will be awfully hard to ask tough, pertinent questions that question the vice president's decision making. Depending then on the witness's role, the lawyer may be cast in different roles. The lawyer may have to take the listening role in some situations and the more talkative, apparently in-control, and dominant role with other witnesses.

With the stereotypical hesitant witness who is intimidated by the status of a lawyer, it is important to work on persuading the witness about his relative status to you. Two persuasion statements that often help are first, where the lawyer describes who he works for and blames that party for having to bother the witness. For example, a lawyer might say, "My supervisor sent me to talk to you. He says you know all about how these things work and what happened. I can't go back to her empty-handed or I'm in real trouble. Can you help me out?" Sharing the perspective of an employee that has an employer telling him what to do can build a good bond with the lay witness. And the best part of it is that it is true. It is your job to find out what happened and you are likely to be evaluated on how well you do it.

Second, you can use a variation of the above with a subtle threat. The technique is called raising the witnesses' expectations by reminding them of their position to know. The lawyer might say to the crossing guard, "The city's records show that you were the crossing guard at that intersection on the day of the car wreck between Brown and Byrd at the time it occurred. I'm sure you must have seen something." In other words, the lawyer's question reminds the witness that the lawyer knows she was there, that she was there as part of her job responsibilities, and that therefore, saying she doesn't know or doesn't remember is not consistent with the expectations of her employer.

5.6.4 Etiquette Barrier

The witness may think that there are certain things that one just does not tell certain other people. Often witnesses are motivated by their protection of another person. They feel that loyalty demands that they not speak ill of another. This can cause all kinds of problems in a case like *Quinlan v. Kane Electronics*. Kane's employees will naturally be protective of him as will employees and business partners of Quinlan. The result for the interviewer is that in the end, the strong loyalties of witnesses toward the opposing parties can leave an impression of what actually occurred that is literally skewed at both ends. Where the truth of the matter might be in the middle, because of strong loyalties to both parties the middle has grown larger, and the truth of the matter harder to discern.

There is again a short story here that may help make the point. Lawyers for the defendants in the Dalkon Shield cases were often baffled by how the product made it to the market when it caused infection, as the plaintiffs proved that it did. In investigating the steps defendants' investigators took in testing the product, they ran into the following repeated behavior. Someone would ask about the testing that was done on the Dalkon Shield. Someone else would make a joke about doing some additional testing on the women at the plant. The embarrassment caused by the joke, combined with the etiquette threat of discussing the testing of the product, made the investigators fail to follow up on their due diligence regarding the testing of the product. As a result, important information went undiscovered.

Whether in domestic disputes or commercial disputes, the motivations of the parties and their behavior often raise conversations that require the lawyer to look impolite if they are pursued. Yet it is the job of the fact investigator to learn how to professionally pursue the answers to these impolite questions. The fact investigator must learn how to stay serious and focused on the subject matter at hand. A series of pointed questions may have the short-term effect of putting off the witness, while at the same time ferreting out important information. If a choice must be made, the lawyer must suffer the anger of the witness to obtain the necessary information. Tone, demeanor, and seriousness of purpose all contribute to success in fact investigation. And it is necessary that they be virtues and behavior lawyers choose to evidence, long before they are responsible for actually asking the questions.

5.6.5 Trauma

The witness's answer to your questions may evoke unpleasant memories. He or she may experience a certain amount of trauma in remembering what happened. If the witness saw the accident, knew the deceased, or helped get a person fired, it may be hard to get a clear understanding of what the witness knows because of all he or she is feeling. For example, the crossing guard at the intersection where the accident underlying *Brown v. Byrd* occurred may have to recall, when asked about the accident, that she almost let a child get away from her and run out into the intersection right before the accident happened. Because memory of that traumatic event is triggered by questions concerning the accident and because the event occurred immediately before the accident, the recollection of the witness about the accident may be difficult to bring to the surface. Likewise, in *State v. Lawrence* the victim, Ms. Fitzgerald, may have a difficult time recalling and relating the traumatic events of her assault. The prosecuting attorney must force those recollections because without Fitzgerald's detailed recollection a conviction cannot be had.

5.6.6 Perceived Irrelevancy

Sometimes the witness doesn't have the energy to summon up the detailed answer the lawyer is looking for, and it is because the witness simply doesn't see how the detail is relevant. The witness may think that there is nothing wrong with dumping used oil down the drain, that it is done all the time. Why should he then mention it during an environmental audit? Similarly, Kane's secretary may deal with hundreds of letters every week that propose some sort of business deal to Kane. As a result, it will be difficult for the secretary to recall the letter that Quinlan says she sent to Kane, and even more difficult to remember the content of that letter and what happened to it. Again the witness is not trying to be evasive, lie, or hide something from the lawyer. He just does not know how it is relevant. Remember that lawyers have an expanded sense of relevance (and plaintiffs' lawyers, of causation) that the witness may not share. It is therefore incumbent upon the lawyer to make the relevance of the questioning known to the witness. By explaining why certain information is important, the lawyer will encourage the witness to search his memory for the sought-after information and make its discovery more likely.

5.6.7 Greater Need

The witness may have a greater need to talk about some subject other than the one on the questioning lawyer's mind at the time. This greater need can also affect the listening skills and the energy level the witness has to summon up the answers to the lawyer's questions. For example, in a child custody case the mother could be more concerned about preventing spousal abuse than focusing on the evidence she has that she is the better parent. The greater the immediate need, the more difficulty the witness will have in attending to the lawyer's questions.

5.6.8 Time and Money

Witnesses can have concerns about their time and the cost of getting involved. They might be unable to afford the time off work that would be necessitated if they were called as a witness to either deposition or trial, or both. They may have child care concerns, or other family priorities that interfere with being able to give the lawyer the time it takes to remember with precision. These are legitimate and important concerns that may have to be addressed with sensitivity and planning in order to overcome the resistance that these inhibitions engender.

As stated above, picking the right time and place can go a long way to alleviating the witness's legitimate concerns about the personal use of time. Yet these might be excuses for some other inhibition that keeps the witness from talking. One way of diagnosing the inhibition is to engage in facilitators with gradually escalating consequences to help you determine the true nature of the inhibition.

For example, the lawyer could first engage in what psychologist call an altruistic appeal. The lawyer could plan to deliver a short, one-paragraph statement of the strengths of the case, and then make an altruistic appeal. For example, the lawyer for Ken Brown in *Brown v. Byrd* might say to a witness:

> I represent Ken Brown, who was the driver of the car that was hit from behind in the accident you saw. Unfortunately, he has some pretty serious injuries that have kept him out of work for several months, and it looks like he'll be out of work for some time. I've agreed to represent Mr. Brown to see that he and his family are compensated for his inability to work

because of this accident. Can you help me with a few minutes of your time, so that I can better understand what happened in this accident?

The power of the persuasive statement on the borderline witness cannot be underestimated. It tells the witness not just what side you are on, but that you are on the side of truth and justice. If you really don't know what you know or haven't yet developed a point of view, such a well-told statement could create a general premise from which you are willing to infer all sorts of things.

If this fails, the lawyer can make time-saving statements. Again the lawyer for Ken Brown might say to a potential witness:

> We are very early in the process of this case and a few minutes of your time now may help us clear up this matter quickly. As you probably know, most car accident cases settle without having to go through the formal litigation process. If you can tell me what you know now, it would go a long way to avoid a full-blown litigation where we would have to call you to a deposition and later a trial. Can we talk now? It would be a great help.

Or, the lawyer may raise the stakes. The lawyer might say:

> Look, you either talk to me now, or I'll have to subpoena you. Then the other lawyers will be present, and you'll be placed under oath, and then you'll have to answer my questions. I don't want that and you don't want that. I don't think this will take too long. Please answer my questions.

Of course threats may backfire. They certainly will dampen any later efforts at establishing rapport. Yet if the lawyer is serious in the need for the information, even more immediate threats might be investigated. If the particular witness has a job (or insurance policy) that requires him to cooperate, this fact can be used as a threat to force the issue. Whether he has already given a statement to the other side should also be explored. It may be that the witness was told not to talk to the lawyer. For example, in the *Lawrence* case, Ms. Fitzgerald may have been told not to talk to defense counsel, or more likely may have interpreted the legitimate advice of the prosecutor that she did not have to talk to the defense lawyer as a directive not to do so. Care should also be taken to record any other impeaching and biasing statements that the witness might make in refusing to talk. Does the witness protest because "she might lose her job," "the target is her friend," "the witness doesn't know anything," "the witness is scared"? Any of these statements are useful for impeachment, if they are preserved in a form that makes them usable at trial.

This raises some additional planning issues before the fact investigator goes to meet the witness. Often the investigator goes armed with an official-looking legal pad and pen, and madly records verbatim what the witness tells him. Yet these techniques increase the likelihood that the investigator won't establish any kind of rapport, or that he will forget to look interested, or nonjudgmental, or maintain eye contact, or head nod, or appropriately respond to what he sees in the witness's face while the witness talks.

Psychologists tell us that communication is a physical act, and that only a small part of it is what we actually say. Often the nuance or subtlety or conflicting feelings come from the hand gestures, or eyes, or expression on the face. These all go unobserved if the investigator's head is buried in his yellow pad. Better for the interviewers to develop habits that allow them "to listen with eyes" rather than just with their ears.

One successful technique is to wait until after the interview and then offer to write up what has been said, "to make sure I've got it right." The witness can then look it over and make any corrections, and then sign the statement. This way witnesses can feel safe and listened to while talking, and further feel that words weren't put in their mouths in that they will have a final say in what they sign. Another technique is to bring along a third person to take notes. A third technique is to tape the conversation. The danger with this last technique is not only that taping can impede the witness in his telling, but that since the lawyer doesn't know yet what the witness will say the lawyer could be preserving damaging testimony against his client. It is most often better to interview first and then record in the form of statement or later deposition, if the need arises. Many jurisdictions criminalize the tape recording of conversation without the consent of all the parties to the conversation. As a result, surreptitious recording of a witness should not be undertaken without resort to local statutes.

5.6.9 Forgetting

It may seem obvious, but memories fade and witnesses forget. To the lawyer who has lived with a case day in and day out for months this fact is, at times, hard to remember. Many lawyers may take the witness's hesitation as evasiveness or cooperation with the other side. Instead it is often neither, but is just a simple failure of memory and concern that he will make a mistake. In fact, in our viewing of hundreds interviews with lawyers and law students, this seems to be a prevalent mistake. They misread the hesitation in the witness as evasiveness and go on the attack, threaten, or cajole, and end up making the witness even more confused and uncertain, and additionally defensive and in no mood to cooperate.

Remember, then, that memory involves at least three things. First it involves the original information, that which was perceived and understood at the time that the event happened. Next it involves the external information, that which the observer later learned or was told but didn't observe himself. Finally there are inferences that a person makes from what he observed which he then comes to know as part of his memory of the event. These inferences, commonly known as filling in, are made on the basis of the experience of the witness. That is, given what the witnesses know about life and what happens in the world, the event must have happened in this way, because that's how events of this sort, in their experience, happen.

When witnesses remember something and tell about it, what they usually are doing is relating their reconstruction of the event. That is, when a person describes a car accident seen several weeks before, that description is a product of the accident, thinking about the accident, the experience of the witness with accidents, and telling about the accident several times. That is, we hardly ever hear from a witness a pure statement of memory, and not because the witness is intentionally misleading. It is for that reason that if there were five witnesses to the accident involved in *Brown v. Byrd,* all five could give different versions of the accident, and wildly so, and if there existed a test that could tell if they were telling the truth, every witness would test as being truthful. It is from such a phenomenon that the phrase "the truth lies somewhere in the middle" comes to life.

All of this leads us to a very important subject in fact investigation, the psychology of memory retrieval, a subject that further complicates the ethical role of lawyer as both researcher and producer of a persuasive story.

5.7 The Psychology of Memory

In recent years there have been significant studies of the effectiveness of eyewitness testimony. One of the leaders in that research is Elizabeth Loftus.[2] She explains that external factors can create distortions that can affect a person's memory of an event. She showed how cross-racial identification can be affected, how photos can be biased, how weapon focus can mislead, how the witness often unconsciously transfers other information directed at another person altogether onto the person he says he saw. She also shows how the witness's previous expectations about what would happen can interfere with memory. And finally, while a certain amount of strong motivation or emotional arousal can heighten accuracy, at some point stress or fear interferes with the ability of the witness to accurately observe an event in the first place.

Yet more important for our purposes, Loftus also has shown how questions (and therefore questioners) themselves can affect memory. She shows that the way a question is phrased can affect estimates people will give.

The question "Do you get headaches frequently, and if so, how often?" produces an average response of 2.2 per week. The question "Do you get headaches occasionally, and if so, how often?" changes the average response to .7 per week. Or "Did you see *a* broken headlight?" versus "Did you see *the* broken headlight?" produces a response to the second question that is more likely to say they saw a broken headlight, even when there was none.

Or, look what happens when the questioner changes the verb:

Verb	Mean Estimate Miles Per Hour
contact	31.8
hit	34.0
bumped	38.1
collided	39.3
smashed	40.8

Loftus also has shown that the way an earlier question is asked can also influence the way later questions are answered. For example, she showed her subjects a movie of an auto accident. After the movie she asked the subjects questions. Some were asked about the collision using the verb "smashed." Some were asked using only the verb "hit." One week later when these same people were asked, "Did you see the broken glass?" sixteen out of fifty of the "smashed" subjects said they saw broken glass. Only seven of fifty of the "hit" people said they saw broken glass. There was no broken glass.

Look what happens when people are asked about seeing stop signs. In a video showing A involved in an auto accident, where A had a stop sign, subjects were asked the following two different questions. How fast was A going when he turned right? How fast was A going when he ran the stop sign? Later in the questionnaire when asked whether they saw a stop sign, 35 percent of the first group said they saw a stop sign, but 53 percent of the second group said they did. The second group's ability to recall seemed to be improved by the earlier question.

In addition, questioners seem to be able to create things in some people's minds. Subjects were shown a film of eight people in a classroom. After the film, half of the subjects were asked, "Was the leader of the twelve people male or female?" Half were asked, "Was the leader of the four people male or female?" One week later the first group was asked how many people were in the class and they said nine; the second group was asked the same question and they said six. They seemed to be averaging in response to the earlier question.

When asked, "Did the demonstrators say anything?" versus "Did the militants say anything?" one week later the groups were more likely to remember violence of some sort.

People even seem to change the colors they see. They will change blue to bluish green if they are asked if they were assuming the color was green.

Finally, Loftus showed that 17.3 percent of subjects will say they saw a barn where there was no barn if asked, "How fast was the car going on the country road when it passed the barn?" Only 2.7 percent will see the barn when asked only, "How fast was the car going on the country road?"

Once people change their impressions it becomes harder and harder for them to change back. Advertisers know it. Ads on behalf of insurance companies which rail against big jury verdicts prove it. If juries have seen these ads, even briefly, their awards are likely to be lowered. They import what they see into their understanding and it interferes with their judgment and view of the facts. Of course this is nothing new, but what Loftus does is place squarely before lawyers the ethical problems of manipulating witnesses into telling different stories about past events.

What Loftus teaches us, then, is to look for ways the memory can be shaped. In the role as a fact finder, the lawyer must be careful his own witness's memory hasn't made him blind to the hard facts that may come back and contradict him later. One fix that Loftus suggests is to use memory flood. If the aim is to get the witnesses to accurately remember what occurred in the past, then they need to be oriented to time and place. Your use of a time line or documents can greatly facilitate this process. Show them the time line, or orient them to time and place by giving them time to recall where they were, who they were with, and what else was going on in order for them to carefully reconstruct what happened. Interestingly enough, the open-ended question that calls for a narrative can be unproductive and, in fact, can lead to inferential confusion. The witnesses might too easily infer what they knew and when they knew it in reference to how they feel about it now, or what they say in a conclusory response to the open-ended question. Better to ask more pointed questions that allow them to orient regarding time and place. The chance that they will be accurate improves greatly.

If, however, the lawyer doesn't want any recollection, the lawyer might reverse-question, but after first evoking the circumstances that might make it difficult for the witness to remember. For example, if it was dark, and things happened fast, or if it was a long time ago, and a lot has happened since then, then suggesting that the witnesses might not recall what happened might produce a response that they don't. From that they might build an inference chain that they don't know other, more specific answers to what people said, heard, or did.

Again, there is no magic here, and there is danger in trying to make a bad fact go away when there are chances that it exists. Still, the advocate in the lawyer with the borderline or hostile witness has an obligation to zealously represent the client where a witness remembers facts that run against the client's memory. As a questioner, the lawyer must look hard for independent verification of the memory: other witnesses, whether the memory was recorded, and if so where and when, and any other facts or circumstances that support the opposing witness's view. (After all, we don't want a witness to later say the plaintiff drove the car to the side of the road if our theory is that he died on impact.) But if there is no independent verification and if the witness's memory could have been affected by external information, it is the role of the advocate to discover that external information and counteract it. What the lawyer needs to be able to do is to move between both roles, to be a rapport-building, listening fact investigator, and a questioning, challenging, and creating advocate. And all of this must be done within the bounds of professional responsibility.

5.8 Professional Responsibility Issues in Witness Interviewing

The Model Rules of Professional Conduct deal with the issue of lawyer contact with witnesses in Rules 4.1 through 4.4. We will deal with each of these rules as it impacts the lawyer's task of witness interviewing.

Rule 4.1, Truthfulness in Statements to Others, provides for the obvious, that in the course of representing a client a lawyer shall not make a false statement of fact or law. In witness interviewing potential violation of this rule may occur in trying to persuade a witness to grant an interview. In setting out altruistic reasons for the witness to grant the interview, the lawyer may overstate the client's case to the point of violating this rule. However, so long as the lawyer makes statements of fact about the nature of the case and the importance of the witness's giving information, violation of this rule is unlikely.

The same possibility for violating Rule 4.1 exists when altruistic appeals to the witness do not work and the lawyer escalates persuasion to the suggestion of formal processes that would compel the appearance of the witness. So long as the process (e.g., deposition) is available, the lawyer will be free to mention it as a possible course of action should the witness fail to cooperate. The problem is, of course, that if the witness's interview produces favorable information, the likelihood of the witness being called upon further increases. That is, a favorable statement by the witness might be preserved in a deposition so as to lock it in for substantive purposes should the recollection of the witness fail at a later time. Similarly, a favorable fact statement in a deposition might very well have greater impact in settlement negotiations than a signed statement or the recollection of the witness interview by the lawyer then negotiating. Still, such statements, designed to obtain witness cooperation in providing truthful statements, are unlikely to rise to the level of falsehood sought to be proscribed by the rule.

MRPC Rule 4.2, Communication with Person Represented by Counsel, governs situations where a lawyer seeks to speak with a witness who is represented by counsel concerning the matter about which information is sought. So long as the lawyer knows that the person is represented, communication with that person cannot be had without the consent of the lawyer representing the person sought to be interviewed. The rule does not, of course, preclude a public prosecutor from communicating with a represented criminal defendant, so long as the defendant waives the right to have counsel present. For example, the prosecutor in *State v. Lawrence* would be allowed to speak with the defendant about the case, so long as Mr. Lawrence agreed to the conversation, even without first contacting Lawrence's lawyer. Although permissible, such contact is unwise, unless the defendant gives a voluntary written waiver of his right to have counsel present during any conversation with representatives of the government.

The potential for running afoul of the rule is much greater in civil practice. And that is so because of the reach of the rule in its definition of "represented persons." When the opposing party is an organization, Comment (4) to Rule 4.2 provides that represented person includes:

1. any person with "managerial responsibility";

2. any person whose "acts or omissions" can be "imputed to the organization for purposes of criminal or civil liability"; or

3. any person whose "statement may constitute an admission on the part of the organization."

It is the third category of "represented person" that creates the most difficulty, as it would include within its reach any current employee of the opposing party no matter what that employee's level is within the company. This is so because Federal Rule of Evidence 801(d)(2)(C) makes statements of any current employees, about matters involved in their employment, admissible against their employers. Given this broad view of party admissions, there is no current employee of a party who knows anything about a matter in litigation who can be interviewed without first getting the consent of counsel for the employer. And it is fairly obvious that once that permission is sought, the employees will be interviewed, if they so consent, with counsel present, thereby diminishing the effectiveness of the interview.

These prohibitions are particularly troublesome for the interviewing lawyer as applied to talking to an opponent's former employee. Contact with former employees is particularly tempting because it may lead to vital information. In addition, it is particularly hard to explain to the lawyer's client why the lawyer can't simply pick up the phone or go visit such a potentially important source of information who is no longer loyal to the employer.

Still, even a former employee could fall under the prohibition against lawyer contact from the opposition. If a former employee committed fraud or illegally dumped toxic wastes while employed, his or her admission could bind the corporation or be imputed to the corporation. Model Rule 4.2 seems to prohibit contact with such a former employee without notifying corporate counsel. But what if the lawyer is approached by the former employee? What then?

Model Rule 4.3 prohibits a lawyer from taking advantage of any confusion the unrepresented witness may have about the lawyer's role, and requires the lawyer to make clear that he is not disinterested or neutral. In these situations, it is best that the lawyer remind the witness and make it clear who he represents. When contacted by a former employee, a lawyer is also prohibited from giving advice regarding the legality of what the employee did. For example, many witnesses will ask a lawyer whether they have any legal problems because of what they did or did not do in the matter about which the interview is conducted. Should the witness seek legal advice from the interviewing lawyer, the *only* advice allowed by the rule is the advice to obtain independent counsel. Any other advice, even if not proscribed directly by Rule 4.3, is likely to involve the lawyer in a Rule 1.7 conflict of interest. Yet it seems clear that to turn down the proffered information from the employee would violate duties of competence and loyalty to the lawyer's client. If asked, then, by the opposing corporate client's former employee whether he or she should talk to the lawyer, the lawyer should make it clear that it is the former employee's choice about whether or not to talk, and that the lawyer cannot advise the former employee one way or the other.

In addition, as a practical matter, if contacted by an opponent's former employee, the lawyer should bring along a witness to their conversation, or seek to record or memorialize it in some way. Otherwise the lawyer may be the only source of what the witness told him and have to withdraw from active representation of the client, because of prohibitions against lawyers' testifying on behalf of their clients.

Rule 4.4, Respect for Rights of Third Persons, provides for both attorney etiquette in conducting interviews and respect for the legal rights of the witness in protecting potential evidence from disclosure. The rule provides that lawyers may not use means that are predominantly designed to "embarrass, delay, or burden" the witness being interviewed. In addition, the lawyer must not attempt to obtain evidence from a witness that has some sort of legal protection. For example, a lawyer may not use the witness's naivete to get the witness to disclose potential evidence in the case that might be protected by some sort of privilege that the witness has against its disclosure.

Other professional responsibility issues that might arise in the context of witness interviewing are covered in MRPC Rule 3.4, Fairness to Opposing Party and Counsel. The issues raised by this rule are most likely to affect a lawyer who has interviewed a favorable witness and would like to keep that witness, or what the witness has to say, from becoming known to opposing counsel. The rule states the obvious—that a lawyer can't obstruct access to witnesses, alter or destroy potential exhibits, falsify evidence, or counsel a witness to falsify evidence. In addition, Rule 3.4(f) precludes a lawyer from requesting that a witness not talk to opposing counsel except when the witness is a relative or employee of a client *and* the witness's interests will not be adversely affected by the refusal to speak with opposing counsel.

As can be seen, the clear thrust of the rules of professional responsibility with regard to witness interviewing is fairness toward the witness, while at the same time respecting the lawyer's need to find information relevant to the client's cause. Disclosure of the lawyer's purpose and client when dealing with witnesses will keep the lawyer on the right side of the professional responsibility rules.

ENDNOTES

1.   David A. Binder, Paul Bergman, and Susan C. Price, *Lawyers as Counselors, A Client Centered Approach* (St. Paul: West Publishing Company, 1991): 83.

2.   Paul Zwier first became aware of Elizabeth Loftus's research when she presented her findings at the University of Richmond School of Law in the spring of 1995. She has presented her work in a variety of books. One particularly useful source is Elizabeth Loftus and Katherine Ketcham, *Witness for the Defense: the Accused, the Eyewitness, and the Expert Who Puts Memory on Trial* (New York: St. Martin's Press, 1991) in which she presents much of her research on how memory works and how it can be affected by interviewing. Mr. Zwier has shared her work with others, including his coauthor.

Chapter 6

Counseling

6.1 Introduction

Of all of the skills necessary to be an effective lawyer, the skill of counseling is the most difficult to learn. Yet in terms of the day-to-day functioning of a lawyer, counseling is probably the most important of all lawyering skills. It is through effective client counseling that the lawyer learns the true goals of the client, the acceptable methods for the client to reach those goals, and finally the decision of the client regarding the ultimate resolution of the case.

Counseling occurs throughout the representation of a client. At the end of the initial interview, it is the skill utilized to clarify the goals of the client representation. Through counseling the lawyer learns what the client wants to accomplish in the relationship, and the client learns from the lawyer a first impression of whether those goals are obtainable. Once the representation is under way, periodic counseling sessions with the client clarify the desires of the client, the methods the lawyer will use to try to attain those goals, and the lawyer's updated evaluation of the course and likely outcome of the matter. At every critical juncture in a client representation, the counseling skills of the lawyer are tested in getting client input and decision making on what the next step should be. And finally, counseling skills will eventually be utilized to determine what the ultimate resolution of the representation will be.

This chapter will explore the skill of counseling by suggesting three different yet overlapping models for client counseling. Reference will be made to the important professional responsibility issues that are intertwined with all of the application of counseling skills. Unlike the skills of client and witness interviewing, where the professional responsibility issues were discussed in a separate section of the respective chapters, we will discuss the professional responsibility issues of counseling in the context in which they occur.

6.2 Three Competing and Interlocking Models

Client autonomy and the lawyer's control of the client are two forces that battle in the attorney-client relationship. Balancing these is the key to skillful ethical litigating. Skillful counseling of the client is crucial for providing the right balance. There are three main models that lawyers use to try to balance client autonomy and lawyer control. First, there is the client-centered model, which attempts a neutral role for the lawyer and tries to ensure that the client makes an informed choice about the objectives of the lawsuit. Second, there is a surrogate or delegation model where the client, in essence, says he doesn't want to be bothered with the lawsuit and turns the lawyer into his surrogate. Under this model, the lawyer is trusted to make decisions on behalf of and in the best interest of the client, informing the client about the client's choices only in the most important and urgent circumstances. Third is a friendship model. As opposed to the first model, it assumes that the lawyer has a say in the choices that the client makes. This model prefers the lawyer take an active role in guiding the client to reach a decision, in much the same way that a wise friend might do. It requires some sense of trust or ongoing relationship between the lawyer and client and allows the lawyer to express his honest personal opinion about what is best.

We will describe each of the three models in more detail below, and make comments about their limitations.

6.2.1 The Client-Centered Approach

A. Preliminary Observations: The Conflict in the Relationship. Consider the traditional view of the relationship between an attorney and client. Many clients take the attitude that it is "their" lawsuit and their life, that they ought to be in control. In order to be in control, they need information that will allow them to reach informed decisions. Their need is for the lawyer to be an information retriever: "Find out what happened, and then analyze it and tell me what risks there are to my options." Even if the client has already done something illegal, he wants to be informed in order to decide how best to proceed. The client is not looking for moral approval from the lawyer. The client is looking for legal information about his options. A client with this point of view would be typical in a criminal case for the defendant and in business or commercial matters with sophisticated clients.

How, or even *should,* the lawyer take control of the situation when he has varying degrees of understanding of what has happened? Even once the lawyer knows his legal theory, factual theory, and theme, how does he inform the client about the persuasiveness of the theory or theme when its persuasiveness is in substantial doubt, or it depends to a great extent on the idiosyncrasies of the judge, jury, and/or negotiation opponent?

Even where the lawyer knows enough about what happened and what the law is, there is still a potential fundamental conflict of interest. If the client has a need and right to control the choices that will have lingering effects on his life, and if he has a right to run his business the way he sees fit, does the lawyer become an accessory to an illegal act where the client so chooses?

Herein lies the problem. Does the client have the right to control what risks he is willing to take, regardless of whether the law says he can take them? For example, what if in *Quinlan v. Kane Electronics*, Kane says to his lawyer, "I know that Quinlan and I had a deal that she would broker my business at the end of our Sunday meeting. Quite frankly, I was surprised that she never memorialized the agreement in writing the way that she said that she would. I must have gotten lucky because apparently she did send me a letter, but I never got it. At the bottom line, I never got the letter, she didn't do anything for me other than make a phone call, and she hasn't earned $300,000 or anything near it. Let's deny the agreement for now, see what evidence she has, and settle it for whatever we have to pay later." Does client autonomy extend that far?

Taking this extreme idea—the client who is willing to engage in borderline illegality, or at least walk over the line between truth and falsity to win—strongly demonstrates the conflict of interest that may exist between lawyer and client. Understanding this conflict should also shed light on the lesser, more usual, conflict between the lawyer's personal values and the legal values of the client.

Before answering this question it is necessary for practitioners to understand what might motivate the client to take this common, yet extreme, autonomy position. Many lawyers report that their clients pressure them to maximize returns at the worst possible time. For example, during deposition prep, or just before trial, clients will (and do) ask, "Who will know? Do we have to tell them? What if they don't ask? It's my life, and I'll decide." Obviously, these clients are responding to the panic and uncertainty of the moment. They are not necessarily thinking clearly and usefully about what is the right thing to do. They are running scared, and their fear must be dealt with.

In addition, modern discovery rules may encourage clients to see litigation as a game. Despite the recent change in the FRCP that provides for local rules regarding mandatory self-disclosure, typical discovery rules do not require that the sides volunteer their own weaknesses.[1] The obligation is on the opposing lawyer to ask the right question or make the right discovery request. It is very easy for the client to get the message that litigation has little to do with what really happened, and instead has to do with "what is the best story we can tell and get away with it?" The client may rationalize that the other side must be hiding quite a lot, because of all that the client is hiding. The objections, motions, and tactics they see from the lawyers during the discovery process itself may help produce the extreme reaction.

Even when the client hasn't expressed an extreme position, the lawyer may assume, because of other pressures, that the client takes the position that the lawyer should obtain the maximum benefit for the client, pushing the law and propriety to the limit to do so. The lawyer may feel pressure to do the spectacular, or magically make the bad fact and bad case go away. The pressure to maximize economic return to the client comes from a couple of different sources. It may initially come from the lawyer's altruistic desires to rescue the "poor client." It may come from the very nature of people who become lawyers: we are a very competitive lot. In addition, winning is the most tangible measure of success for the litigator, and as Vince Lombardi said, "Winning isn't everything, it's the only thing." If the lawyer wants to stand out above the crowd, even "winning" a majority of cases may not be enough. After all, any lawyer can win a case with favorable facts. The really good lawyer wins when no one else could. To some lawyers, the best compliment is for another lawyer to say, "If I'm ever in real trouble, I want you on my side." The implication is the best lawyers get results, even when the facts don't support them.

In any event, the lawyer's pressure to win may lead to false assumptions about the client's wishes and desires. This is one of the most common complaints about litigators. They assume that the client wants a no-holds-barred fight. If the fight ends up keeping clients from resolving their differences amicably and quickly, or once the client gets the bill and nets out the expenses, he may think better of the litigation tactics used and complain about his attorney, and all attorneys. In the language of economics, the client may have suddenly become "risk averse." In noneconomic terms, the clients may simply view the risks to their other relationships as more important than strictly the economic return.

On the other hand, there are significant market pressures that do legitimately drive the litigator to push for one-sided, win-at-all-cost results. If a client settles a case then finds out that he could have gotten more, or that other lawyers did better for a client in a "similar" situation, the litigator will often hear about it from the client. Personal injury lawyers are familiar with clients who compare what the lawyer says they should settle for with what the newspaper said someone else got. Also, the particular client may have high expectations. In the lingo of the law and economics literature, some clients are "risk preferrers." They may be willing to risk more than is "rational" for a shot at the large gain. In other words, assuming a "zeal-ous" representation posture may be partly driven by experi-ence with a particular client's expectations and desires.

In addition, the Kanes (clients who want to fight) of the world are not at all unusual. Many clients prefer to fight all comers in order to discourage others from filing suit. This is the successful position taken by some insurance companies. Their stringent position may make sense if they are seeking to maxi-mize their economic gain over the long run. To some clients, their legal position is a matter of judging the risks of getting caught in a particular mistake, as compared with the long-term costs of appearing weak.

The point is that the forces acting on the lawyer and the cli-ent during the counseling session are complex and partly incon-sistent. If the litigator *assumes* a particular motivation drives the client and gets it wrong, the client is very unhappy and feels that his autonomy and dignity have been violated. The real dan-ger in counseling the client about what risks he ought to take is in failure to communicate clearly and failure to find out about what motivates the client, and describe comprehensively the po-tential consequences of the client's proposed behavior.

How can the litigator balance client autonomy and the need for attorney control? How can the litigator act ethically, and still please the client?

B. Model Code of Professional Responsibility and Model Rules of Professional Conduct. While the model is clear, under Canon 7, about the lawyer's obligation to represent the client's objectives zealously, the question of who controls what is left to the Ethical Considerations. EC 7-7 reads:

> In certain areas of legal representation not affecting the merits of the cause or substantially prejudicing the rights of a client, a lawyer is entitled to make decisions on his own. But otherwise the authority to make decisions is exclusively that of the client, and if made within the framework of the law, such decisions are binding on his lawyer.

The same EC describes settlement offers, affirmative defenses, and pleas as examples of what the client controls. While not in the form of a Disciplinary Rule, the Code places the ultimate decision-making power with the client. And the Code's position is consistent with general agency principles that the agent must act in the best interests of the principal. Presumably the best interests of the principal are best determined by the principal herself.

The Model Rules of Professional Conduct clear up any potential ambiguity over whether the EC was meant to be mandatory with Rule 1.2, which amplifies the EC and provides:

> (a) A lawyer shall abide by a client's decisions concerning the objectives of representation subject to paragraphs (c), (d) and (e).

(c) deals with the lawyer's ability to limit client's objectives after consent with consultation, (d) deals with the lawyer's inability to consult with regard to criminal or fraudulent activity, (e) deals with the lawyer's inability to assist the client with conduct in violation of rules of professional conduct or contrary to law) and states that the lawyer "<u>shall consult with the client as to the means by which they are to be pursued</u>." (Our emphasis.)

Model Rule 1.2 contains a radical provision. The Model Rule is remarkable for the obligation it places on the lawyer with regard to counseling, including a requirement to counsel the client with regard to the means to be pursued in the representation. It forces the lawyer to consult with the client both as to objectives and means, and subjects the lawyer to discipline for failing to do so.

Before getting to the *means* issue in litigation, the conflict within 1.2 itself must be discussed. Model Rule 1.2 (d) provides the countervailing pressure:

(d) A lawyer shall not counsel a client to engage, or assist a client, in conduct that the lawyer knows is criminal or fraudulent, but a lawyer may discuss the legal consequences of any proposed course of conduct with a client and may counsel or assist a client to make a good faith effort to determine the validity, scope, meaning or application of the law.

One of the most difficult aspects of 1.2(d) is defining "counseling" or "assisting." The lawyer is told that he can discuss the legal consequences of proposed courses of conduct, but that he can't counsel or assist the illegal conduct. How can a lawyer provide the client information without assisting him to commit an illegal act?

Consider the following:

1. You represent Kane Electronics. Kane has discovered some old oil drums in the woods behind one of his sales installations. Kane asks you to tell him the amount of fines in this and surrounding jurisdictions for dumping without a permit. (Imagine that he has already estimated the costs of transporting various kinds of waste material and dumping the wastes into the appropriate dumps. He tells you he wants to have a cost comparison to determine if he will dump illegally.)

Comment 6 to the Model Rule gives only this guidance:

A lawyer is required to give an honest opinion about the actual consequences that appear likely to result from a client's conduct. The fact that a client uses advice in a course of action that is criminal or fraudulent does not, of itself, make a lawyer a party to the course of action. However, a lawyer may not knowingly assist a client in criminal or fraudulent conduct. There is a critical distinction between presenting an analysis of legal aspects of questionable conduct and recommending the means by which a crime or fraud might be committed with impunity. (Emphasis added)

Apply Comment 6 to the above example. The lawyer might feel that telling the client the amount of the fines allows him to make a cost comparison to determine whether (using economic savings only) to obey the law or not. Is the lawyer recommending the *means* by which the crime can be carried out? Probably not.

Yet the lawyer may feel uncomfortable that by providing the information he is empowering the client. The lawyer is giving the client legal knowledge that he otherwise might fear was more than sufficient to argue against the illegal choice. He may be increasing the chances that the client will do the illegal act. Isn't giving information assisting the client in committing an illegal act? For instance, where a client may be contemplating murder and planning an escape, should he be able to find out what countries do not have extradition treaties with the United States?

While the comment tells the lawyer there is an important distinction between counseling and assisting, what exactly is the distinction?

The issue for the lawyer is whether he must give the information that may increase the chances that his client will do the illegal thing. How does the lawyer make this decision? On the one hand, he can fall back on the Binder et al. distinction between consequences and alternatives, and give up to the client the freedom to chose the illegal and fraudulent choice. On the other hand, he can refuse to give the information if he feels strongly that the law ought to be obeyed.[2] And there is a third alternative. The lawyer could give the information, but engage in counseling to explore the morality of the decision. If the lawyer and client don't see eye to eye and the conflict would prohibit zealous representation by the lawyer, he can withdraw.

Under the second course of action, the lawyer ensures that the client follows the law. The result is paramount to the lawyer. Consider, however, how the contemplated action may affect the consistency with which a lawyer decides not to give the client information that encourages illegality. Consider the often-given example of the client/retail merchant who is deciding whether to stay open on Sunday in violation of the county's blue laws. The client wants to know what the fine amount is in order to determine whether to stay open on Sunday and risk the fine. In this instance, many lawyers and law students opt for giving the information. If pressed, they admit that they favor doing away with the blue laws because they force a particular religious observance on those who may not share the same religion. They favor "maximizing" client autonomy.

The implication, however, is that the lawyer is making his decision with reference to whether he agrees with the law. Where the decision criterion is whether the lawyer agrees with the law, he is saying something about his view of the law itself, morality, and ethics, for that matter.[3] If different lawyers feel different pressures, desires, or values moving them to give or withhold information, then different clients will certainly have different values, and even a different jurisprudence, that drive their willingness to obey or disobey the law. And it reveals how the lawyer's view of different types of laws can lead to a willingness to subvert the law. The lawyer appeals to some higher law (whether an interpretation of the Constitution, religious law, or natural law). In any event, his view of the worth of the blue law is important to the resolution of one of lawyering's most difficult questions: "How should the lawyer counsel the client about ethical and moral choices?" Tell the client, and leave it to the client.

Assuming for a moment that lawyers share a distrust for certain types of law, the question becomes why they do not tell their clients about a general obligation to obey the law, and how law is necessary for orderly management of the community's affairs. The consequence on society of disobeying the law is not discussed, presumably because it is a matter of personal morality. On the other hand, where the lawyer feels the law is important to society, the lawyer denies the client the ability to make the personal moral choice.

There are further reasons why the lawyer may choose only between telling and leaving it to the client, or not telling and keeping the client from making the decision. After all, how exactly does a lawyer counsel someone about morality? The whys and wherefores of moral counseling are often left undiscussed for two major reasons. First, morality, values, and religion are all believed to be matters of personal choice and personal freedom. Second, there may be no shared language for discussion of value choice.

Some lawyers, however, do try to talk at least on a basic level. Most situations of ethics and morality can be examined at the level of whether the decision maker is likely to be caught or found out, and thereafter pay in some way for his choice. The reference point assumes a personal egoist utilitarian ethic, balancing personal cost and personal gain. But what of other ethical systems of making moral choices? How are these systems to be discussed?

To determine whether to do "moral counseling," the lawyer must be clear on the nature of all counseling, whether legal, economic, psychological, or social. Once the lawyer has a clear model for other types of counseling, moral counseling shouldn't be much different or more difficult. As we shall see, it is often a matter of knowing what questions to ask, and how to draw the client into examining his decision comprehensively.

Whether the information is the lawyer's opinion (and should be kept to himself) or legal fact is often beside the point. A conflict between the lawyer and the client is most often due to a conflict over values. The ethical dilemma is most difficult where the lawyer's and client's values differ. The question is, How do the lawyer and client communicate to each other about their different value systems? Let's look at three different models and how they may answer the question.

6.2.1.1 Stages of the Client-Centered Approach

The Model Rules and Code are clear that the client "owns" the lawsuit and the lawyer serves the client's objectives. One viewpoint on the lawyer's job requires the lawyer to be centered on the client's problem, rather than on self-gains or societal goals. The lawyer is an aid in solving the problem, not the problem solver by himself. Under this view, the problem solver needs to be client-centered in order for the counseling to be truly professional.

- **Interviewing**

The first step in client-centered counseling is getting information. In this regard, dividing the skills of interviewing and counseling is somewhat artificial. Before any counseling can be done, the lawyer needs to be aware of all the relevant facts and feelings of both the client and himself. In addition, counseling will often lead to further interviewing, and further interviewing will often necessitate new or modified counseling.

- **Discussing Options and Alternatives**

Assuming, however, that the lawyer has gathered all the legally relevant information, there comes a time in the relationship when the information gathering stops and the lawyer and client turn their attention to problem solving. The Model Rules are the starting place for ethical problem solving through counseling. Model Rule 1.4(b) requires that a lawyer explain a matter to the extent reasonably necessary to permit the client to make informed decisions regarding the representation. In order for the client to make the decision, the lawyer must give the client his reasonable options or alternatives, and then try to predict the various consequences from each alternative.

To offer one alternative only is to substantially reduce the chances that the client will be the chooser. By analogy to the informed consent issue in medical malpractice, a doctor may be liable for battery when an operation is performed without making the patient aware of the treatment options and the side effects. Similarly, when faced with a series of choices (i.e., trial, negotiation, arbitration, mediation, or "drop-the-lawsuit"), simply presenting one option—going to trial, for instance—does not provide the client with the meaningful options to make an informed litigation decision.

Simply talking to the client in terms of options and alternatives, however, may not be ethically sufficient either. During the process of identifying options the lawyer may unconsciously take the decision away from the client. Imagine that the lawyer in a case involving a personal injury plaintiff leads off the counseling session as follows:

> Now, Mr. Brown, we could negotiate or we could go to trial. If you negotiate, you could save yourself a whole lot of grief and expense, not to mention the unpredictability of a jury, and you'll probably get close to what the jury is likely to give you (and I only get one third, as opposed to 40 percent if we try the case). But if you want to try the case, I'm ready. It's your choice.

Clearly, the lawyer favors settlement. But what is wrong with him giving his opinion? Isn't that what the client is paying for? The problem is that in cases where the client is not a strong-willed individual, he may not feel he can stand up to the lawyer and disagree. It's in these situations that the lawyer should be particularly careful to make sure the client both understands his options and makes the choice. Otherwise, the client may be very unhappy with the results and turn on the lawyer at a later date.

Imagine, for instance, that Mr. Brown really wants a chance to tell the judge and jury what happened. He's got medical insurance that covered his bills. What he wants is to make the defendant stop his behavior in the future, and he feels that a full trial will bring this about. His true "values" conflict with the lawyer's assumptions about what motivates his lawsuit. Money is of lesser importance to him than principle.

But if the client disagrees with the lawyer, why doesn't he say so? The client may be intimidated or may feel that the lawyer will not really try hard if he disagrees. Maybe he doesn't know can disagree. Whatever the reason, the danger of the lawyer imposing his judgment on the client is significant.

Importantly, the danger can be easily avoided. With very little effort, the lawyer can make sure that the decision is the client's own and avoid making incorrect assumptions. What follows is a series of suggestions for keeping the decision with the client:

- **Suggestions for Making the Client Own the Decision**

1. Describe to the client the agenda for the counseling session. If the lawyer's role is described, the client will be less likely to read too much meaning into what the lawyer is saying. The lawyer can make this clear by saying, for instance:

> Mr. Brown, I thought we could spend some time getting clear about where you want to head from here. My experience has been that if we can fully explore your options and the consequences of each option, then you will feel more comfortable with the way the litigation is resolved. What I suggest is that you and I identify your options, and then we brainstorm about which option is the best one.

2. Identify the options, ask if the client sees any others, and ask the client to choose which one he wants to talk about. For instance, the lawyer might say:

> I see three options. We can proceed to trial, negotiate, or drop the suit. Do you see any others? Okay, which one do you want to talk about?

By adopting the above as standard operating procedure, the lawyer can keep his own opinions from the client, once the client accepts the fact that he needs to make the decision and starts to work at solving it. The client, however, may not buy the lawyer's agenda. He may not have the time or interest for making the decision and may (and often does) ask, "Well, what do you think I ought to do?"

A word of caution is important here. Before the lawyer jumps in and takes over the decision, he should recognize what motivates the question. Many people hate to make tough decisions. They would just as soon have someone else to blame. Or they don't like the stress of making a decision, or how they feel when they have to make one.

On the other hand, they may misunderstand and perceive that the lawyer is trying to sell them something. They want information, and then they want to go home where they can make the decision in private or with friends and family. In this case, the lawyer needs to be their partner, friend, and counselor to whom they turn when they make tough decisions. The lawyer has both information and experience with helping people reach decisions. He is the ideal person to pick up pieces of misinformation, calm the overemotional response, and help the client to look at the situation comprehensively.

Some clients, though fewer than most lawyers assume, are in control, for the most part, of their litigation problem and only want legal information. They only want the lawyer's frank input, and they will go away and make the decision on their own. Some like a good adversarial give-and-take to help them clarify their thinking. They want the lawyer to take a position against which they can argue. After the "fight" with the lawyer over what should be done, the client is more ready to make the decision. Once again, this kind of client is rare.

When the client does want the lawyer's opinion, it is important to find out why. Different levels of sophistication, behavioral preferences for making decisions, or different client values require different responses from the lawyer. If the client simply wants to put the decision off on the lawyer without taking ownership of the problem, then the lawyer may want to "make" the client work some first before giving his opinion. If the client is strong-willed and simply wants the lawyer's opinion in order to judge the lawyer's bias in the information that will follow, then giving the opinion will not interfere with taking ownership of the decision.

One option for dealing with the client's expectation is for the lawyer to give his opinion but explain how it may be biased. This option falls in the general advice category "if in doubt, honesty isn't a bad place to start." For instance, the lawyer might say

> Mr. Brown, if it were my lawsuit, I'd try to reach a settlement, but you need to understand that I'm looking at this partly from time savings versus dollar return to me. I'm wondering whether the increased trial preparation time will produce a sufficiently greater return at trial than what we can get now. On the other hand, only you know how you would feel if you gave up going to trial. So let's consider my opinion for what it is, just my opinion, and talk about what is likely to happen, assuming you pick various alternatives. After all, it's your decision to live with, not mine, and my job is to work as hard as I can to see you get what you want.

3. Plan to Identify and Discuss Legal, Economic, and Social/Psychological Consequences

Do some planning and preparation before your counseling session. First and foremost you should identify areas where the client has superior information about the effects of the various decisions.

Binder, Bergman, and Price, in their book *Lawyer as Counselor*, suggest that lawyers look for categories of information about which the client has superior information. While the lawyer has the superior information base about the law and the legal setting, the client usually has superior knowledge about the economic, social, psychological, and moral/religious effects of the decision.

Binder et al. suggest a prepared chart for that purpose with alternatives running along the side, and legal, economic, and social/other factors running across the top. Whether you develop, chart, and write down things that the client says in the appropriate box, or simply ensure that each factor is discussed is a matter of interviewing preference. What is essential is for the lawyer to see that the economic impact of the decision is something about which the client usually has much better information.

While the lawyer may be able to predict the dollar value of the litigation, usually only the client knows the cash flow effect, how the litigation affects other sources of income he might have, what the tax effect will be, how money spent on litigation affects other opportunities the client may have, etc. The client may, however, be seeking economic information. The client may want to know what the jury will award, or what the judge will order by way of a fine. The lawyer, in this case, is giving quasi-legal advice that depends for its legitimacy on the lawyer's experience in similar matters, or information sources that help predict the economic consequences.

Binder et al. point out, given this economic/legal information, that the client often already possesses superior information concerning the economic consequences of various choices. The client may know better what an order granting him child custody will cause in the way of expenses. Or, the client may know how a product recall will affect his company's bottom line. For the lawyer to assume he has greater information about economic consequences can lead to embarrassing and bad advice.

The lawyer is not without a role, however. The lawyer's job in this area is to clarify the client's thinking about the economic consequences. The client may not be thinking comprehensively about the problem. His emotions or preoccupation with one aspect of the problem may cause him to lose sight of the big picture. The lawyer should look out for this possibility, and if he is surprised by the outcome or finds some of the client's reasoning inappropriate and irrational, seek to clarify the client's understanding of the problem.

It is important at this stage for the lawyer to be clear with the client about what the lawyer is doing. Without an explanation of the lawyer's clarifying role, the client could take the lawyer's questions as disagreement with the client's choice. If Kane says, "I never want to settle" and the lawyer responds, "Why do you say that?" Kane may "hear" that his lawyer disagrees with his statement. To protect against being misunderstood, the lawyer must first describe his questioning role and ask the client to clarify his reasoning in order to help the client to be careful and comprehensive in his thinking. The lawyer can ask questions such as, "Won't a fair settlement send an effective message to the market? What amount might do that short of a trial? What is the value of an apology? What if it were public?" In other words, "Is your picture of settlements too narrowly drawn?"

5. Discuss Psychological and Moral Consequences through Discussion of Feelings

Ask how the client feels about an option, as well as what he thinks about it. Often what drives an initial emotional, passionate decision to litigate is a fear of the economic effect of the opposition's behavior. Depending on whether that economic impact is actualized, the passion for the litigation may either increase (where the economic situation becomes more desperate), or decrease (where the supposed costs of the opposition's behavior never materialize, or other opportunities make the significance of litigation diminish). The client's emotional feelings are key to understanding his position.

In addition, the lawyer must realize that the client bears the primary social, psychological, and even moral/religious effects of the litigation. After all, it is the client who must live with having sued and received nothing, or having settled for a moderate sum which runs out when college tuition costs are higher than expected. It is the client who must decide whether spousal support should be higher, or whether child support should be higher and risk a custody fight. Each of these decisions affects the client's family, social, and psychological welfare, as well as the client's economic welfare. Asking how each option will affect significant relationships, family, friends, business, or community will clarify these other concerns for the client.

In addition, we come full circle to the earlier issue of counseling about morality and religious issues. But now we should have a model in place for discussing these topics. The lawyer should gain access to this information by asking how the clients feel about their decisions, as well as how they think about them. This will produce a jumble of social, psychological, and moral and religious reasoning. This reasoning needs to be clarified for the benefit of the clients, so that they understand the effects of their choices, and come to "know" what is right for them to do. Just as the medical profession needs to respect the religious patient who doesn't want a blood transfusion, and sets up procedures to identify these patients, lawyers should be on the lookout for feelings, beliefs, and attitudes that change the set of solutions that are available to their clients. Just as in the area of economic consequences, it would be wrong for the lawyer to think that he brings no information to the counseling session on social, moral, and psychological issues. The lawyer, as he practices law, should be learning from experience the effects that clients' decisions have on their later level of satisfaction. The lawyer should be able to offer advice based on what he has experienced or been told of the reaction clients may have to trial or to dropping or settling cases. In fact, referring to this experience, or referring to what the lawyer has been told, is key to raising some of the important social and moral issues and helping clients to clarify their thinking. The lawyer might say

> My experience has been (or, in discussions with other legal counselors, I've heard) that some clients wished that they hadn't gone ahead with trial. They feel that taking the witness stand made them destroy all chances to reconcile with the other side. They now wish they had sought a settlement. How do you think you would feel if you did win at trial? Would there be any costs to your future relationship with the other side that you would be worried about?

To borrow from the language of decision-making theory, the lawyer facilitates the client's decision by getting the client to imagine that he has made each decision and is living with the consequences. The counselor enables the client to "try on" the decision, to see if it feels right and fits.

Binder and Berman suggest that the lawyer see his role as both giving and clarifying information. The lawyer's purpose is not to manipulate the client to reach the decision the lawyer thinks is right for the client. The lawyer primarily gives information about the legal consequences of the client's various choices, but also helps the client clarify his own values in order to increase chances that he will get maximum satisfaction from his decision.

6.2.1.2 Problems Using the Client-Centered Approach

There are, however a number of problems that develop when lawyers use the client-centered model. These are not necessarily problems with the model but they are brought about by the unreflective and rote use of any allegedly objective and neutral informed-consent model.[4] A description of some of the more obvious problems that may develop follows.

1. The Problem of Lawyer Lowballing

The lawyer must be careful neither to lowball the client, nor overvalue the client's legal position. Of the two potential problems, lowballing is the more common ethical pitfall. Lowballing refers to some lawyers' practice of telling clients that their chances of success in court are very low in order to please the client when the lawyer reaches a negotiated settlement of more than what he initially said the case was worth. The negotiated settlement makes the lawyer look like a tough bargainer, and the client is thankful and surprised by the amount of settlement. The lawyer guards against the possibility of valuing the case too optimistically, which may result in the client being disappointed and the lawyer looking like he failed. To protect against client disappointment, some lawyers lowball.

Lowballing denies the client his ability to make his own decision about the lawsuit. The lawyer has, in effect, made the decision for him. Without an accurate assessment of the legal status of the case, the client may be too willing to settle, and decide to settle too low. The decision to settle is not informed.

2. Giving the Client the Bad News

Another ethical problem can arise because the litigator doesn't want to be the bearer of bad news. In fact, this is likely with a client like Kane. After all, Kane may have come to the interview to test the lawyer and the law firm to see if it was tough enough to handle his litigation. Imagine that Kane had been dissatisfied with his previous law firm in his case against Quinlan. They thought he should settle for around $200,000. Their recommendation led to Kane's leaving that firm and bringing the representation to the current firm. After the case has been litigated, it looks like the old firm's evaluation of the lawsuit was about right. How does the lawyer deliver this "bad news" without losing the client?

The lawyer may be severely tempted to let the lawsuit run its course, so that the bad news comes from the court and jury rather than from the lawyer. And, despite the well-known advice to the contrary, sometimes people do kill the messenger. Once again, the lawyer needs to understand that the client has a right to the information so he can make an informed choice. And the skillful counselor should be able to give the information in a way that doesn't risk the relationship. To do this, the lawyer needs to make sure that the client understands that the litigation is the client's, brought about by the client's actions. The client needs to see the lawyer as a counselor, not the judge. The lawyer can make these roles clear by describing the counseling process (see section 6.2.1.1.), and by taking care with his language. He needs to be careful to both develop his language of prediction, and transfer any value judgments to be made onto the backs of the true decision makers. For instance, the lawyer might say:

> Mr. Kane, I would predict three likely outcomes at trial. First, and this in my judgment is most likely, the jury could decide against you, probably in the range of $200,000 to $250,000 and the judge and/or Court of Appeals would uphold their decision. I would estimate our total litigation costs for trial and appeal, including attorney's fees, to be about $90,000. On the other hand, if we can convince the jury that Ms. Quinlan never had any agreement with you, that she had virtually nothing to do with the sale of your company, and that she is trying to take advantage of happenstance, the jury could side with us completely. As the case stands right now, I'd say we don't really have the goods on that, and it would depend on how the jury viewed both you and Ms. Quinlan and I should say she appeared to be a witness the jury would find believable during her deposition. Finally, there is a chance that the jury

and judge could side completely with Quinlan and decide that you acted in a fraudulent way in this matter and really hit you with big damages, one to two million dollars, maybe more. The other side may be able to make you out to be a cutthroat businessman trying to take advantage of a hard-working woman like Ms. Quinlan who did put you together with the company that bought you out. I'd say the chances of the first result are about 60 percent, and the chances of the second two are about 20 percent each.

Of course, some lawyers would be uncomfortable putting percentages on the outcome. They might prefer to talk in terms of "most likely" and "least likely" results. In either case, the client has been given the lawyer's frank opinion about what will happen at trial so the client can decide what risks he wants to take. Or, with Lawrence in a criminal case, the lawyer might say:

Mr. Lawrence, I would say your chances of a not guilty verdict are about 50/50. On the one hand, the jury could decide that the victim was too scared to be able to identify you. We will show how dark it was and how quickly it happened. Because of your criminal record, I'd recommend you not take the stand. Their case comes down to a very shaky identification and suggestive lineup. On the other hand, the prosecution will get the jury to be frightened by the theft, and believe the victim, who is very forthright, even though the identification was suggestive.

The language of prediction is also related to the jury's role in the decision. The lawyer remains neutral. In addition, the lawyer is not attacking the client's values, but the opposition is. It is the opposing attorney who is calling Kane fraudulent, not Kane's lawyer, at least not yet. Similarly, it is the prosecutor, not the lawyer, who is making the case against the client. The client is thereafter drawn into a discussion of the lawyer's reasoning and prediction process, and is given the chance to understand the lawyer's calculations of the outcome at trial. A key technique to the discussion is for it not to be about who is right about the value of the case, but to be future-looking and to identify the third-party decision maker who will ultimately decide.

The lawyer's goal need not be to bring to the client a total understanding of his reasoning. After all, part of the reasoning process is three years of legal education and more years of practice experience. Yet the client is entitled to substantial understanding of the forces that go into the lawyer's opinion. Just as the patient should be encouraged to inquire into why the doctor is recommending an option, similarly, the client should have the same opportunity to inquire of the lawyer. The patient doesn't need to know exactly the basis of the doctor's "percentage of recovery" opinion, whether based on epidemiological studies or on some other basis. The client doesn't need to know, either, unless he asks whether the jury prediction comes from a comparison of similar cases, or from jury verdict research, or from the attorney's intuition. The client does need to have some information about where the lawyer predicts the case will end up and why. That is what the client is paying for.

The client may force the issue further. The client might ask why the lawyer feels that the jury might see Kane as lying. The client might express a willingness to improve his story to help the case. Or, Lawrence might say, "How about if I get my girlfriend to say I was with her at the time of the theft." Then what is the lawyer to do?

3. Taking Ethical Control of the Case

While we have discussed certain philosophical arguments about the difficulties of counseling a client who wants to do something illegal or at least unethical, the lawyer must understand the particular risks of counseling or assisting a client in borderline illegal activity. At the risk of stating the obvious, if the Model Rules won't get you, malpractice and criminal actions will. Recent litigation demonstrates that when clients get caught doing something illegal, one option is for them to blame their lawyers for advising them that it was all right to do so. The files are opened, and the client tries to prove his lawyer was to blame. In addition, in the area of criminal law practice involving drugs and drug defendants, the client might even be a plant—an undercover law enforcement officer who is testing the lawyer's ethics. The risk to the lawyer is real and great—his license and more can hang in the balance.

If the client's values have been clarified to the extent that they express a willingness to do whatever is necessary to win, then the lawyer ought to have no hesitation in taking control. The lawyer doesn't need to be angry or "holier than thou," just clear. He can start with self-interest appeals, move to altruistic appeals, and finally make threats, as ways of persuading the client. The lawyer might say:

> Mr. Kane, are you saying that you would be willing to lie or ask someone else to lie to win the lawsuit? Mr. Kane, I need to be clear with you about this from here on out. You don't want to commit perjury. Not only is it my experience that the jury will know, and that the other side will make you pay during their cross-examination, but you risk a criminal prosecution. You risk your reputation and good standing in the community.

> [If this doesn't bring ready agreement from the client] In addition, Mr. Kane, you surely don't want to unfairly deny to Ms. Quinlan her right to a fair trial; after all, you have made quite a lot in selling your business and Ms. Quinlan's claimed fee is less than you could have paid a broker.

> [If this doesn't do it] Mr. Kane, I risk losing my license if I put either of you on the stand when I know you are going to lie. While your case is important, I'm sure you understand that I have other obligations, like continued employment and reputation, that I have to look out for. If you insist on taking the stand and lying, I have to withdraw right now.

Similarly, with Mr. Lawrence, the lawyer needs to be clear: "I can't suborn perjury. If she gets up and I know she'll tell I lie, I have to tell the court. Then where are we?"

The Model Rules and Code each provide that the lawyer must take ethical control of the litigation to protect the integrity of the process. Model Rule 3.4 (b) reads:

> A lawyer shall not:

> (b) falsify evidence, counsel or assist a witness to testify falsely, or offer an inducement to a witness that is prohibited by law;

DR 7-102 (A)(6) reads,

> (6) . . . a lawyer shall not participate in the creation or preservation of evidence when he knows or it is obvious that the evidence is false.

The Code and Model Rules raise the obligation to withdraw before suborning perjury. And the Comments to the Model Rules of Professional Conduct make clear that the ultimate loyalty of the lawyer in such a circumstance is to the judicial system. If the lawyer cannot persuade the client to do the right thing, the lawyer must withdraw, and if withdrawal is not allowed by the judge, the lawyer cannot participate in the creation of false testimony. If false testimony is nonetheless given, the lawyer must inform the judge as to what has occurred.

The problem is that lawsuits have bad facts in them. Each side has them. That is often why there is a lawsuit in the first place. The lawyers' job is to characterize and argue zealously about the meaning of their clients' facts. But they must take control and draw the line at the creation of new facts.

There is one last litigation way out of the dilemma of the bad fact. While the obligation to tell the truth applies at trial, what about during the negotiation? Can the lawyer hide the bad facts of the full story during the negotiation, and settle his way out of the problem?

Whether the lawyer has an obligation to tell the other lawyer about bad facts, he should tell his own client during the prenegotiation counseling session. Without full disclosure, the client can't make an informed decision on the amount he is willing to settle for.

4. The Client May Want More from the Lawyer

There is a greater need from some clients for the lawyer to be more than just a neutral information provider and/or warrior for the client. The client may want the lawyer to actually care about whether the client is doing the "right" thing. The client may want "wisdom" from the lawyer. After all, the lawyer presumably has experience with clients who have been in similar situations. How did these clients feel after their suits? Were these clients' victories hollow? Did a win in a lawsuit have repercussions that the clients need to know about in order to make a truly informed decision? Did they win the lawsuit but lose market share? Did they win short-term market share, but lose customer loyalty? In the case of Kane, did he defend the lawsuit successfully only to be unable to enter into informal business relations with others after the lawsuit? In litigation between business partners, is it better for a party to win the case but lose a valuable business relationship? A lawsuit may actually present an opportunity to become closer business allies, rather than deadly enemies.

Many clients want their lawyers to care about these questions. They want to be engaged in a conversation with a person who really understands their business and can speak wisely and forcefully about the choices that matter most to the client. They want a lawyer who shares with them a different model for their working relationship. One danger to the client-centered model is for the lawyer to "wash his hands" of the client's decision too early.

6.2.2 Surrogate or Delegation Model

A second model for lawyer-client decision making is for the clients to simply delegate to the lawyer the power to make decisions for them, "in their best interests." Consider the very reasonable position that clients simply don't want to know or worry about the litigation. "You, the lawyer, are getting paid a lot of money to handle my legal matters. I have other things to worry about. You make the decisions that arise out of the legal issues and just keep me informed as we go along. I'll pay you to do my worrying, and I'll get some sleep tonight."

There is a real, but open question whether a client can actually delegate to a lawyer the right to make decisions regarding the objective of a representation, or whether he can expressly or impliedly waive the MRPC Rule 1.4 right to be counseled regarding decisions to be made in a representation. But the seeking of this kind of relationship is not uncommon. It can arise in the federal regulatory area, where clients simply want the government to interfere with their business as little as possible. They hire lawyers who will fight to get the EPA, SEC, FTC off their backs. They have been accused of violating some regulation and they want the lawyer to make it go away.

The surrogate model can affect, dramatically, what information you present the client and whether one of the lawyer's legitimate concerns is protecting the client from knowing too much. This kind of relationship, however, runs some real risks. Its exact nature needs to be well documented. Even then, when particular issues arise that go to the very heart of the client's needs, the lawyer must be careful that he is up-to-date on the client's best interests. To the extent that the client's interests in the marketplace may change, or the client's method and persona may have to vary, depending on the particular person he is dealing with, the lawyer runs the risk of getting away from the delegated authority he presumes he has.

6.2.2.1 Risks in Using the Surrogate Model
1. Accentuating the Game of Hiding Information

Clients may also see it is to their advantage to have an advocate who doesn't know what is really going on. Such knowledge of the "bad" facts or sloppy management may affect the lawyer's willingness to fight vigorously for the client. Not telling all to the lawyers also protects the lawyers from knowing that they are lying when they are asked questions by the government about what the client knows or is or has done. These situations are analogous to the criminal defense lawyer who starts off his interview with his client by saying, "I don't want to know what happened, I just want to know what story you want me to tell." The interviewing techniques accentuate the client's view that lying is permissible and may be partly responsible for giving all criminal attorneys a bad name.

2. Difficulty Investigating Internally

Many lawyers who are treated as surrogate/warriors report that they have a hard time getting information from the client about who knows what and when they knew it. Their relationship with in-house counsel is crucial. In-house counsel feed the litigator what he needs, and can closely control the lawyer's access to information.

3. Lawyer Being Seen as a Warrior Who Fights More for Self Than for the Client

Again, there is a certain logic to the delegation/surrogate model. The clients could rightfully believe that they get their wise counseling from in-house counsel. They have also done the business calculation and determined that it is better to fight than build relationships. The management may believe that it is always better to fight aggressively in "these kinds of cases" so that they have a policy in place that doesn't need to be rethought each time they are involved in litigation. Yet the unintended effect on the lawyer-client relationship can be profound. The lawyer can believe that his continued success with the client is to win at all costs. He may have not been privy to the thinking behind the policy to fight and therefore assume that the clients are amoral at best, and affirmatively sociopathic, at worst. This can lead to the lawyer/associates not understanding or respecting the client's thinking, which can in turn lead to an undue focus on winning at all costs. After a while it may be hard to get sufficient meaning and reward from "criminal defense" work. The hired-gun mentality can take over. Economic reward can become the sole reward for the lawyer, which can be insufficient for long-term lawyer satisfaction about what the lawyer is doing.

The lawyer can be affected in another way. The lawyer may in turn start giving the client limited options with limited information. The lawyer may become a "yes man," because even where he's wrong the lawyer wins by increasing control. Or the lawyer becomes unreasonably risk-averse in order to show how much he's protecting the client. In these ways the lawyer can take the delegation of authority and use it to his own economic advantage.

These unintended long-term effects on the lawyer and client have to be watched carefully and continually monitored. It may be why there is substantial dissatisfaction among lawyers in what it is that they do. It may also be why the Model Rules require the lawyer to keep the client reasonably informed about the means and objectives of the lawsuit.

These are not hypothetical matters. Federal Judge Ann Williams reports her repeated experience with clients who have stopped listening to their lawyers. The attitude she sees from the corporate client is too often a "not on my watch" attitude. In other words, "I pay you lawyers a lot of money to make sure that I don't look bad. Make the litigation go away so I won't get in trouble with the board." Often, then, the judge must play the role of the legal adviser. She must be the one that says, "You have real exposure here and you need to go to your board and tell them so." Somehow the client hasn't been able to hear this advice from his lawyer, either because the lawyer has been unwilling to be the bearer of bad news or because the management simply doesn't see their lawyer as being an unbiased advice giver.

If the lawyer becomes too much of a lone ranger, the lawyer may not have a sufficient relationship with the client to be heard when he has to give the client independent advice that the client needs to hear.

6.2.3 Friendship Model

A final model that can structure the lawyer-client relationship is lawyer as friend. We first describe some of its underlying assumptions. Second, we describe what techniques the lawyer might use in counseling the client. Finally, we will describe some of its uses, benefits, and risks.

6.2.3.1 Some Underlying Assumptions

Many have argued that the previous two models for the lawyer-client relationship are inadequate, and unduly constrain the relationship. The criticisms are basically threefold: First, the earlier models assume that the client is unable to make decisions for himself because neither lawyer nor client can truly understand each other's motives. Second, the earlier models cause each of the parties to overly distrust the opposing party. Third, the earlier models underestimate the client's altruistic motives.

But how does thinking of the lawyer as the friend, rather than as a lawyer/problem solver, help to resolve some of these difficulties? To answer that question takes some imagination, and some new assumptions.[5] Let's see where they might lead.

First, imagine yourself in need of a listener, not a problem solver. Imagine that you have a moral or ethical dilemma, and you want someone to be your mirror or sounding board in order for you to clarify your own thinking about a particular problem. Imagine that there are no laws that constrain your behavior. Imagine instead that you could make out your own solutions to your dilemma, once you had thought comprehensively about it and fully informed yourself about the matter. How would you then come to a solution to your problem and what skills would you need to assist someone else to do so?

6.2.3.2 Four Steps to Friendly Counseling
1. Get/Listen

Psychiatrist Tom Rusk contends that the skill of listening is essential to ethical and effective counseling. The issue is whether listening can be taught. The first thing to do is persuade yourself that listening is of vital importance to reaching an understanding of the client's situation, and that reaching an understanding of another's point of view is crucial to friendship. There are a number of reasons why listening is important. First, it may be your most important tool for showing your intelligence. Maude Pervere reports that studies in leadership at Stanford found that study participants most highly correlated a leader's ability to listen with his or her intelligence. This makes sense, in a narcissistic way. Doesn't it make sense that we would believe someone else was intelligent who listened to what we had to say and considered it valuable? How often have you heard the advice that when you are seeking a job you should ask a lot of questions so that the interviewer fondly recalls the interview with you because he did all of the talking? Think how flattered you are when a teacher remembers, in class, something you said or wrote. Similarly, your ability to demonstrate that you have listened carefully to what the client has said implies that you have some wise characteristics:

1. gather information before you rush to judgment;
2. think comprehensively before expressing an opinion;
3. manage your own emotional reactions; and
4. focus carefully on the task at hand.

In other words, you exhibit wisdom.

In addition, listening serves a client/relationship purpose. It allows for catharsis. It respects the problem-solving abilities of the speaker. It shares the responsibility for the problem with the one who owns it.

It is important to analyze what gets in the way of listening. Our tendency is to blame the speaker or teacher for our own failure. And at times the responsibility does reside with the client speaker. But major problems lie with the listener. They can be summarized as "self-consciousness." Most important is the fear of failure. We are afraid we will not be able to help, or that our incompetence will be discovered. Additionally, we deal with personal distractions, conflicts of interest and value conflicts, perceived irrelevancies, case threat, ego threat, etiquette barriers, and role expectations.

One way to deal with these distractions is to reorient yourself at the counseling/interviewing stage about who owns the problem. Consider how differently you would react if the client simply said, "Look, what I want is for you to just listen. I don't want your advice. I don't want you to solve my problem for me. All I want is for you to act as my mirror. Help me hear back what I think, and how I feel about my situation. You can do this best by simply listening to what I have to say."

Of course, in the end, many clients do not want this. But many do. And most do in the initial stages of their relationship with you. They are often unsure about what they should do, and that comes from their lack of knowledge about the legal system and from their lack of knowledge about themselves as part of the legal problem they are dealing with.

Consider your own vulnerability when you go to make a major purchase—for example, a home or a car. What do you want? What do you need? What can you afford? What are the differences among these three? What role does your view of yourself and all its complexity play in your answer to these questions? If the decision is truly yours to make, think what little help you need from the real estate agent or the car salesman, at least in that part of the decision which involves what to do.

If the problem-solving role is removed, what listening characteristics start to surface? First, the listener can better quiet fears of inadequacy. After all, the problem is not his to solve. The listener need only attend to whether the speaker is clear, consistent, specific, or conflicted, and attend to how he is feeling about the matter. It is often within the emotional responses that information that the client will need most help in sorting out is found.

Think of the range of emotions clients might have concerning their various legal problems. How might their different emotional states affect the direction they might take in resolving their particular problems? The following chart is taken from Madelyn Burly-Allen's *Listening, The Forgotten Skill*, 2d ed. (1995), p. 131.

	Anger	Elation	Depression	Fear
Mild	Annoyed Bothered Bugged Peeved Irritated	Glad Pleased Amused Contented Comfortable Surprised Relieved Confident	Unsure Confused Bored Resigned Disappointed Discontented Apathetic Hurt	Uneasy Tense Concerned Anxious Apprehensive Worried
Moderate	Disgusted Harassed Resentful Mad Put upon Set up	Cheerful Delighted Happy Up Elated Great Hopeful Eager Anticipating	Discouraged Drained Distressed Down Unhappy Burdened Sad	Alarmed Shook Threatened Afraid Scared Frightened
Intense	Angry Contemptuous Hostile Hot Burned Furious	Joyful Excited Enthusiastic Turned on Moved Enthralled Free Proud Fulfilled Fascinated Titillated Engrossing Absorbing	Miserable Ashamed Crushed Humiliated Hopeless Despairing Anguished	Panicky Overwhelmed Petrified Terrified Terror- stricken

Here, we encounter advanced empathy. In order to hear, see, and feel these emotions in others, lawyers need to be skilled in:

Quieting the self
Being attentive
Listening with ears, eyes, and insides
Clarifying
Restating
Reflecting
Summarizing
Validating
Encouraging

They need to resist the temptation to take over and problem-solve by:

Turning off the filters

Not agreeing

Not advising

Not arguing

Not correcting

Not questioning

So what does this mean during a counseling session? Dr. Tom Rusk, in *The Power of Ethical Persuasion*, argues that the ability to listen is the key to reaching an ethical understanding with another person. Friends seek ethical understanding from each other. Rusk suggests that you confine yourself strictly to the following tasks:

1. Establish that your immediate goal is mutual understanding, not problem solving.

2. Elicit the other person's thoughts, feelings, and desires about the subject at hand.

3. Ask for the other person's help in understanding him or her. Try not to defend or disagree.

4. Repeat the other person's position in your own words to show you understand.

5. Ask the other person to correct your understanding, and keep restating his or her position.

6. Refer back to your position only to keep things going.

7. Repeat steps 1 through 6 until the other person unreservedly agrees that you understand his or her position.

2. Give

The next part of the friendship model is for the friend to care enough to give his perspective on the problem. This model is different from the standard objective presentation of alternatives and consequences. It requires instead subjective input on the part of the lawyer. It requires that the lawyer "care" whether the client reaches the "right" decision for the client.

What exactly is the "care perspective," and what are its benefits?[6] "Care perspective" is described as a moral orientation and a mode of moral thinking that stands in contrast to the justice orientation. The language of the care perspective is still evolving and is admittedly fuzzy. A succinct description comes from A. L. Carse. Carse says that, according to Carol Gilligan,

[T]he justice orientation construes the moral point of view as [1] an impartial point of view, [2] which understands particular moral judgments as derived from abstract and universal principles, [3] which sees moral judgment as essentially dispassionate rather than passionate, and [4] it emphasizes individual rights and norms of formal equality and reciprocity in modeling our moral relationships. By contrast, the care orientation [1] rejects impartiality as an essential mark of the moral, [2] understands moral judgments as situation-attuned perceptions sensitive to others' needs and to the dynamics of particular relationships, [3] construes moral reasoning as involving empathy and concern, and [4] emphasizes norms of responsiveness and responsibility in our relationships with others.[7]

What would a decision-making process that is modeled on care look like, and how would such a process resist the constraints that arise from the role-playing hierarchical model? An individual approaching the previous case from the care perspective would proceed as follows.[8] First, the provider/counselor would identify the persons involved in interdependent relationships in this situation. For the legal practitioner, it violates an exclusive focus on the client. The opinions of all persons in significant relationships with the one cared for are considered. The lawyer's opinion is also included, because he's also in a significant relationship by virtue of his involvement with the client.

The second step of the friend/decision-making process is the most radical. It identifies the central issue of care, and addresses what caring demands in this particular situation, with these particular persons, to strengthen (or at least maintain) their primary relationships and avoid hurt and harm. This step can only be taken after identifying the interdependent parties and their primary relationships. One then considers the view of both the client and those in the other relationships—customers, employees, suppliers, shareholders, family, or friends.

These steps provide for a subjectivity that friendship requires. It allows for moral self-expression. It necessitates a true understanding of, and reflection upon, the feelings of others, yet doesn't designate to one individual or another the moral responsibility for the decision. The role taken by the lawyer is more of a facilitator of the discussion, or consensus builder, than problem solver.

3. Merge

Third, a friend should discuss and think through all possible alternative activities to determine which are "loving and just" to those who are involved. They should ask how the action will affect each person's life, including their shared life together. The perspective of the friend/counselor arises from this attempt to enter into and understand the context of the situation. The friend/counselor enters the situation and participates as one caring, whose view is to be communicated to the parties involved and carefully considered. Again, any actions proposed, and the consequences of proposed alternatives, are evaluated in terms of whether they are "loving and just" for the individuals and their shared life.[9]

A friend/counselor doesn't necessarily go along with the client's decision. In this model, the friend takes moral responsibility for whether he joins the client's decision. If the friend cannot, then he withdraws from the partnership. The friendship model protects the lawyer from necessarily joining in every client's ventures. It allows for the moral self to discuss, and disagree, on courses of action.

4. Go

Finally, assuming a successful merger has been reached, the involved parties should jointly select an acceptable alternative, anticipate objections and answer them, and devise a workable plan for carrying out the proposed solution.[10] After the decision is carried out, it is also helpful to evaluate its adequacy. The friendship/lawyer model assumes that this "Listen, Give, Merge, Go" model will create more meaningful lawyer-client relationships, which will better represent the holistic client and build more shared decision making. The aim is that both the practice of law and client satisfaction will be more enhanced.[11]

**Four Steps to
Friendship Counseling**

1. Get/Listen
2. Give
3. Merge
4. Go

6.3 Choosing the Right Model for the Client and the Situation

It is important to recognize that, beyond their practical limitations, surrogate and friendship models have Code of Professional Responsibility limitations. The Model Rules of Responsibility, Rule 1. 2, prohibit the extreme power structure of a "hired gun surrogate" model by requiring that a lawyer "consult with the client as to the means by which [client objectives] are to be pursued." Rule 1.4 also states that a lawyer (a) "shall keep a client reasonably informed about the status of a matter" and (b) "shall explain a matter to the extent reasonably necessary to permit the client to make informed decisions regarding the representation." Of course, if the client doesn't want to know, who is to complain? But if the client changes his mind, then the Model Rules become a sword against the lawyer, a risk of which the surrogate lawyer should be particularly wary.

Regarding the friendship model, the lawyer's concern about gathering salient facts and getting input from various other parties in relationships with the client shouldn't overstep client confidentiality requirements. Model Rule 1.6 obligates the lawyer to protect the confidences of the client. Comment 1 to Model Rule 1.3 also limits the friendship model: "A lawyer should pursue a matter on behalf of a client despite opposition, obstruction or personal inconvenience to the lawyer, and may take whatever lawful and ethical measures are required to vindicate a client's cause or endeavor. A lawyer should act with commitment and dedication to the interests of the client and with zeal in advocacy upon the client's behalf." In other words, the merger must not produce lukewarm, half-hearted representation, nor be a heavy-handed attempt by the lawyer to impose his morality on the client.

Having said this, the friendship model can be an attractive alternative for some clients. The new or burgeoning business client is a prime example. Many of these clients have long been interested in having more from their lawyers than just technical legal advice. They want them to be partners; to care whether the business succeeds in the long term; to understand what is really important to the client, which is often more than short-term, bottom-line profits.

A subset of the business lawyer setting, where friendship seems to be in vogue, is the in-house counsel, or the lawyer who heads a corporate acquisition team. These lawyers must be able not only to advocate the client's interests but to understand them well enough to move in a strong way when the interests of the client demand creative, responsive action. The friend analogy, where deep trust has been built on the basis of understanding and moral discussion, explains why the lawyer can act so forcefully and accurately for the client.

Interestingly enough, the same is true of a good domestic relations lawyer. Some clients want, first and foremost, a trusting relationship. They want someone who understands not only what they think, but how they feel. They need both emotional support and tough love. They need to be "bucked up" when they are momentarily depressed, and brought into touch with reality when they are feeling unrealistically powerful and in control. In other words, they would rather have a friend who made the occasional mistake than the dispassionate, disinterested analysis of a hired gun.

In summary, the "friendship model" should be explored in a number of areas. The first of these is, wherever the lawyer is asked to deal with individuals who are, or will be, in long-term relationships with each other. In the commercial arena, for example, lawyers are often asked to be lawyers for "the deal," in the drafting of corporate documents for small, closely held corporations, or in drafting partnership agreements that could affect the parties for years to come. These situations always seem to put the lawyers in an impossible situation. They continually need to trade short-term risk and gain for long-term gain and building relationships of trust. The ethic of care, and the friendship model, can structure the lawyer's role, and provide guidance about what to do and say. Similarly, he should consider it when he acts as trustee for trusts with multiple beneficiaries. Family legal problems, problems with the placement and care of children, situations involving bioethical issues, and those involving the elderly also seem to be potentially useful.

On the other hand, the friendship model is probably not for problems between strangers where the concept of the wed of relatedness doesn't seem to fit. For example, questions of torts,[12] products liability, and crimes between strangers seem less promising. When impartial issues of justice and fairness are the heart of the conflict, the rights-based model may be more appropriate and thus preferable. But where the situation involves individuals in strong relationships with each other, it only makes sense that early involvement of these others is crucial, both to gathering accurate information and to understanding what care demands of the people involved. It requires the lawyer to break the bounds of rights analysis, and seek particularized, human solutions that better fit the people involved.

6.4 Counseling the Client to Obtain Settlement Authority

Every lawyer knows the dangers of prediction. Predicting victory can raise false expectations in the client, making the client spend the money before the client gets it. It also subjects the lawyer to the "But you said . . ." from the client when the prediction does not come true. Still, the client is entitled to make an informed decision when giving the lawyer settlement authority for negotiation purposes. And the question is whether economic models which use probabilities provide the useful language of prediction in order for the client to make informed decisions. In fact, the question of whether to use probabilities may be moot because clients seem to be demanding as much. Certainly business clients and/or client insurers want a probability of success in order to set up reserves. And consumers demand it of their doctors, so why not of their lawyers?

The beauty of economic analysis is that for every real-world problem that makes prediction impossible, the lawyer simply makes an assumption. And the result is a mathematic-like formula that gives the appearance of a scientific method, or certainty, and of objectivity. For these purposes, the assumption that the economist makes is that jurors are rational. The economist also assumes perfect information about a case will be produced by the litigation process. The question is whether these assumptions are false and will cloud any probabilities so as to make the probabilities misleading rather than helpful. On the other hand, the lawyer needs to start someplace, and with these two assumptions in mind, the lawyer can start to calculate how jurors will likely calculate damages in a given case. Rationally speaking, the lawyers might be able to create a formula that will make them more precise in valuing the case, and better inform the client about what to expect. Simultaneously it will make the lawyers more persuasive in their negotiations about what the case is worth, and provide the language to move the opponents off their position (provided the reasoning does not open up counterarguments to their disadvantage).

Let's look at it from the perspective of the jury. First (assuming the jury has perfect information, as presented through the trial process), the jury will need to determine the percentage of fault of each party. It then adds up the fault attributed to the defendants (depending on joint and several liability rules) and subtracts the amount of fault attributed to the plaintiff to come up with percentages of liability. Of course, in a jurisdiction that is not a "pure comparative" this works, but figuring close cases in 50 percent jurisdictions (where the plaintiff is barred from recovery where the plaintiff's fault is equal to or greater than the defendant's), then the jurors may lean toward the plaintiff to make sure the plaintiff gets something . . . at least if they know about the results of finding 49 or 50 percent liability on the part of the plaintiff. Some jurisdictions do not tell the jury.

Second, if the jury determines there is compensable liability, then it needs to figure damages. Damages are made up of "hard damages," such as past medicals and past lost income figures and then move to "softer damages," including predictions on future medical expenses and future lost income, to "softest damages," for pain and suffering, humiliation and mental anguish, loss of consortium, "hedonic" damages (e.g., loss of the pleasure of playing the piano), and/or punitive damages. These send a message to defendants to deter future behavior.

Third, the jury will need to multiply the percentage of fault times the total amount of damages found. Or, depending on joint and several liability rules, the jury simply takes the total damages and subtracts the percentage of fault attributed to the plaintiff to come up with a figure for damages.

Yet in predicting what the jury will actually do in such a case, the lawyer knows that there are a lot of "nonrational" factors the jury may take into account. The particular judge may exercise a lot of subtle control of the process. Marginally relevant good or bad facts may significantly affect the outcome (e.g., evidence that one of the parties is a saint, or that one is not a nice person). The jury may consciously or subconsciously take into account race, age, or sex, or may be biased against corporations, or angry at institutions and governments who make their lives difficult—especially where injury occurs to protected classes like the elderly, pregnant women, children, etc. Also, jury verdicts of city/minority jurors tend to give more to some plaintiffs, and rural or suburban jurors and/or upper/middle class jurors may give less.

To try and factor these biases into any economic calculation, lawyers may try to determine a *multiplier*—that amount which they multiply times the "hard" economic damages in the case, to come up with a prediction as to what the jury will do. And so certain jurisdictions try to keep tabs on how much juries give in relation to the "hard" damages in the case. Historically, Philadelphia or New York may have a multiplier of 4.5 to 5. Chesterfield, Virginia, may have a multiplier of 2 to 3. Of course, any given case can and should be distinguished from the average verdicts (just as with any jury verdict service), arguing even about what are hard damages, whether future loss income should be counted as hard in a particular case, and whether the pain and suffering is either greater or lesser. Still, the multiplier can be a way of predicting how much over the hard damages the jury might pay in a given jurisdiction.

In a given case, a lawyer might value a case as follows:

	30,000	hospital
	60,000	future hospital*
	50,000	lost wages (+ int)
	500,000	future lost wages*
Total Specials	640,000	
Multiplier 4.5	**2,880,000**	

* Discount factor

The difference is presumably made up in pain and suffering, emotional distress, and the like.

Now the attorney needs to predict percentage of liability to plaintiff, say 30 percent.

30 percent of 2,880,000 is 864,000

Net Damages   **2,016,000**

Now, assuming that the probability figure is accurate, $2,016,000 is the lawyer's prediction of the most likely jury damages award. Of course, here is where the lawyer must be careful. In counseling, the plaintiff should be told how this figure depends on persuading the jury about a number of key elements of the case, including duty, breach, proximate cause, and damages. For example, the plaintiff needs to be told that the jury may see future hospital bills as potentially curing the ailment, or the plaintiff finding another job somewhere, or that the chances of the jury's attributing 30 percent to the plaintiff depends on the court's excluding evidence of plaintiff's drinking (since the result of the Breathalyzer test was under the legal limit, or if this fails, of keeping people who are religiously opposed to drinking off the jury).

Some attorneys also find helpful knowing the latest percentages of plaintiff success once a case goes to a jury. For example, recent plaintiffs' lawyers quote a 70 percent win rate in front of Los Angeles County juries. Medical malpractice defense lawyers quote recent Center for State Courts statistics showing that doctors sued for malpractice win over 50 percent of the time when the case goes to jury. (In fact, the Center's statistics seemed to indicate that plaintiffs have a better chance to win if they try their case just to a judge.) These percentages can again add information to a client to help him realize the predictive nature of the attorney's case evaluation, but still assess the biasing factors.

Defendants' lawyers like to argue in negotiation that, economically speaking, the rational thing to do is weight by percentage each decision the jury needs to make. So weighting duty, breach, proximate cause, and some damage would mathematically result in a better understanding of the probabilities involved. Instead of giving a probability to the chances of winning, they give a probability to each element of the cause of action, and multiply them together. For example, if proving a duty existed was .9, breach was .5, proximate cause was .7, and proving some damage was .9, then the probability of plaintiff success would be .2835.

Yet, probability weighting could be more sophisticated still. The plaintiff might argue that if breach is proven, then proximate cause and damages are certainties. So the true probability in the case above is .45 (duty times breach). Plaintiffs would cite to attitudinal studies which seem to indicate that accountability for one's behavior is the number one value in the United States today, according to a *Time Magazine* poll, Spring 2000. The thinking would be that the jury would focus in on one tough decision, the blameworthiness of the defendant, and then simply do what was required after they made that decision.

There is some support for plaintiffs' arguments in Donald E. Vinson's *Jury Trials,* "The Psychology of Winning Strategy," 1–46, that jurors think deductively from certain strongly held values. This would mean that giving a single probability on liability

may make some sense. For the purpose of early case evaluation, then, focus groups may provide the quickest and most accurate prediction of what attitudes the jurors may have that
are outcome determinative—and as a result, the case's chance
of success before a jury. Pay $15 an hour to twelve persons the
lawyer assembles who meet the demographics of the jury, present opening statements on both sides, and see where they come
out. Of course, where they have questions and proof can be obtained, the lawyer might refine his theories and themes in the
process, but for purposes of telling the client what the case is
worth, the focus group could be a pretty good predictor of how
the jury might respond to the case. Of course, the credibility of
the witness will not be tested, but attitudinal values of the
likely jurors could be surveyed to determine what the likely result would be.

Some lawyers like to summarize all the variables of prediction by giving a percentage chance of winning and include giving a best possible alternative, a most likely alternative, a
likely alternative, and a worst likely alternative. In the example above, the lawyer might then add two figures (in addition to
the $2,880,000 best possible), $2,016,000 most likely, $100,000
as a likely alternative, as the figure that covers the plaintiff's
out-of-pocket losses, and that may give something to cover
plaintiff's attorney's fees, and $0 as the worst alternative. The
plaintiff might even weight these outcomes by percentage.

Best possible	20%	$2,880,000
Most likely	50%	$2,016,000
Likely	30%	$100,000
Worst possible	20%	$0

In any event, the client is armed with substantially better
information to make an informed decision, and the negotiator
is more precise about what he thinks the case is worth and
why.

Finally, for the purpose of developing settlement authority
from the client, there are three additional economic forces that
need to be figured: (1) the expense already incurred and expense involved in further trial preparation, (2) expense of the
trial itself, (3) a discount factor till trial. (It will be assumed

that the lawyer has already figured in the discount rate for determining the present value of future income streams. Of course, if the jurisdiction does not discount—reasoning that inflation and discount balance out—then do not discount.) Dealing with (3) first, in some jurisdictions trial could still be a long way off, though if discovery is completed, as in the typical case, this is not likely a big factor. On the other hand, if payment is going to be made over a significant period of time, as with structure payments, then plaintiff needs to be familiar with the present-value-of-money calculations to advise the client about settlement authority.

And so an economic value of a case for developing client settlement authority would include total damages, subtraction of plaintiff fault, a weighing of this figure on percentage chance of winning and proving damages as predicted, any discounting for present value, and costs yet to be incurred in producing the result, and/or minus lawyer's contingency.

Total damages (X) % Fault to defendants (X) % Chance of winning at all (-) Disc for PV (-) Costs incurred and yet to be Incurred (-) Contingency fee (=) Legal and economic case value

---

Using this formula with your clients as a foundation for discussing the legal and economic consequences of a decision will help the lawyer be more prepared and more precise in informing the client in order to develop settlement authority. It will also help prepare him to be more persuasive during settlement negotiations. Of course, counseling clients also includes counseling as to other factors—social, psychological, moral, and/or preferences for risk, which are discussed elsewhere. Suffice it to say, a particular settlement's effects on other cases and/or other relationships, including with employees, stockholders, the market, etc. could produce a settlement different from the legal value of any one particular case.

ENDNOTES

1. Of course, under the new Federal Rules of Civil Procedure there is an affirmative duty to disclose. However, many jurisdictions have opted out from under the affirmative disclosure duties. It also remains an open question whether parties, in doing so, are revealing written information that would be damaging to their case.

2. One's jurisprudence can lead to different beliefs about whether a client ought to obey the law. Many lawyers share the Platonic/Aristotelian view that places the law in very high regard. Lawyers who view the law this way may withhold information that would result in the breaking of the law because not to do so would simply be wrong . . . end of discussion. These lawyers have little to discuss because their legal philosophy doesn't require any further discussion. Violating the law is wrong, period, without regard to the consequences of *not* violating the law.

Others are more willing to examine the consequences of violating laws. They view the law as normative, and as having a purpose to bring about a greater good for society. Law serves man, not man the law. These lawyers are willing to discuss whether following the law will produce a greater good for society. If they don't believe the law will be useful to society, then they will discuss disobeying it. The question of whether to discuss the alternative of disobeying the law is made with reference to the lawyer's agreement or disagreement with it.

What if the law will serve society as a whole, but at a disproportionate cost to the client? Whether one is a positivist, a realist, a Marxist, or a feminist might make a difference, depending on the precise case and client. In any event, one's view of the law will determine the lawyer's willingness to give information, or withhold it.

If different lawyers feel different pressures, desires, or values moving them to give or withhold information, then different clients will certainly have different values, and even a different jurisprudence, that drive their willingness to obey or disobey the law.

3. Paul Zwier has written elsewhere in criticism of the prevailing model. See Hamric and Zwier, *The Ethics of Care and Reimagining the Lawyer / Client Relationship*, 22 J. Contemp. L. 383 (1996).

4. Much of what follows comes from ideas and discussion that came out of a NITA program called "Reinventing the Lawyer/Client Relationship." The intellectual leaders of that group included Maude Pevere and Janeen Kerper. Maude first discussed with us the four-step counseling model, Get, Give, Merge, Go. She and Janeen also first described to me Tom Rusk's book *The Power of Ethical Persuasion: From Conflict to Partnership at Work and in Private Life*, (New York: Viking, 1993), which informs much of my thinking. Again,

these ideas are more than "just ideas" but have been tested, taught, and used by lawyers in a variety of settings and situations.

5.   *See* Ann Hamric, *Using the Care Perspective in Case Analysis*, article in preparation. *See, cites supra, note 5. See* Donald P. Judges, *Taking Care Seriously*, 73 N.C. L. Rev. 1323, 1390 (1995). Judges writes:

> Noddings argues that moral philosophy's reliance on traditional Kantian criteria of universality and objectivity "has led to a serious imbalance in moral discussion." The universals of Nodding's ethic are attitudinal and motivation, rather than behavioral. Caring and relatedness thus are desirable ends in themselves; caring is not an obligation that one must discharge to achieve morality. To the contrary, "[w]e want to be moral in order to remain in the caring relation and to enhance the ideal of ourselves" as persons who care. Morality under this view derives from a natural desire to become and to remain related, which gradually unfolds in a succession of caring relations. Such relations allow "identity-conferring commitments" that reveal personal integrity; provide the sense that one's life has meaning, foundation, and a place in the community; and elicit the values of patience, trust, and moderation of manipulative striving.
>
> While the caring relation is the ethical ideal, even when the empathic connection is strong, and a motivation to act naturally arises, the individual can choose whether to accept and act upon, or reject the feeling. Furthermore, in some personal encounters such sentiments either do not arise naturally at all, or do so only faintly, and are displaced by other feelings such as hostility or revulsion. In such cases, an individual may summon motivation from remembrance of his or her own natural caring and being cared for, to take care of his or her ethical self. Noddings refers to this process as "Ethical caring."
>
> An ethic of care thus "is a natural derivative of the desire to be related. It springs from our experience of caring and the inevitable assessment of this relation as 'good'. What we seek in caring is not payment or reciprocity in kind, but the special reciprocity that connotes completion." This ethic of care leads to self-fulfillment; it does not require self-sacrifice on the altar of an abstract altruistic ideal. Moreover, the roles of caring and being cared for are neither static nor predetermined, but shift over time and betwen persons.
>
> A caring attitude is not enough, though; there must be connection. *Id* at 1389–92.

6.   *See* A.L. Carse, "The 'Voice of Care': Implications for Bioethical Education", *Journal of Medicine and Philosophy,* 16 (1991): 5–6.

7.   *See* Ann Hamric, *Using the Care Perspective in Case Analysis* (article in preparation).

8.   Again, Rusk has three steps to creating resolutions. They are:
    1. Affirm your mutual understanding and confirm that you are both ready to consider options for resolution.
    2. Brainstorm multiple options.
    3. If a mutually agreeable solution is not obvious, try one or more of the following:
        a. Take time out to reconsider, consult, exchange proposals and reconvene.
        b. Agree to neutral arbitration, mediation, or counseling.
        c. Compromise between alternative solutions.
        d. Take turns between alternative solutions.
        e. Yield (for now) once your position is thoroughly and respectfully considered.
        f. Assert your positional power after thoroughly and respectfully considering their position.

9.   As a possible final step, the counselor might consider drafting an agreement which can memorialize the agreed-upon solutions. Such a process suggests bargaining over the rights and duties of the parties. At least one commentator feels that bargaining is not a useful tool, and is antihetical to a care perspective. *See* Annette Baier, *Trust and Antitrust,* 96 Ethics 231 (1986). (Baier criticizes contractarians because they ignore the costs to relationships from adversarial self-interested bargaining.)

10.   This role can best be summed up by a Shoshone Indian saying:
    Oh, the comfort, the inexpressible comfort of feeling safe with a person; having neither to weight thought nor measure words, but pouring them all right out, just as they are, chaff and grain together, certain that a faithful hand will take and sift them, keep what is worth keeping, and with a breath of kindness, blow the rest away.

11.   *See* Steven Toulmin, *The Tyranny of Principles,* Hastings Center Report (1981). Toulmin writes
    So in the ethics of strangers, respect for rules is all, and the opportunities for discretion are few. In the ethics of intimacy, discretion is all, and the relevance of strict rules is minimal. *Id.* at 35.

Toulmin also critiques Rawls' theory as exaggerated in the direction of strangers with its emphasis on impartiality. *See also* Margaret Urban Walker, *Moral Understanding: Alternative Epistemology for a Feminist Ethics*, 4 Hypatia 23 (1989). Walker cautions against being tempted to create separate spheres for justice and care. She writes:

> The alternative picture also invites us not to be too tempted by the "separate spheres" move of endorsing particularism for personal or intimate relations, universalism for the large-scale or genuinely administrative context, or for dealings with unknown or little-known personas. While principled generalized treatments may really be the best we can resort to in many cases of the latter sort, it is well to preserve a lively sense of the *moral incompleteness* or inadequacy of these resorts. This is partly to defend ourselves against disposition to keep strangers strange and outsiders outside, but it is also to prevent our becoming comfortable with essentially distancing, depersonalizing, or paternalistic attitudes which may not really be the only resorts if roles and institutions can be shaped to embody expressive and communicative possibilities. It is often claimed that more humanly responsive institutions are not practical (read: instrumentally efficient). But if moral-practical intelligence is understood consistently in the alternative way discussed (the way appropriate to relations among persons), it may instead be correct to say that certain incorrigibly impersonal or depersonalizing institutions are too morally impractical to be tolerated. It is crucial to examine how structural features of institutionalized relations—medical personnel, patients and families; teachers, students and parents; case workers and clients, for example—combine with typical situations to enable or deform the abilities of all concerned to hear and to be heard. Some characteristically modern forms of universalist thinking may project a sort of "moral colonialism" ("the 'subjects' of my moral decisions disappear behind uniform 'polices' I must impartially 'apply' ") precisely because they were forged historically with an eye to actual colonization—industrial or imperial.

12. *cf.* Leslie Bender, *From Gender Difference to Feminist Solidarity: Using Carol Gilligan and An Ethic of Care in Law*, 15 Vt. L. Rev. 1 (1990); Leslie Bender, *A Lawyer's Primer on Feminist Theory and Tort,* 38 J. Legal Educ. 3 (1988).

Appendix

Selected Model Rules of Professional Conduct

Rule 1.2 Scope of Representation

(a) A lawyer shall abide by a client's decisions concerning the objectives of representation subject to paragraphs (c), (d) and (e), and shall consult with the client as to the means by which they are to be pursued. A lawyer shall abide by a client's decision whether to accept an offer of settlement of a matter. In a criminal case, the lawyer shall abide by the client's decision, after consultation with the lawyer, as to a plea to be entered, whether to waive jury trial and whether the client will testify.

(b) A lawyer's representation of a client, including representation by appointment, does not constitute an endorsement of the client's political, economic, social or moral views or activities.

(c) A lawyer may limit the objectives of the representation if the client consents after consultation.

(d) A lawyer shall not counsel a client to engage, or assist a client, in conduct that the lawyer knows is criminal or fraudulent, but a lawyer may discuss the legal consequences of any proposed course of conduct with a client and may counsel or assist a client to make a good faith effort to determine the validity, scope, meaning or application of the law.

(e) When a lawyer knows that a client expects assistance not permitted by the rules of professional conduct or other law, the lawyer shall consult with the client regarding the relevant limitations on the lawyer's conduct.

Comment

Scope of Representation

[1] Both lawyer and client have authority and responsibility in the objectives and means of representation. The client

has ultimate authority to determine the purposes to be served by legal representation, within the limits imposed by law and the lawyer's professional obligations. Within those limits, a client also has a right to consult with the lawyer about the means to be used in pursuing those objectives. At the same time, a lawyer is not required to pursue objectives or employ means simply because the client may wish that a lawyer do so. A clear distinction between objectives and means sometimes cannot be drawn, and in many cases the client-lawyer relationship partakes of a joint undertaking. In questions of means, the lawyer should assume responsibility for technical and legal tactical issues, but should defer to the client regarding such questions as the expense to be incurred and concern for third persons who might be adversely affected. Law defining the lawyer's scope of authority in litigation varies among jurisdictions.

[2] In a case in which the client appears to be suffering mental disability, the lawyer's duty to abide by the client's decisions is to be guided by reference to Rule 1.14 .

Independence from Client's Views or Activities

[3] Legal representation should not be denied to people who are unable to afford legal services, or whose cause is controversial or the subject of popular disapproval. By the same token, representing a client does not constitute approval of a client's views or activities.

Services Limited in Objectives or Means

[4] The objectives or scope of services provided by a lawyer may be limited by agreement with the client or by the terms under which the lawyer's services are made available to the client. For example, a retainer may be for a specifically defined purpose. Representation provided through a legal aid agency may be subject to limitations on the types of cases the agency handles. When a lawyer has been retained by an insurer to represent an insured, the representation may be limited to matters related to the insurance coverage. The terms upon which representation is undertaken may exclude specific objectives or means. Such limitations may exclude objectives or means that the lawyer regards as repugnant or imprudent.

[5] An agreement concerning the scope of representation must accord with the Rules of Professional Conduct and other law. Thus, the client may not be asked to agree to representation so limited in scope as to violate Rule 1.1 , or to surrender the right to terminate the lawyer's services or the right to settle litigation that the lawyer might wish to continue.

Criminal, Fraudulent and Prohibited Transactions

[6] A lawyer is required to give an honest opinion about the actual consequences that appear likely to result from a client's conduct. The fact that a client uses advice in a course of action that is criminal or fraudulent does not, of itself, make a lawyer a party to the course of action. However, a lawyer may not knowingly assist a client in criminal or fraudulent conduct. There is a critical distinction between presenting an analysis of legal aspects of questionable conduct and recommending the means by which a crime or fraud might be committed with impunity.

[7] When the client's course of action has already begun and is continuing, the lawyer's responsibility is especially delicate. The lawyer is not permitted to reveal the client's wrongdoing, except where permitted by Rule 1.6. However, the lawyer is required to avoid furthering the purpose, for example, by suggesting how it might be concealed. A lawyer may not continue assisting a client in conduct that the lawyer originally supposes is legally proper but then discovers is criminal or fraudulent. Withdrawal from the representation, therefore, may be required.

[8] Where the client is a fiduciary, the lawyer may be charged with special obligations in dealings with a beneficiary.

[9] Paragraph (d) applies whether or not the defrauded party is a party to the transaction. Hence, a lawyer should not participate in a sham transaction; for example, a transaction to effectuate criminal or fraudulent escape of tax liability. Paragraph (d) does not preclude undertaking a criminal defense incident to a general retainer for legal services to a lawful enterprise. The last clause of paragraph (d) recognizes that determining the validity or interpretation of a statute or regulation may require a course of action involving disobedience of the statute or regulation or of the interpretation placed upon it by governmental authorities.

Model Code Comparison

Paragraph (a) has no counterpart in the Disciplinary Rules of the Model Code. EC 7-7 stated: "In certain areas of legal representation not affecting the merits of the cause or substantially prejudicing the rights of a client, a lawyer is entitled to make decisions on his own. But otherwise the authority to make decisions is exclusively that of the client . . . ." EC 7-8 stated that "[I]n the final analysis, however, the . . . decision whether to forego legally available objectives or methods because of nonlegal factors is ultimately for the client . . . . In the event that the client in a nonadjudicatory matter insists upon a course of conduct that is contrary to the judgment and advice of the lawyer but not prohibited by Disciplinary Rules, the lawyer may withdraw form the employment." DR 7-101(A)(1) provided that a lawyer "shall not intentionally . . . fail to seek the lawful objectives of his client through reasonably available means permitted by law . . . . A lawyer does not violate this Disciplinary Rule, however, by . . . avoiding offensive tactics . . . ."

Paragraph (b) has no counterpart in the Model Code.

With regard to Paragraph (c), DR 7-102(B)(1) provided that a lawyer may, "where permissible, exercise his professional judgment to waive or fail to assert a right or position of his client."

With regard to Paragraph (d), DR 7-102(A)(7) provided that a lawyer shall not "counsel or assist his client in conduct that the lawyer knows to be illegal or fraudulent." DR 7-102(A)(6) provided that a lawyer shall not "participate in the creation or preservation of evidence when he knows or it is obvious that the evidence is false."

DR 7-106 provided that a lawyer shall not "advise his client to disregard a standing rule of a tribunal or a ruling of a tribunal . . . but he may take appropriate steps in good faith to test the validity of such a rule or ruling." EC 7-5 stated that a lawyer "should never encourage or aid his client to commit criminal acts or counsel his client on how to violate the law and avoid punishment therefor."

With regard to Paragraph (e), DR 2-110(C)(1)(c) provided that a lawyer may withdraw from representation if a client "insists" that the lawyer engage in "conduct that is illegal or that is prohibited under the Disciplinary Rules."

DR 9-101(C) provided that "a lawyer shall not state or imply that he is able to influence improperly . . . Any tribunal, legislative body or public official."

Rule 1.3 Diligence

A lawyer shall act with reasonable diligence and promptness in representing a client.

Comment

[1] A lawyer should pursue a matter on behalf of a client despite opposition, obstruction or personal inconvenience to the lawyer, and may take whatever lawful and ethical measures

are required to vindicate a client's cause or endeavor. A lawyer should act with commitment and dedication to the interests of the client and with zeal in advocacy upon the client's behalf. However, a lawyer is not bound to press for every advantage that might be realized for a client. A lawyer has professional discretion in determining the means by which a matter should be pursued. See Rule 1.2 . A lawyer's work load should be controlled so that each matter can be handled adequately.

[2] Perhaps no professional shortcoming is more widely resented than procrastination. A client's interests often can be adversely affected by the passage of time or the change of conditions; in extreme instances, as when a lawyer overlooks a statute of limitations, the client's legal position may be destroyed. Even when the client's interests are not affected in substance, however, unreasonable delay can cause a client needless anxiety and undermine confidence in the lawyer's trustworthiness.

[3] Unless the relationship is terminated as provided in Rule 1.16 , a lawyer should carry through to conclusion all matters undertaken for a client. If a lawyer's employment is limited to a specific matter, the relationship terminates when the matter has been resolved. If a lawyer has served a client over a substantial period in a variety of matters, the client sometimes may assume that the lawyer will continue to serve on a continuing basis unless the lawyer gives notice of withdrawal. Doubt about whether a client-lawyer relationship still exists should be clarified by the lawyer, preferably in writing, so that the client will not mistakenly suppose the lawyer is looking after the client's affairs when the lawyer has ceased to do so. For example, if a lawyer has handled a judicial or administrative proceeding that produced a result adverse to the client but has not been specifically instructed concerning pursuit of an appeal, the lawyer should advise the client of the possibility of appeal before relinquishing responsibility for the matter.

Model Code Comparison

DR 6-101(A)(3) required that a lawyer not "[n]eglect a legal matter entrusted to him." EC 6-4 stated that a lawyer should "give appropriate attention to his legal work." Canon 7 stated that "a lawyer should represent a client zealously within the bounds of the law." DR 7-101(A)(1) provided that a lawyer "shall not intentionally . . . fail to seek the lawful objectives of his client through reasonably available means permitted by law and the Disciplinary Rules. . . ." DR 7-101(A)(3) provided that a lawyer "shall not intentionally . . . [p]rejudice or damage his client during the course of the relationship. . . ."

Rule 1.4 Communication

(a) A lawyer shall keep a client reasonably informed about the status of a matter and promptly comply with reasonable requests for information.

(b) A lawyer shall explain a matter to the extent reasonably necessary to permit the client to make informed decisions regarding the representation.

[1] The client should have sufficient information to participate intelligently in decisions concerning the objectives of the representation and the means by which they are to be pursued, to the extent the client is willing and able to do so. For example, a lawyer negotiating on behalf of a client should provide the client with facts relevant to the matter, inform the client of communications from another party and take other reasonable steps that permit the client to make a decision regarding a serious offer from another party. A lawyer who receives from opposing counsel an offer of settlement in a civil controversy or a proffered plea bargain in a criminal case should promptly inform the client of its substance unless prior discussions with the client have left it clear that the proposal will be unacceptable. See Rule 1.2(a). Even when a client delegates authority to the lawyer, the client should be kept advised of the status of the matter.

[2] Adequacy of communication depends in part on the kind of advice or assistance involved. For example, in negotiations where there is time to explain a proposal, the lawyer should review all important provisions with the client before proceeding to an agreement. In litigation a lawyer should explain the general strategy and prospects of success and ordinarily should consult the client on tactics that might injure or coerce others. On the other hand, a lawyer ordinarily cannot be expected to describe trial or negotiation strategy in detail. The guiding principle is that the lawyer should fulfill reasonable client expectations for information consistent with the duty to act in the client's best interests, and the client's overall requirements as to the character of representation.

[3] Ordinarily, the information to be provided is that appropriate for a client who is a comprehending and responsible adult. However, fully informing the client according to this standard may be impracticable, for example, where the client is a child or suffers from mental disability. See Rule 1.14. When

the client is an organization or group, it is often impossible or inappropriate to inform every one of its members about its legal affairs; ordinarily, the lawyer should address communications to the appropriate officials of the organization. See Rule 1.13. Where many routine matters are involved, a system of limited or occasional reporting may be arranged with the client. Practical exigency may also require a lawyer to act for a client without prior consultation.

Withholding Information

[4] In some circumstances, a lawyer may be justified in delaying transmission of information when the client would be likely to react imprudently to an immediate communication. Thus, a lawyer might withhold a psychiatric diagnosis of a client when the examining psychiatrist indicates that disclosure would harm the client. A lawyer may not withhold information to serve the lawyer's own interest or convenience. Rules or court orders governing litigation may provide that information supplied to a lawyer may not be disclosed to the client. Rule 3.4(c) directs compliance with such rules or orders.

Model Code Comparison

Rule 1.4 has no direct counterpart in the Disciplinary Rules of the Model Code. DR 6-101(A)(3) provided that a lawyer shall not "[n]eglect a legal matter entrusted to him." DR 9-102(B)(1) provided that a lawyer shall "[p]romptly notify a client of the receipt of his funds, securities, or other properties." EC 7-8 stated that a lawyer "should exert his best efforts to insure that decisions of his client are made only after the client has been informed of relevant considerations." EC 9-2 stated that "a lawyer should fully and promptly inform his client of material developments in the matters being handled for the client."

Rule 1.5 Fees

(a) A lawyer's fee shall be reasonable. The factors to be considered in determining the reasonableness of a fee include the following:

(1) the time and labor required, the novelty and difficulty of the questions involved, and the skill requisite to perform the legal service properly;

(2) the likelihood, if apparent to the client, that the acceptance of the particular employment will preclude other employment by the lawyer;

(3) the fee customarily charged in the locality for similar legal services;

(4) the amount involved and the result obtained;

(5) the time limitations imposed by the client or by the circumstances;

(6) the nature and length of the professional relationship with the client;

(7) the experience, reputation, and ability of the lawyer or lawyers performing the services; and

(8) whether the fee is fixed or contingent.

(b) When the lawyer has not regularly represented the client, the basis or rate of the fee shall be communicated to the client, preferably in writing, before or within a reasonable time after commencing the representation.

(c) A fee may be contingent on the outcome of the matter for which the service is rendered, except in a matter in which a contingent fee is prohibited by paragraph (d) or other law. A contingent fee agreement shall be in writing and shall state the method by which the fee is to be determined, including the percentage or percentages that shall accrue to the lawyer in the event of settlement, trial or appeal, litigation and other expenses to be deduced from the recovery, and whether such expenses are to be deduced before or after the contingent fee is calculated. Upon conclusion of a contingent fee matter, the lawyer shall provide the client with a written statement stating the outcome of the matter and, if there is a recovery, showing the remittance to the client and the method of its determination.

(d) A lawyer shall not enter into an arrangement for, charge, or collect:

(1) any fee in a domestic relations matter, the payment or amount of which is contingent upon the securing of a divorce or upon the amount of alimony or support, or property settlement in lieu thereof; or

(2) a contingent fee for representing a defendant in a criminal case.

(e) A division of a fee between lawyers who are not in the same firm may be made only if:

(1) the division is in proportion to the service performed by each lawyer or, by written agreement with the client, each lawyer assumes joint responsibility for the representation;

(2) the client is advised of and does not object to the participation of all the lawyers involved; and

(3) the total fee is reasonable.

Comment

Basis or Rate of Fee

[1] When the lawyer has regularly represented a client, they ordinarily will have evolved an understanding concerning the basis or rate of the fee. In a new client-lawyer relationship, however, an understanding as to the fee should be promptly established. It is not necessary to recite all the factors that underlie the basis of the fee, but only those that are directly involved in its computation. It is sufficient, for example, to state that the basic rate is an hourly charge or a fixed amount or an estimated amount, or to identify the factors that may be taken into account in finally fixing the fee. When developments occur during the representation that render an earlier estimate substantially inaccurate, a revised estimate should be provided to the client. A written statement concerning the fee reduces the possibility of misunderstanding. Furnishing the client with a simple memorandum or a copy of the lawyer's customary fee schedule is sufficient if the basis or rate of the fee is set forth.

Terms of Payment

[2] A lawyer may require advance payment of a fee, but is obliged to return any unearned portion. See Rule 1.16(d). A lawyer may accept property in payment for services, such as an ownership interest in an enterprise, providing this does not involve acquisition of a proprietary interest in the cause of action or subject matter of the litigation contrary to Rule 1.8(j). However, a fee paid in property instead of money may be subject to special scrutiny because it involves questions concerning both the value of the services and the lawyer's special knowledge of the value of the property.

[3] An agreement may not be made whose terms might induce the lawyer improperly to curtail services for the client or perform them in a way contrary to the client's interest. For example, a lawyer should not enter into an agreement whereby services are to be provided only up to a stated amount when it is foreseeable that more extensive services probably will be required, unless the situation is adequately explained to the client. Otherwise, the client might have to bargain for further assistance in the midst of a proceeding or transaction. However, it is proper to define the extent of services in light of the client's ability to pay. A lawyer should not exploit a fee arrangement based primarily on hourly charges by using wasteful procedures. When there is doubt whether a contingent fee is

consistent with the client's best interest, the lawyer should offer the client alternative bases for the fee and explain their implications. Applicable law may impose limitations on contingent fees, such as a ceiling on the percentage.

Division of Fee

[4] A division of fee is a single billing to a client covering the fee of two or more lawyers who are not in the same firm. A division of fee facilitates association of more than one lawyer in a matter in which neither alone could serve the client as well, and most often is used when the fee is contingent and the division is between a referring lawyer and a trial specialist. Paragraph (e) permits the lawyers to divide a fee on either the basis of the proportion of services they render or by agreement between the participating lawyers if all assume responsibility for the representation as a whole and the client is advised and does not object. It does not require disclosure to the client of the share that each lawyer is to receive. Joint responsibility for the representation entails the obligations stated in Rule 5.1 for purposes of the matter involved.

Disputes over Fees

[5] If a procedure has been established for resolution of fee disputes, such as an arbitration or mediation procedure established by the bar, the lawyer should conscientiously consider submitting to it. Law may prescribe a procedure for determining a lawyer's fee, for example, in representation of an executor or administrator, a class or a person entitled to a reasonable fee as part of the measure of damages. The lawyer entitled to such a fee and a lawyer representing another party concerned with the fee should comply with the prescribed procedure.

Model Code Comparison

DR 2-106(A) provided that a lawyer "shall not enter into an agreement for, charge, or collect an illegal or clearly excessive fee." DR 2-106(B) provided that a fee is "clearly excessive when, after a review of the facts, a lawyer of ordinary prudence would be left with a definite and firm conviction that the fee is in excess of a reasonable fee." The factors of a reasonable fee in Rule 1.5(a) are substantially identical to those listed in DR 2-106(B). EC 2-17 states that a lawyer "should not charge more than a reasonable fee. . . ."

There was no counterpart to paragraph (b) in the Disciplinary Rules of the Model Code. EC 2-19 stated that it is "usually beneficial to reduce to writing the understanding of the parties regarding the fee, particularly when it is contingent."

There was also no counterpart to paragraph (c) in the Disciplinary Rules of the Model Code. EC 2-20 provided that "[c]ontingent fee arrangements in civil cases have long been commonly accepted in the United States," but that "a lawyer generally should decline to accept employment on a contingent fee basis by one who is able to pay a reasonable fixed fee. . . ."

With regard to paragraph (d), DR 2-106(C) prohibited "a contingent fee in a criminal case." EC 2-20 provided that "contingent fee arrangements in domestic relation cases are rarely justified."

With regard to paragraph (e), DR 2-107(A) permitted division of fees only if: "(1) The client consents to employment of the other lawyer after a full disclosure that a division of fees will be made. (2) The division is in proportion to the services performed and responsibility assumed by each. (3) The total fee does not exceed clearly reasonable compensation. . . ." Paragraph (e) permits division without regard to the services rendered by each lawyer if they assume joint responsibility for the representation.

Rule 1.6 Confidentiality of Information

(a) A lawyer shall not reveal information relating to representation of a client unless the client consents after consultation, except for disclosures that are impliedly authorized in order to carry out the representation, and except as stated in paragraph (b).

(b) A lawyer may reveal such information to the extent the lawyer reasonably believes necessary:

(1) to prevent the client from committing a criminal act that the lawyer believes is likely to result in imminent death or substantial bodily harm; or

(2) to establish a claim or defense on behalf of the lawyer in a controversy between the lawyer and the client, to establish a defense to a criminal charge or civil claim against the lawyer based upon conduct in which the client was involved, or to respond to allegations in any proceeding concerning the lawyer's representation of a client.

Comment

[1] The lawyer is part of a judicial system charged with upholding the law. One of the lawyer's functions is to advise clients so that they avoid any violation of the law in the proper exercise of their rights.

[2] The observance of the ethical obligation of a lawyer to hold inviolate confidential information of the client not only facilitates the full development of facts essential to proper representation of the client but also encourages people to seek early legal assistance.

[3] Almost without exception, clients come to lawyers in order to determine what their rights are and what is, in the maze of laws and regulations, deemed to be legal and correct. The common law recognizes the client's confidences must be protected from disclosure. Based upon experience, lawyers know that almost all clients follow the advice given, and the law is upheld.

[4] A fundamental principle in the client-lawyer relationship is that the lawyer maintain confidentiality of information relating to the representation. The client is thereby encouraged to communicate fully and frankly with the lawyer even as to embarrassing or legally damaging subject matter.

[5] The principle of confidentiality is given effect in two related bodies of law, the attorney-client privilege (which includes the work product doctrine) in the law of evidence and the rule of confidentiality established in professional ethics. The attorney-client privilege applies in judicial and other proceedings in which a lawyer may be called as a witness or otherwise required to produce evidence concerning a client. The rule of client-lawyer confidentiality applies in situations other than those where evidence is sought from the lawyer through compulsion of law. The confidentiality rule applies not merely to matters communicated in confidence by the client but also to all information relating to the representation, whatever its source. A lawyer may not disclose such information except as authorized or required by the Rules of Professional Conduct or other law. See also Scope .

[6] The requirement of maintaining confidentiality of information relating to representation applies to government lawyers who may disagree with the policy goals that their representation is designed to advance.

Authorized Disclosure

[7] A lawyer is impliedly authorized to make disclosures about a client when appropriate in carrying out the representation, except to the extent that the client's instructions or special circumstances limit that authority. In litigation, for example, a lawyer may disclose information by admitting a

fact that cannot properly be disputed, or in negotiation by making a disclosure that facilitates a satisfactory conclusion.

[8] Lawyers in a firm, may in the course of the firm's practice, disclose to each other information relating to a client of the firm, unless the client has instructed that particular information be confined to specified lawyers.

Rule 1.7 Conflict of Interest: General Rule

(a) A lawyer shall not represent a client if the representation of that client will be directly adverse to another client, unless:

(1) the lawyer reasonably believes the representation will not adversely affect the relationship with the other client; and

(2) each client consents after consultation.

(b) A lawyer shall not represent a client if the representation of that client may be materially limited by the lawyer's responsibilities to another client or to a third person, or by the lawyer's own interests, unless:

(1) the lawyer reasonably believes the representation will not be adversely affected; and

(2) the client consents after consultation. When representation of multiple clients in a single matter is undertaken, the consultation shall include explanation of the implications of the common representation and the advantages and risks involved.

Comment

Disclosure Adverse to Client

[9] The confidentiality rule is subject to limited exceptions. In becoming privy to information about a client, a lawyer may foresee that the client intends serious harm to another person. However, to the extent a lawyer is required or permitted to disclose a client's purposes, the client will be inhibited from revealing facts which would enable the lawyer to counsel against a wrongful course of action. The public is better protected if full and open communication by the client is encouraged than if it is inhibited.

[10] Several situations must be distinguished. First, the lawyer may not counsel or assist a client in conduct that is criminal or fraudulent. See Rule 1.2(d). Similarly, a lawyer has a duty under Rule 3.3(a)(4) not to use false evidence. This duty is essentially a special instance of the duty prescribed in Rule

1.2(d) to avoid assisting a client in criminal or fraudulent conduct.

[11] Second, the lawyer may have been innocently involved in past conduct by the client that was criminal or fraudulent. In such a situation the lawyer has not violated Rule 1.2(d), because to "counsel or assist" criminal or fraudulent conduct requires knowing that the conduct is of that character.

[12] Third, the lawyer may learn that a client intends prospective conduct that is criminal and likely to result in imminent death or substantial bodily harm. As stated in paragraph (b)(1), the lawyer has professional discretion to reveal information in order to prevent such consequences. The lawyer may make a disclosure in order to prevent homicide or serious bodily injury which the lawyer reasonably believes is intended by a client. It is very difficult for a lawyer to "know" when such a heinous purpose will actually be carried out, for the client may have a change of mind.

[13] The lawyer's exercise of discretion requires consideration of such factors as the nature of the lawyer's relationship with the client and with those who might be injured by the client, the lawyer's own involvement in the transaction and factors that may extenuate the conduct in question. Where practical, the lawyer should seek to persuade the client to take suitable action. In any case, a disclosure adverse to the client's interest should be no greater than the lawyer reasonably believes necessary to the purpose. A lawyer's decision not to take preventive action permitted by paragraph (b)(1) does not violate this Rule.

Withdrawal

[14] If the lawyer's services will be used by the client in materially furthering a course of criminal or fraudulent conduct, the lawyer must withdraw, as stated in Rule 1.16(a)(1).

[15] After withdrawal the lawyer is required to refrain from making disclosure of the clients' confidences, except as otherwise provided in Rule 1.6. Neither this Rule nor Rule 1.8(b) nor Rule 1.16(d) prevents the lawyer from giving notice of the fact of withdrawal, and the lawyer may also withdraw or disaffirm any opinion, document, affirmation, or the like.

[16] Where the client is an organization, the lawyer may be in doubt whether contemplated conduct will actually be carried out by the organization. Where necessary to guide conduct in connection with this Rule, the lawyer may make inquiry within the organization as indicated in Rule 1.13(b).

Dispute Concerning Lawyer's Conduct

[17] Where a legal claim or disciplinary charge alleges complicity of the lawyer in a client's conduct or other misconduct of the lawyer involving representation of the client, the lawyer may respond to the extent the lawyer reasonably believes necessary to establish a defense. The same is true with respect to a claim involving the conduct or representation of a former client. The lawyer's right to respond arises when an assertion of such complicity has been made. Paragraph (b)(2) does not require the lawyer to await the commencement of an action or proceeding that charges such complicity, so that the defense may be established by responding directly to a third party who has made such an assertion. The right to defend, of course, applies where a proceeding has been commenced. Where practicable and not prejudicial to the lawyer's ability to establish the defense, the lawyer should advise the client of the third party's assertion and request that the client respond appropriately. In any event, disclosure should be no greater than the lawyer reasonably believes is necessary to vindicate innocence, the disclosure should be made in a manner which limits access to the information to the tribunal or other persons having a need to know it, and appropriate protective orders or other arrangements should be sought by the lawyer to the fullest extent practicable.

[18] If the lawyer is charged with wrongdoing in which the client's conduct is implicated, the rule of confidentiality should not prevent the lawyer from defending against the charge. Such a charge can arise in a civil, criminal or professional disciplinary proceeding, and can be based on a wrong allegedly committed by the lawyer against the client, or on a wrong alleged by a third person; for example, a person claiming to have been defrauded by the lawyer and client acting together. A lawyer entitled to a fee is permitted by paragraph (b)(2) to prove the services rendered in an action to collect it. This aspect of the rule expresses the principle that the beneficiary of a fiduciary relationship may not exploit it to the detriment of the fiduciary. As stated above, the lawyer must make every effort practicable to avoid unnecessary disclosure of information relating to a representation, to limit disclosure to those having the need to know it, and to obtain protective orders or make other arrangements minimizing the risk of disclosure.

Disclosures Otherwise Required or Authorized

[19] The attorney-client privilege is differently defined in various jurisdictions. If a lawyer is called as a witness to give testimony concerning a client, absent waiver by the client, paragraph (a) requires the lawyer to invoke the privilege when it is applicable. The lawyer must comply with the final orders of a court or other tribunal of competent jurisdiction requiring the lawyer to give information about the client.

[20] The Rules of Professional Conduct in various circumstances permit or require a lawyer to disclose information relating to the representation. See Rules 2.2, 2.3, 3.3 and 4.1. In addition to these provisions, a lawyer may be obligated or permitted by other provisions of law to give information about a client. Whether another provision of law supersedes Rule 1.6 is a matter of interpretation beyond the scope of these Rules, but a presumption should exist against such a supersession.

Former Client

[21] The duty of confidentiality continues after the client - lawyer relationship has terminated.

Model Code Comparison

Rule 1.6 eliminates the two-pronged duty under the Model Code in favor of a single standard protecting all information about a client "relating to representation." Under DR 4-101, the requirement applied to information protected by the attorney-client privilege and to information "gained in" the professional relationship that "the client has requested be held inviolate or the disclosure of which would be embarrassing or would be likely to be detrimental to the client." EC 4-4 added that the duty differed from the evidentiary privilege in that it existed "without regard to the nature or source of information or the fact that others share the knowledge." Rule 1.6 imposes confidentiality on information relating to the representation even it is acquired before or after the relationship existed. It does not require the client to indicate information that is to be confidential, or permit the lawyer to speculate whether particular information might be embarrassing or detrimental.

Paragraph (a) permits a lawyer to disclose information where impliedly authorized to do so in order to carry out the representation. Under DR 4-101 (B) and (C), a lawyer was not permitted to reveal "confidences" unless the client first consented after disclosure.

Loyalty to a Client

[1] Loyalty is an essential element in the lawyer's relationship to a client. An impermissible conflict of interest may exist before representation is undertaken, in which event the representation should be declined. The lawyer should adopt reasonable procedures, appropriate for the size and type of firm and practice, to determine in both litigation and non-litigation matters the parties and issues involved and to determine whether there are actual or potential conflicts of interest.

[2] If such a conflict arises after representation has been undertaken, the lawyer should withdraw from the representation. See Rule 1.16. Where more than one client is involved and the lawyer withdraws because a conflict arises after representation, whether the lawyer may continue to represent any of the clients is determined by Rule 1.9. See also Rule 2.2(c). As to whether a client-lawyer relationship exists or, having once been established, is continuing, see Comment to Rule 1.3 and Scope.

[3] As a general proposition, loyalty to a client prohibits undertaking representation directly adverse to that client without that client's consent. Paragraph (a) expresses that general rule. Thus, a lawyer ordinarily may not act as advocate against a person the lawyer represents in some other matter, even if it is wholly unrelated. On the other hand, simultaneous representation in unrelated matters of clients whose interests are only generally adverse, such as competing economic enterprises, does not require consent of the respective clients. Paragraph (a) applies only when the representation of one client would be directly adverse to the other.

[4] Loyalty to a client is also impaired when a lawyer cannot consider, recommend or carry out an appropriate course of action for the client because of the lawyer's other responsibilities or interests. The conflict in effect forecloses alternatives that would otherwise be available to the client. Paragraph (b) addresses such situations. A possible conflict does not itself preclude the representation. The critical questions are the likelihood that a conflict will eventuate and, if it does, whether it will materially interfere with the lawyer's independent professional judgment in considering alternatives or foreclose courses of action that reasonably should be pursued on behalf of the client. Consideration should be given to whether the client wishes to accommodate the other interest involved.

Consultation and Consent

[5] A client may consent to representation notwithstanding a conflict. However, as indicated in paragraph (a)(1) with respect to representation directly adverse to a client, and paragraph (b)(1) with respect to material limitations on representation of a client, when a disinterested lawyer would conclude that the client should not agree to the representation under the circumstances, the lawyer involved cannot properly ask for such agreement or provide representation on the basis of the client's consent. When more than one client is involved, the question of conflict must be resolved as to each client. Moreover, there may be circumstances where it is impossible to make the disclosure necessary to obtain consent. For example, when the lawyer represents different clients in related matters and one of the clients refuses to consent to the disclosure necessary to permit the other client to make an informed decision, the lawyer cannot properly ask the latter to consent.

Lawyer's Interests

[6] The lawyer's own interests should not be permitted to have an adverse effect on representation of a client. For example, a lawyer's need for income should not lead the lawyer to undertake matters that cannot be handled competently and at a reasonable fee. See Rules 1.1 and 1.5. If the probity of a lawyer's own conduct in a transaction is in serious question, it may be difficult or impossible for the lawyer to give a client detached advice. A lawyer may not allow related business interests to affect representation, for example, by referring clients to an enterprise in which the lawyer has an undisclosed interest.

Conflicts in Litigation

[7] Paragraph (a) prohibits representation of opposing parties in litigation. Simultaneous representation of parties whose interests in litigation may conflict, such as coplaintiffs or codefendants, is governed by paragraph (b). An impermissible conflict may exist by reason of substantial discrepancy in the parties' testimony, incompatibility in positions in relation to an opposing party or the fact that there are substantially different possibilities of settlement of the claims or liabilities in question. Such conflicts can arise in criminal cases as well as civil. The potential for conflict of interest in representing multiple defendants in a criminal case is so grave that ordinarily a lawyer should decline to represent more than one codefendant. On the other hand, common representation of persons having

similar interests is proper if the risk of adverse effect is minimal and the requirements of paragraph (b) are met. Compare Rule 2.2 involving intermediation between clients.

[8] Ordinarily, a lawyer may not act as advocate against a client the lawyer represents in some other matter, even if the other matter is wholly unrelated. However, there are circumstances in which a lawyer may act as advocate against a client. For example, a lawyer representing an enterprise with diverse operations may accept employment as an advocate against the enterprise in an unrelated matter if doing so will not adversely affect the lawyer's relationship with the enterprise or conduct of the suit and if both clients consent upon consultation. By the same token, government lawyers in some circumstances may represent government employees in proceedings in which a government agency is the opposing party. The propriety of concurrent representation can depend on the nature of the litigation. For example, a suit charging fraud entails conflict to a degree not involved in a suit for a declaratory judgment concerning statutory interpretation.

[9] A lawyer may represent parties having antagonistic positions on a legal question that has arisen in different cases, unless representation of either client would be adversely affected. Thus, it is ordinarily not improper to assert such positions in cases pending in different trial courts, but it may be improper to do so in cases pending at the same time in an appellate court.

Interest of Person Paying for a Lawyer's Service

[10] A lawyer may be paid from a source other than the client, if the client is informed of that fact and consents and the arrangement does not compromise the lawyer's duty of loyalty to the client. See Rule 1.8(f). For example, when an insurer and its insured have conflicting interests in a matter arising from a liability insurance agreement, and the insurer is required to provide special counsel for the insured, the arrangement should assure the special counsel's professional independence. So also, when a corporation and its directors or employees are involved in a controversy in which they have conflicting interests, the corporation may provide funds for separate legal representation of the directors or employees, if the clients consent after consultation and the arrangement ensures the lawyer's professional independence.

Other Conflict Situations

[11] Conflicts of interest in contexts other than litigation sometimes may be difficult to assess. Relevant factors in determining whether there is potential for adverse effect include the duration and intimacy of the lawyer's relationship with the client or clients involved, the functions being performed by the lawyer, the likelihood that actual conflict will arise and the likely prejudice to the client from the conflict if it does arise. The question is often one of proximity and degree.

[12] For example, a lawyer may not represent multiple parties to a negotiation whose interests are fundamentally antagonistic to each other, but common representation is permissible where the clients are generally aligned in interest even though there is some difference of interest among them.

[13] Conflict questions may also arise in estate planning and estate administration. A lawyer may be called upon to prepare wills for several family members, such as husband and wife, and, depending upon the circumstances, a conflict of interest may arise. In estate administration the identity of the client may be unclear under the law of a particular jurisdiction. Under one view, the client is the fiduciary; under another view the client is the estate or trust, including its beneficiaries. The lawyer should make clear the relationship to the parties involved.

[14] A lawyer for a corporation or other organization who is also a member of its board of directors should determine whether the responsibilities of the two roles may conflict. The lawyer may be called on to advise the corporation in matters involving actions of the directors. Consideration should be given to the frequency with which such situations may arise, the potential intensity of the conflict, the effect of the lawyer's resignation from the board and the possibility of the corporation's obtaining legal advice from another lawyer in such situations. If there is material risk that the dual role will compromise the lawyer's independence of professional judgment, the lawyer should not serve as a director.

Conflict Charged by an Opposing Party

[15] Resolving questions of conflict of interest is primarily the responsibility of the lawyer undertaking the representation. In litigation, a court may raise the question when there is reason to infer that the lawyer has neglected the responsibility. In a criminal case, inquiry by the court is generally required when a lawyer represents multiple defendants. Where the conflict is

such as clearly to call in question the fair or efficient administration of justice, opposing counsel may properly raise the question. Such an objection should be viewed with caution, however, for it can be misused as a technique of harassment. See Scope.

Model Code Comparison

DR 5-101 (A) provided that "[e]xcept with the consent of his client after full disclosure, a lawyer shall not accept employment if the exercise of his professional judgment on behalf of the client will be or reasonably may be affected by his own financial business, property, or personal interests." DR 5-105(A) provided that a lawyer "shall decline proffered employment if the exercise of his independent professional judgment in behalf of a client will be or is likely to be adversely affected by the acceptance of the proffered employment, or if it would be likely to involve him in representing differing interests, except to the extent permitted under DR 5-105(C)." DR 5-105(C) provided that "a lawyer may represent multiple clients if it is obvious that he can adequately represent the interest of each and if each consents to the representation after full disclosure of the possible effects of such representation on the exercise of his independent professional judgment on behalf of each." DR 5-107(B) provided that a lawyer "shall not permit a person who recommends, employs, or pays him to render legal services for another to direct or regulate his professional judgment in rendering such services."

Rule 1.7 clarifies DR 5-105(A) by requiring that, when the lawyer's other interest are involved, not only must the client consent after consultation but also that, independent of such consent, the representation reasonably appears not to be adversely affected by the lawyer's other interests. This requirement appears to be the intended meaning of the provision in DR 5-105(C) that "it is obvious that he can adequately represent" the client, and was implicit in EC 5-2, which stated that a lawyer "should not accept proffered employment if his personal interests or desires will, or there is a reasonable probability that they will, affect adversely the advice to be given or services to be rendered the prospective client."

Rule 1.8 Conflict of Interest: Prohibited Transactions

(a) A lawyer shall not enter into a business transaction with a client or knowingly acquire an ownership, possessory, security or other pecuniary interest adverse to a client unless:

(1) the transaction and terms on which the lawyer acquires the interest are fair and reasonable to the client and are fully disclosed and transmitted in writing to the client in a manner which can be reasonably understood by the client;

(2) the client is given a reasonable opportunity to seek the advice of independent counsel in the transaction; and

(3) the client consents in writing thereto.

(b) A lawyer shall not use information relating to representation of a client to the disadvantage of the client unless the client consents after consultation, except as permitted or required by Rule 1.6 or Rule 3.3.

(c) A lawyer shall not prepare an instrument giving the lawyer or a person related to the lawyer as parent, child, sibling, or spouse any substantial gift from a client, including a testamentary gift, except where the client is related to the donee.

(d) Prior to the conclusion of representation of a client, a lawyer shall not make or negotiate an agreement giving the lawyer literary or media rights to a portrayal or account based in substantial part on information relating to the representation.

(e) A lawyer shall not provide financial assistance to a client in connection with pending or contemplated litigation, except that:

(1) a lawyer may advance court costs and expenses of litigation, the repayment of which may be contingent on the outcome of the matter; and

(2) a lawyer representing an indigent client may pay court costs and expenses of litigation on behalf of the client.

(f) A lawyer shall not accept compensation for representing a client from one other than the client unless:

(1) the client consents after consultation;

(2) there is not interference with the lawyer's independence of professional judgement or with the client-lawyer relationship; and

(3) information relating to representation of a client is protected as required by Rule 1.6.

(g) A lawyer who represents two or more clients shall not participate in making an aggregate settlement of the claims of or against the clients, or in a criminal case an aggregated agreement as to guilty or nolo contendere pleas, unless each client consents after consultation, including disclosure of the existence and nature of all the claims or pleas involved and of the participation of each person in the settlement.

(h) A lawyer shall not make an agreement prospectively limiting the lawyer's liability to a client for malpractice unless permitted by law and the client is independently represented in making the agreement, or settle a claim for such liability with an unrepresented client or former client without first advising that person in writing that independent representation is appropriate in connection therewith.

(i) A lawyer related to another lawyer as parent, child, sibling or spouse shall not represent a client in a representation directly adverse to a person who the lawyer knows is represented by the other lawyer except upon consent by the client after consultation regarding the relationship.

(j) A lawyer shall not acquire a proprietary interest in a cause of action or subject matter of litigation the lawyer is conducting for a client, except that the lawyer may:

(1) acquire a lien granted by law to secure the lawyer's fee or expenses; and

(2) contract with a client for a reasonable contingent fee in a civil case.

Comment

Transactions Between Client and Lawyer

[1] As a general principle, all transactions between client and lawyer should be fair and reasonable to the client. In such transactions a review by independent counsel on behalf of the client is often advisable. Furthermore, a lawyer may not exploit information relating to the representation to the client's disadvantage. For example, a lawyer who has learned that the client is investing in specific real estate may not, without the client's consent, seek to acquire nearby property where doing so would adversely affect the client's plan for investment. Paragraph (a) does not, however, apply to standard commercial transactions between the lawyer and the client for products or services that the client generally markets to others, for example, banking or brokerage services, medical services, products manufactured or distributed by the client, and utilities' services. In such transactions, the lawyer has no advantage in dealing with the client, and the restrictions in paragraph (a) are unnecessary and impracticable.

[2] A lawyer may accept a gift from a client, if the transaction meets general standards of fairness. For example, a simple

gift such as a present given at a holiday or as a token of appreciation is permitted. If effectuation of a substantial gift requires preparing a legal instrument such as a will or conveyance, however, the client should have the detached advice that another lawyer can provide. Paragraph (c) recognizes an exception where the client is a relative of the donee or the gift is not substantial.

Literary Rights

[3] An agreement by which a lawyer acquires literary or media rights concerning the conduct of the representation creates a conflict between the interests of the client and the personal interests of the lawyer. Measures suitable in the representation of the client may detract from the publication value of an account of the representation. Paragraph (d) does not prohibit a lawyer representing a client in a transaction concerning literary property from agreeing that the lawyer's fee shall consist of a share in ownership in the property, if the arrangement conforms to Rule 1.5 and paragraph (j).

Person Paying for a Lawyer's Services

[4] Paragraph (f) requires disclosure of the fact that the lawyer's services are being paid for by a third party. Such an arrangement must also conform to the requirements of Rule 1.6 concerning confidentiality and Rule 1.7 concerning conflict of interest. Where the client is a class, consent may be obtained on behalf of the class by court-supervised procedure.

Limiting Liability

[5] Paragraph (h) is not intended to apply to customary qualifications and limitations in legal opinions and memoranda.

Family Relationships Between Lawyers

[6] Paragraph (i) applies to related lawyers who are in different firms. Related lawyers in the same firm are governed by Rules 1.7, 1.9, and 1.10. The disqualification stated in paragraph (i) is personal and is not imputed to members of firms with whom the lawyers are associated.

Acquisition of Interest in Litigation

[7] Paragraph (j) states the traditional general rule that lawyers are prohibited from acquiring a proprietary interest in litigation. This general rule, which has its basis in common law champerty and maintenance, is subject to specific exceptions developed in decisional law and continued in these Rules, such as the exception for reasonable contingent fees set forth in Rule

1.5 and the exception for certain advances of the costs of litigation set forth in paragraph (e).

Model Code Comparison

With regard to paragraph (a), DR 5-104(A) provided that a lawyer "shall not enter into a business transaction with a client if they have differing interests therein and if the client expects the lawyer to exercise his professional judgment therein for the protection of the client, unless the client has consented after full disclosure." EC 5-3 stated that a lawyer "should not seek to persuade his client to permit him to invest in an undertaking of his client nor make improper use of his professional relationship to influence his client to invest in an enterprise in which the lawyer is interested."

With regard to paragraph (b), DR 4-101(B)(3) provided that a lawyer should not use "a confidence or secret of his client for the advantage of himself, or of a third person, unless the client consents after full disclosure."

There was no counterpart to paragraph (c) in the Disciplinary Rules of the Model Code. EC 5-5 stated that a lawyer "should not suggest to his client that a gift be made to himself or for his benefit. If a lawyer accepts a gift from his client, he is peculiarly susceptible to the charge that he unduly influenced or overreached the client. If a client voluntarily offers to make a gift to his lawyer, the lawyer may accept the gift, but before doing so, he should urge that the client secure disinterested advice from an independent, competent person who is cognizant of all the circumstances. Other than in exceptional circumstances, a lawyer should insist that an instrument in which his client desires to name him beneficially be prepared by another lawyer selected by the client."

Paragraph (d) is substantially similar to DR 5-104(B), but refers to "literary or media" rights, a more generally inclusive term than "publication" rights.

Paragraph (e)(1) is similar to DR 5-103(B), but eliminates the requirement "that the client remains ultimately liable for such expenses."

Paragraph (e)(2) has no counterpart in the Model Code.

Paragraph (f) is substantially identical to DR 5-107(A)(1).

Paragraph (g) is substantially identical to DR 5-106.

The first clause of paragraph (h) is similar to DR 6-102(A). There was no counterpart in the Model Code to the second clause of paragraph (h).

Paragraph (i) has no counterpart in the Model Code.

Paragraph (j) is substantially identical to DR 5-103(A).

Rule 1.9 Conflict of Interest: Former Client

(a) A lawyer who has formerly represented a client in a matter shall not thereafter represent another person in the same or substantially related matter in which that person's interests are materially adverse to the interests of the former client unless the former client consents after consultation.

(b) A lawyer shall not knowingly represent a person in the same or substantially related matter in which a firm with which the lawyer formerly was associated had previously represented a client,

(1) whose interests are materially adverse to that person; and

(2) about whom the lawyer has acquired information protected by Rule 1.6 and 1.9(c) that is material to the matter; unless the former client consents after consultation.

(c) A lawyer who has formerly represented a client in a matter or whose present or former firm has formerly represented a client in a matter shall not thereafter:

(1) use information relating to the representation to the disadvantage of the former client except as Rule 1.6 or 3.3 would permit or require with respect to a client, or when the information has become generally known; or

(2) reveal information relating to the representation except as Rule 1.6 or 3.3 would permit or require with respect to a client.

Comment

[1] After termination of a client-lawyer relationship, a lawyer may not represent another client except in conformity with this Rule. The principles in Rule 1.7 determine whether the interests of the present and former client are adverse. Thus, a lawyer could not properly seek to rescind on behalf of a new client a contract drafted on behalf of the former client. So also a lawyer who has prosecuted an accused person could not properly represent the accused in a subsequent civil action against the government concerning the same transaction.

[2] The scope of a "matter" for purposes of this Rule may depend on the facts of a particular situation or transaction. The lawyer's involvement in a matter can also be a question of degree. When a lawyer has been directly involved in a specific transaction, subsequent representation of other clients with materially

adverse interests clearly is prohibited. On the other hand, a lawyer who recurrently handled a type of problem for a former client is not precluded from later representing another client in a wholly distinct problem of that type even though the subsequent representation involves a position adverse to the prior client. Similar considerations can apply to the reassignment of military lawyers between defense and prosecution functions within the same military jurisdiction. The underlying question is whether the lawyer was so involved in the matter that the subsequent representation can be justly regarded as a changing of sides in the matter in question.

Lawyers Moving Between Firms

[3] When lawyers have been associated within a firm but then end their association, the question of whether a lawyer should undertake representation is more complicated. There are several competing considerations. First, the client previously represented by the former firm must be reasonably assured that the principle of loyalty to the client is not compromised. Second, the rule should not be so broadly cast as to preclude other persons from having reasonable choice of legal counsel. Third, the rule should not unreasonably hamper lawyers from forming new associations and taking on new clients after having left a previous association. In this connection, it should be recognized that today many lawyers practice in firms, that many lawyers to some degree limit their practice to one field or another, and that many move from one association to another several times in their careers. If the concept of imputation were applied with unqualified rigor, the result would be radical curtailment of the opportunity of lawyers to move from one practice setting to another and of the opportunity of clients to change counsel.

[4] Reconciliation of these competing principles in the past has been attempted under two rubrics. One approach has been to seek per se rules of disqualification. For example, it has been held that a partner in a law firm is conclusively presumed to have access to all confidences concerning all clients of the firm. Under this analysis, if a lawyer has been a partner in one law firm and then becomes a partner in another law firm, there may be a presumption that all confidences known by the partner in the first firm are known to all partners in the second firm. This presumption might properly be applied in some circumstances, especially where the client has been extensively represented, but may be unrealistic where the client

was represented only for limited purposes. Furthermore, such a rigid rule exaggerates the difference between a partner and an associate in modern law firms.

[5] The other rubric formerly used for dealing with disqualification is the appearance of impropriety proscribed in Canon 9 of the ABA Model Code of Professional Responsibility. This rubric has a two-fold problem. First, the appearance of impropriety can be taken to include any new client-lawyer relationship that might make a former client feel anxious. If that meaning were adopted, disqualification would become little more than a question of subjective judgment by the former client. Second, since "impropriety" is undefined, the term "appearance of impropriety" is question-begging. It therefore has to be recognized that the problem of disqualification cannot be properly resolved either by simple analogy to a lawyer practicing alone or by the very general concept of appearance of impropriety.

Confidentiality

[6] Preserving confidentiality is a question of access to information. Access to information, in turn, is essentially a question of fact in particular circumstances, aided by inferences, deductions or working presumptions that reasonably may be made about the way in which lawyers work together. A lawyer may have general access to files of all clients of a law firm and may regularly participate in discussions of their affairs; it should be inferred that such a lawyer in fact is privy to all information about all the firm's clients. In contrast, another lawyer may have access to the files of only a limited number of clients and participate in discussions of the affairs of no other clients; in the absence of information to the contrary, it should be inferred that such a lawyer in fact is privy to information about the clients actually served but not those of other clients.

[7] Application of paragraph (b) depends on a situation's particular facts. In such an inquiry the burden of proof should rest upon the firm whose disqualification is sought.

[8] Paragraph (b) operates to disqualify the lawyer only when the lawyer involved has actual knowledge of information protected by Rules 1.6 and 1.9(b). Thus, if a lawyer while with one firm acquired no knowledge or information relating to a particular client of the firm, and that lawyer later joined another firm, neither the lawyer individually nor the second firm is disqualified from representing another client in the same or a related matter even though the interests of the two clients

conflict. See Rule 1.10(b) for the restrictions on a firm once a lawyer has terminated association with the firm.

[9] Independent of the question of disqualification of a firm, a lawyer changing professional association has a continuing duty to preserve confidentiality of information about a client formerly represented. See Rules 1.6 and 1.9.

Adverse Positions

[10] The second aspect of loyalty to a client is the lawyer's obligation to decline subsequent representations involving positions adverse to a former client arising in substantially related matters. This obligation requires abstention from adverse representation by the individual lawyer involved, but does not properly entail abstention of other lawyers through imputed disqualification. Hence, this aspect of the problem is governed by Rule 1.9(a). Thus, if a lawyer left one firm for another, the new affiliation would not preclude the firms involved from continuing to represent clients with adverse interests in the same or related matters, so long as the conditions of paragraphs (b) and (c) concerning confidentiality have been met.

[11] Information acquired by the lawyer in the course of representing a client may not subsequently be used or revealed by the lawyer to the disadvantage of the client. However, the fact that a lawyer has once served a client does not preclude the lawyer from using generally known information about that client when later representing another client.

[12] Disqualification from subsequent representation is for the protection of former clients and can be waived by them. A waiver is effective only if there is disclosure of the circumstances, including the lawyer's intended role in behalf of the new client.

[13] With regard to an opposing party's raising a question of conflict of interest, see Comment to Rule 1.7. With regard to disqualification of a firm with which a lawyer is or was formerly associated, see Rule 1.10.

Model Code Comparison

There was no counterpart to this Rule in the Disciplinary Rules of the Model Code. Representation adverse to a former client was sometimes dealt with under the rubric of Canon 9 of the Model Code, which provided: "A lawyer should avoid even the appearance of impropriety." Also applicable were EC 4-6 which stated that the "obligation of a lawyer to preserve the confidences and secrets of his client continues after the termination of his employment" and Canon 5 which stated that "[a] lawyer should exercise independent professional judgment on behalf of a client."

The provision for waiver by the former client in paragraphs (a) and (b) is similar to DR 5-105(C).

The exception in the last clause of paragraph (c)(1) permits a lawyer to use information relating to a former client that is in the "public domain," a use that was also not prohibited by the Model Code, which protected only "confidences and secrets." Since the scope of paragraphs (a) and (b) is much broader than "confidences and secrets," it is necessary to define when a lawyer may make use of information about a client after the client-lawyer relationship has terminated.

Rule 1.10 Imputed Disqualification: General Rule

(a) While lawyers are associated in a firm, none of them shall knowingly represent a client when any one of them practicing alone would be prohibited from doing so by Rule 1.7, 1.8(c), 1.9 or 2.2.

(b) When a lawyer has terminated an association with a firm, the firm is not prohibited from thereafter representing a person with interests materially adverse to those of a client represented by the formerly associated lawyer, and not currently represented by the firm, unless:

(1) the matter is the same or substantially related to that in which the formerly associated lawyer represented the client; and

(2) any lawyer remaining in the firm has information protected by Rules 1.6 and 1.9(c) that is material to the matter.

(c) A disqualification prescribed by this Rule may be waived by the affected client under the conditions stated in Rule 1.7.

Comment

Definition of "Firm"

[1] For purposes of the Rules of Professional Conduct, the term "firm" includes lawyers in a private firm, and lawyers in the legal department of a corporation or other organization, or in a legal services organization. Whether two or more lawyers constitute a firm within this definition can depend on the specific facts. For example, two practitioners who share office space and occasionally consult or assist each other ordinarily would not be regarded as constituting a firm. However, if they present themselves to the public in a way suggesting that they are a firm or conduct themselves as a firm, they should be regarded as a firm

for purposes of the Rules. The terms of any formal agreement between associated lawyers are relevant in determining whether they are a firm, as is the fact that they have mutual access to information concerning the clients they serve. Furthermore, it is relevant in doubtful cases to consider the underlying purpose of the Rule that is involved. A group of lawyers could be regarded as a firm for purposes of the rule that the same lawyer should not represent opposing parties in litigation, while it might not be so regarded for purposes of the rule that information acquired by one lawyer is attributed to the other.

[2] With respect to the law department of an organization, there is ordinarily no question that the members of the department constitute a firm within the meaning of the Rules of Professional Conduct. However, there can be uncertainty as to the identity of the client. For example, it may not be clear whether the law department of a corporation represents a subsidiary or an affiliated corporation, as well as the corporation by which the members of the department are directly employed. A similar question can arise concerning an unincorporated association and its local affiliates.

[3] Similar questions can also arise with respect to lawyers in legal aid. Lawyers employed in the same unit of a legal service organization constitute a firm, but not necessarily those employed in separate units. As in the case of independent practitioners, whether the lawyers should be treated as associated with each other can depend on the particular rule that is involved, and on the specific facts of the situation.

[4] Where a lawyer has joined a private firm after having represented the government, the situation is governed by Rule 1.11(a) and (b); where a lawyer represents the government after having served private clients, the situation is governed by Rule 1.11(c)(1). The individual lawyer involved is bound by the Rules generally, including Rules 1.6 , 1.7 and 1.9.

[5] Different provisions are thus made for movement of a lawyer from one private firm to another and for movement of a lawyer between a private firm and the government. The government is entitled to protection of its client confidences and, therefore, to the protections provided in Rules 1.6, 1.9 and 1.11. However, if the more extensive disqualification in Rule 1.10 were applied to former government lawyers, the potential effect on the government would be unduly burdensome. The government deals with all private citizens and organizations and, thus, has a much wider circle of adverse legal interests than

does any private law firm. In these circumstances, the government's recruitment of lawyers would be seriously impaired if Rule 1.10 were applied to the government.

On balance, therefore, the government is better served in the long run by the protections stated in Rule 1.11.

Principles of Imputed Disqualification

[6] The rule of imputed disqualification stated in paragraph (a) gives effect to the principle of loyalty to the client as it applies to lawyers who practice in a law firm. Such situations can be considered from the premise that a firm of lawyers is essentially one lawyer for purposes of the rules governing loyalty to the client, or from the premise that each lawyer is vicariously bound by the obligation of loyalty owed by each lawyer with whom the lawyer is associated. Paragraph (a) operates only among the lawyers currently associated in a firm. When a lawyer moves from one firm to another, the situation is governed by Rules 1.9(b) and 1.10(b).

[7] Rule 1.10(b) operates to permit a law firm, under certain circumstances, to represent a person with interests directly adverse to those of a client represented by a lawyer who formerly was associated with the firm. The Rule applies regardless of when the formerly associated lawyer represented the client. However, the law firm may not represent a person with interests adverse to those of a present client of the firm, which would violate Rule 1.7. Moreover, the firm may not represent the person where the matter is the same or substantially related to that in which the formerly associated lawyer represented the client and any other lawyer currently in the firm has material information protected by Rules 1.6 and 1.9(c).

Model Code Comparison

DR 5-105(D) provided that "[i]f a lawyer is required to decline or to withdraw from employment under a Disciplinary Rule, no partner, or associate, or any other lawyer affiliated with him or his firm, may accept or continue such employment."

Rule 1.16 Declining or Terminating Representation

(a) Except as stated in paragraph (c), a lawyer shall not represent a client or, where representation has commenced, shall withdraw from the representation of a client if:

(1) the representation will result in violation of the rules of professional conduct or other law;

(2) the lawyer's physical or mental condition materially impairs the lawyer's ability to represent the client; or

(3) the lawyer is discharged.

(b) Except as stated in paragraph (3), a lawyer may withdraw from representing a client if withdrawal can be accomplished without material adverse effect on the interests of the client, or if:

(1) the client persists in a course of action involving the lawyer's services that the lawyer reasonably believes is criminal or fraudulent;

(2) the client has used the lawyer's services to perpetrate a crime or fraud;

(3) a client insists upon pursuing an objective that the lawyer considers repugnant or imprudent;

(4) the client fails substantially to fulfill an obligation to the lawyer regarding the lawyer's services and has been given reasonable warning that the lawyer will withdraw unless the obligation is fulfilled;

(5) the representation will result in an unreasonable financial burden on the lawyer or has been rendered unreasonably difficult by the client; or

(6) other good cause for withdrawal exists.

(c) when ordered to do so by a tribunal, a lawyer shall continue representation notwithstanding good cause for terminating the representation.

(d) Upon termination of representation, a lawyer shall take steps to the extent reasonably practicable to protect a client's interest, such as giving reasonable notice to the client, allowing time for employment of other counsel, surrendering papers and property to which the client is entitled and refunding any advance payment of fee that has not been earned. The lawyer may retain papers relating to the client to the extent permitted by other law.

Comment

[1] A lawyer should not accept representation in a matter unless it can be performed competently, promptly, without improper conflict of interest and to completion.

Mandatory Withdrawal

[2] A lawyer ordinarily must decline or withdraw from representation if the client demands that the lawyer engage in conduct that is illegal or violates the Rules of Professional Conduct or other law. The lawyer is not obliged to decline or withdraw

simply because the client suggests such a course of conduct; a client may make such a suggestion in the hope that a lawyer will not be constrained by a professional obligation.

[3] When a lawyer has been appointed to represent a client, withdrawal ordinarily requires approval of the appointing authority. See also Rule 6.2. Difficulty may be encountered if withdrawal is based on the client's demand that the lawyer engage in unprofessional conduct. The court may wish an explanation for the withdrawal, while the lawyer may be bound to keep confidential the facts that would constitute such an explanation. The lawyer's statement that professional considerations require termination of the representation ordinarily should be accepted as sufficient.

Discharge

[4] A client has a right to discharge a lawyer at any time, with or without cause, subject to liability for payment for the lawyer's services. Where future dispute about the withdrawal may be anticipated, it may be advisable to prepare a written statement reciting the circumstances.

[5] Whether a client can discharge appointed counsel may depend on applicable law. A client seeking to do so should be given a full explanation of the consequences. These consequences may include a decision by the appointing authority that appointment of successor counsel is unjustified, thus requiring the client to represent himself.

[6] If the client is mentally incompetent, the client may lack the legal capacity to discharge the lawyer, and in any event the discharge may be seriously adverse to the client's interests. The lawyer should make special effort to help the client consider the consequences and, in an extreme case, may initiate proceedings for a conservatorship or similar protection of the client. See Rule 1.14.

Optional Withdrawal

[7] A lawyer may withdraw from representation in some circumstances. The lawyer has the option to withdraw if it can be accomplished without material adverse effect on the client's interests. Withdrawal is also justified if the client persists in a course of action that the lawyer reasonably believes is criminal or fraudulent, for a lawyer is not required to be associated with such conduct even if the lawyer does not further it. Withdrawal is also permitted if the lawyer's services were misused in the past even if that would materially prejudice the client. The

lawyer also may withdraw where the client insists on a repugnant or imprudent objective.

[8] A lawyer may withdraw if the client refuses to abide by the terms of an agreement relating to the representation, such as an agreement concerning fees or court costs or an agreement limiting the objectives of the representation.

Assisting the Client upon Withdrawal

[9] Even if the lawyer has been unfairly discharged by the client, a lawyer must take all reasonable steps to mitigate the consequences to the client. The lawyer may retain papers as security for a fee only to the extent permitted by law.

[10] Whether or not a lawyer for an organization may under certain unusual circumstances have a legal obligation to the organization after withdrawing or being discharged by the organization's highest authority is beyond the scope of these Rules.

Model Code Comparison

With regard to paragraph (a), DR 2-109(A) provided that a lawyer "shall not accept employment . . . if he knows or it is obvious that [the prospective client] wishes to . . . [b]ring a legal action . . . or otherwise have steps taken for him, merely for the purpose of harassing or maliciously injuring any person . . . ." Nor may a lawyer accept employment if the lawyer is aware that the prospective client wishes to "[p]resent a claim or defense . . . that is not warranted under existing law, unless it can be supported by good faith argument for an extension, modification, or reversal of existing law." DR 2-110(B) provided that a lawyer "shall withdraw from employment . . . if:

"(1) He knows or it is obvious that his client is bringing the legal action . . . or is otherwise having steps taken for him, merely for the purpose of harassing or maliciously injuring any person.

"(2) He knows or it is obvious that his continued employment will result in violation of a Disciplinary Rule.

"(3) His mental or physical condition renders it unreasonably difficult for him to carry out the employment effectively.

"(4) He is discharged by his client."

With regard to paragraph (b), DR 2-110(C) permitted withdrawal regardless of the effect on the client if:

"(1) His client: (a) Insists upon presenting a claim or defense that is not warranted under existing law and cannot be supported by good faith argument for an extension, modification, or reversal of existing law; (b) Personally seeks to pursue an illegal course of conduct; (c) Insists that the lawyer pursue a course of conduct that is illegal or that is prohibited under the Disciplinary Rules; (d) By other conduct renders it unreasonably difficult for the lawyer to carry out his employment effectively; (e) Insists, in a matter not pending before a tribunal, that the lawyer engage in conduct that is contrary to the judgment and advice of the lawyer but not prohibited under the Disciplinary Rules; (f) Deliberately disregards an agreement or obligation to the lawyer as to expenses and fees.

"(2) His continued employment is likely to result in a violation of a Disciplinary Rule.

"(3) His inability to work with co-counsel indicates that the best interest of the client likely will be served by withdrawal.

"(4) His mental or physical condition renders it difficult for him to carry out the employment effectively.

"(5) His client knowingly and freely assents to termination of his employment.

"(6) He believes in good faith, in a proceeding pending before a tribunal, that the tribunal will find the existence of other good cause for withdrawal."

With regard to paragraph (c), DR 2-110(A)(1) provided: "If permission for withdrawal from employment is required by the rules of a tribunal, the lawyer shall not withdraw . . . without its permission."

The provisions of paragraph (d) are substantially identical to DR 2-110(A)(2) and (3).

3.3 Candor Toward the Tribunal

(a) A lawyer shall not knowingly:

(1) make a false statement of material fact or law to a tribunal;

(2) fail to disclose a material fact to a tribunal when disclosure is necessary to avoid assisting a criminal or fraudulent act by the client;

(3) fail to disclose to the tribunal legal authority in the controlling jurisdiction known to the lawyer to be directly adverse to the position of the client and not disclosed by opposing counsel; or

(4) offer evidence that the lawyer knows to be false. If a lawyer has offered material evidence and comes to know

of its falsity, the lawyer shall take reasonable remedial measures.

(b) The duties stated in paragraph (a) continue to the conclusion of the proceeding, and apply even if compliance requires disclosure of information otherwise protected by Rule 1.6.

(c) A lawyer may refuse to offer evidence that the lawyer reasonably believes is false.

(d) In an ex parte proceeding, a lawyer shall inform the tribunal of all material facts known to the lawyer which will enable the tribunal to make an informed decision, whether or not the facts are adverse.

Comment

[1] The advocate's task is to present the client's case with persuasive force. Performance of that duty while maintaining confidences of the client is qualified by the advocate's duty of candor to the tribunal. However, an advocate does not vouch for the evidence submitted in a cause; the tribunal is responsible for assessing its probative value.

Representations by a Lawyer

[2] An advocate is responsible for pleadings and other documents prepared for litigation, but is usually not required to have personal knowledge of matters asserted therein, for litigation documents ordinarily present assertions by the client, or by someone on the client's behalf, and not assertions by the lawyer. Compare Rule 3.1. However, an assertion purporting to be on the lawyer's own knowledge, as in an affidavit by the lawyer or in a statement in open court, may properly be made only when the lawyer knows the assertion is true or believes it to be true on the basis of a reasonably diligent inquiry. There are circumstances where failure to make a disclosure is the equivalent of an affirmative misrepresentation. The obligation prescribed in Rule 1.2(d) not to counsel a client to commit or assist the client in committing a fraud applies in litigation. Regarding compliance with Rule 1.2(d), see the Comment to that Rule. See also the Comment to Rule 8.4(b).

Misleading Legal Argument

[3] Legal argument based on a knowingly false representation of law constitutes dishonesty toward the tribunal. A lawyer is not required to make a disinterested exposition of the law, but must recognize the existence of pertinent legal authorities. Furthermore, as stated in paragraph (a)(3), an advocate

has a duty to disclose directly adverse authority in the controlling jurisdiction which has not been disclosed by the opposing party. The underlying concept is that legal argument is a discussion seeking to determine the legal premises properly applicable to the case.

False Evidence

[4] When evidence that a lawyer knows to be false is provided by a person who is not the client, the lawyer must refuse to offer it regardless of the client's wishes.

[5] When false evidence is offered by the client, however, a conflict may arise between the lawyer's duty to keep the client's revelations confidential and the duty of candor to the court. Upon ascertaining that material evidence is false, the lawyer should seek to persuade the client that the evidence should not be offered or, if it has been offered, that its false character should immediately be disclosed. If the persuasion is ineffective, the lawyer must take reasonable remedial measures.

[6] Except in the defense of a criminal accused, the rule generally recognized is that, if necessary to rectify the situation, an advocate must disclose the existence of the client's deception to the court or to the other party. Such a disclosure can result in grave consequences to the client, including not only a sense of betrayal but also loss of the case and perhaps a prosecution for perjury. But the alternative is that the lawyer cooperate in deceiving the court, thereby subverting the truth-finding process which the adversary system is designed to implement. See Rule 1.2(d). Furthermore, unless it is clearly understood that the lawyer will act upon the duty to disclose the existence of false evidence, the client can simply reject the lawyer's advice to reveal the false evidence and insist that the lawyer keep silent. Thus the client could in effect coerce the lawyer into being a party to fraud on the court.

Perjury by a Criminal Defendant

[7] Whether an advocate for a criminally accused has the same duty of disclosure has been intensely debated. While it is agreed that the lawyer should seek to persuade the client to refrain from perjurious testimony, there has been dispute concerning the lawyer's duty when that persuasion fails. If the confrontation with the client occurs before trial, the lawyer ordinarily can withdraw. Withdrawal before trial may not be possible, however, either because trial is imminent, or because the

confrontation with the client does not take place until the trial itself, or because no other counsel is available.

[8] The most difficult situation, therefore, arises in a criminal case where the accused insists on testifying when the lawyer knows that the testimony is perjurious. The lawyer's effort to rectify the situation can increase the likelihood of the client's being convicted as well as opening the possibility of a prosecution for perjury. On the other hand, if the lawyer does not exercise control over the proof, the lawyer participates, although in a merely passive way, in deception of the court.

[9] Three resolutions of this dilemma have been proposed. One is to permit the accused to testify by a narrative without guidance through the lawyer's questioning. This compromises both contending principles; it exempts the lawyer from the duty to disclose false evidence but subjects the client to an implicit disclosure of information imparted to counsel. Another suggested resolution, of relatively recent origin, is that the advocate be entirely excused from the duty to reveal perjury if the perjury is that of the client. This is a coherent solution but makes the advocate a knowing instrument of perjury.

[10] The other resolution of the dilemma is that the lawyer must reveal the client's perjury if necessary to rectify the situation. A criminal accused has a right to the assistance of an advocate, a right to testify and a right of confidential communication with counsel. However, an accused should not have a right to assistance of counsel in committing perjury. Furthermore, an advocate has an obligation, not only in professional ethics but under the law as well, to avoid implication in the commission of perjury or other falsification of evidence. See Rule 1.2(d).

Remedial Measures

[11] If perjured testimony or false evidence has been offered, the advocate's proper course ordinarily is to remonstrate with the client confidentially. If that fails, the advocate should seek to withdraw if that will remedy the situation. If withdrawal will not remedy the situation or is impossible, the advocate should make disclosure to the court. It is for the court then to determine what should be done—making a statement about the matter to the trier of fact, ordering a mistrial or perhaps nothing. If the false testimony was that of the client, the client may controvert the lawyer's version of their communication when the lawyer discloses the situation to the court. If there is an issue whether the client has committed perjury, the lawyer

cannot represent the client in resolution of the issue, and a mistrial may be unavoidable. An unscrupulous client might in this way attempt to produce a series of mistrials and thus escape prosecution. However, a second such encounter could be construed as a deliberate abuse of the right to counsel and as such a waiver of the right to further representation.

Constitutional Requirements

[12] The general rule—that an advocate must disclose the existence of perjury with respect to a material fact, even that of a client—applies to defense counsel in criminal cases, as well as in other instances. However, the definition of the lawyer's ethical duty in such a situation may be qualified by constitutional provisions for due process and the right to counsel in criminal cases. In some jurisdictions these provisions have been construed to require that counsel present an accused as a witness if the accused wishes to testify, even if counsel knows the testimony will be false. The obligation of the advocate under these Rules is subordinate to such a constitutional requirement.

Duration of Obligation

[13] A practical time limit on the obligation to rectify the presentation of false evidence has to be established. The conclusion of the proceeding is a reasonably definite point for the termination of the obligation.

Refusing to Offer Proof Believed to Be False

[14] Generally speaking, a lawyer has authority to refuse to offer testimony or other proof that the lawyer believes is untrustworthy. Offering such proof may reflect adversely on the lawyer's ability to discriminate in the quality of evidence and thus impair the lawyer's effectiveness as an advocate. In criminal cases, however, a lawyer may, in some jurisdictions, be denied this authority by constitutional requirements governing the right to counsel.

Ex Parte Proceedings

[15] Ordinarily, an advocate has the limited responsibility of presenting one side of the matters that a tribunal should consider in reaching a decision; the conflicting position is expected to be presented by the opposing party. However, in any ex parte proceeding, such as an application for a temporary restraining order, there is no balance of presentation by opposing advocates. The object of an ex parte proceeding is nevertheless to yield a substantially just result. The judge has an affirmative responsibility to accord the absent party just consideration. The

lawyer for the represented party has the correlative duty to make disclosures of material facts known to the lawyer and that the lawyer reasonably believes are necessary to an informed decision.

Model Code Comparison

Paragraph (a)(1) is substantially identical to DR 7-102(A)(5), which provided that a lawyer shall not "knowingly make a false statement of law or fact."

Paragraph (a)(2) is implicit in DR 7-102(A)(3), which provided that "a lawyer shall not ... knowingly fail to disclose that which he is required by law to reveal."

Paragraph (a)(3) is substantially identical to DR 7-106(B)(1).

With regard to paragraph (a)(4), the first sentence of this subparagraph is similar to DR 7-102(A)(4), which provided that a lawyer shall not "knowingly use" perjured testimony or false evidence. The second sentence of paragraph (a)(4) resolves an ambiguity in the Model Code concerning the action required of a lawyer who discovers that the lawyer has offered perjured testimony or false evidence. DR 7-102(A)(4), quoted above, did not expressly deal with this situation, but the prohibition against "use" of false evidence can be construed to preclude carrying through with a case based on such evidence when that fact has become known during the trial. DR 7-102(B)(1), also noted in connection with Rule 1.6 , provided that a lawyer "who receives information clearly establishing that ... [h]is client has ... perpetrated a fraud upon ... a tribunal shall [if the client does not rectify the situation] ... reveal the fraud to the ... tribunal. ...." Since use of perjured testimony or false evidence is usually regarded as "fraud" upon the court, DR 7-102(B)(1) apparently required disclosure by the lawyer in such circumstances. However, some states have amended DR 7-102(B)(1) in conformity with an ABA-recommended amendment to provide that the duty of disclosure does not apply when the "information is protected as a privileged communication." This qualification may be empty, for the rule of attorney-client privilege has been construed to exclude communications that further a crime, including the crime of perjury. On this interpretation of DR 7-102(B)(1), the lawyer had a duty to disclose the perjury.

Paragraph (c) confers discretion on the lawyer to refuse to offer evidence that the lawyer "reasonably believes" is false. This gives the lawyer more latitude than DR 7-102(A)(4), which prohibited the lawyer from offering evidence the lawyer "knows" is false.

There was no counterpart in the Model Code to paragraph (d).

Rule 3.4 Fairness to Opposing Party and Counsel

A lawyer shall not:

(a) unlawfully obstruct another party's access to evidence or unlawfully alter, destroy or conceal a document or other material having potential evidentiary value. A lawyer shall not counsel or assist another person to do any such act;

(b) falsify evidence, counsel or assist a witness to testify falsely, or offer an inducement to a witness that is prohibited by law;

(c) knowingly disobey an obligation under the rules of a tribunal except for an open refusal based on an assertion that no valid obligation exists;

(d) in pretrial procedure, make a frivolous discovery request or fail to make reasonably diligent effort to comply with a legally proper discovery request by an opposing party;

(e) in trial, allude to any matter that the lawyer does not reasonably believe is relevant or that will not be supported by admissible evidence, assert personal knowledge of facts in issue except when testifying as a witness, or state a personal opinion as to the justness of a cause, the credibility of a witness, the culpability of a civil litigant or the guilt or innocence of an accused; or

(f) request a person other than a client to refrain from voluntarily giving relevant information to another party unless:

(1) the person is a relative or an employee or other agent of a client; and

(2) the lawyer reasonably believes that the person's interests will not be adversely affected by refraining from giving such information.

Comment

[1] The procedure of the adversary system contemplates that the evidence in a case is to be marshalled competitively by the contending parties. Fair competition in the adversary system is secured by prohibitions against destruction or concealment of evidence, improperly influencing witnesses, obstructive tactics in discovery procedure, and the like.

[2] Documents and other items of evidence are often essential to establish a claim or defense. Subject to evidentiary privileges, the right of an opposing party, including the government, to obtain evidence through discovery or subpoena is an important procedural right. The exercise of that right can be frustrated if relevant material is altered, concealed or destroyed. Applicable law in many jurisdictions makes it an offense to destroy material for the purpose of impairing its availability in a pending proceeding or one whose commencement can be foreseen. Falsifying evidence is also generally a criminal offense. Paragraph (a) applies to evidentiary material generally, including computerized information.

[3] With regard to paragraph (b), it is not improper to pay a witness's expenses or to compensate an expert witness on terms permitted by law. The common law rule in most jurisdictions is that it is improper to pay an occurrence witness any fee for testifying and that it is improper to pay an expert witness a contingent fee.

[4] Paragraph (f) permits a lawyer to advise employees of a client to refrain from giving information to another party, for the employees may identify their interests with those of the client. See also Rule 4.2.

Model Code Comparison

With regard to paragraph (a), DR 7-109(A) provided that a lawyer "shall not suppress any evidence that he or his client has a legal obligation to reveal." DR 7-109(B) provided that a lawyer "shall not advise or cause a person to secrete himself... for the purpose of making him unavailable as a witness. . . ." DR 7-106(C)(7) provided that a lawyer shall not "[i]ntentionally or habitually violate any established rule of procedure or of evidence."

With regard to paragraph (b), DR 7-102(A)(6) provided that a lawyer shall not participate "in the creation or preservation of evidence when he knows or it is obvious that the evidence is false." DR 7-109(C) provided that a lawyer "shall not pay, offer to pay, or acquiesce in the payment of compensation to a witness contingent upon the content of his testimony or the outcome of the case. But a lawyer may advance, guarantee or acquiesce in the payment of: (1) Expenses reasonably incurred by a witness in attending or testifying; (2) Reasonable compensation to a witness for his loss of time in attending or testifying; (or) (3) A reasonable fee for the professional services of an expert witness." EC 7-28 stated that witnesses "should always

testify truthfully and should be free from any financial induce-
ments that might tempt them to do otherwise."

Paragraph (c) is substantially similar to DR 7-106(A),
which provided that "A lawyer shall not disregard . . . a standing rule of a tribunal or a ruling of a tribunal made in the
course of a proceeding, but he may take appropriate steps in
good faith to test the validity of such rule or ruling."

Paragraph (d) has no counterpart in the Model Code.

Paragraph (e) substantially incorporates DR 7-106(C)(1),
(2), (3) and (4). DR 7-106(C)(2) proscribed asking a question
"intended to degrade a witness or other person," a matter dealt
with in Rule 4.4 . DR 7-106(C)(5), providing that a lawyer shall
not "fail to comply with known local customs of courtesy or
practice," was too vague to be a rule of conduct enforceable as
law.

With regard to paragraph (f), DR 7-104(A)(2) provided that
a lawyer shall not "give advice to a person who is not represented . . . other than the advice to secure counsel, if the interests of such person are or have a reasonable possibility of being
in conflict with the interests of his client."

Rule 4.1 Truthfulness in Statements to Others

In the course of representing a client a lawyer shall not
knowingly:

(a) make a false statement of material fact or law to a third
person; or

(b) fail to disclose a material fact to a third person when disclosure is necessary to avoid assisting a criminal or fraudulent
act by a client, unless disclosure is prohibited by Rule 1.6.

Comment

Misrepresentation

[1] A lawyer is required to be truthful when dealing with
others on a client's behalf, but generally has no affirmative
duty to inform an opposing party of relevant facts. A misrepresentation can occur if the lawyer incorporates or affirms a
statement of another person that the lawyer knows is false.
Misrepresentations can also occur by failure to act.

Statements of Fact

[2] This Rule refers to statements of fact. Whether a particular statement should be regarded as one of fact can depend on
the circumstances. Under generally accepted conventions in
negotiation, certain types of statements ordinarily are not

taken as statements of material fact. Estimates of price or value placed on the subject of a transaction and a party's intentions as to an acceptable settlement of a claim are in this category, and so is the existence of an undisclosed principal except where nondisclosure of the principal would constitute fraud.

Fraud by Client

[3] Paragraph (b) recognizes that substantive law may require a lawyer to disclose certain information to avoid being deemed to have assisted the client's crime or fraud. The requirement of disclosure created by this paragraph is, however, subject to the obligations created by Rule 1.6.

Model Code Comparison

Paragraph (a) is substantially similar to DR 7-102(A)(5), which stated that "[i]n his representation of a client, a lawyer shall not . . . [k]nowingly make a false statement of law or fact."

With regard to paragraph (b), DR 7-102(A)(3) provided that a lawyer shall not "[c]onceal or knowingly fail to disclose that which he is required by law to reveal."

Rule 4.2 Communication with Person Represented by Counsel

In representing a client, a lawyer shall not communicate about the subject of the representation with a party the lawyer knows to be represented by another lawyer in the matter, unless the lawyer has the consent of the other lawyer or is authorized by law to do so.

Comment

[1] This Rule does not prohibit communication with a represented person, or an employee or agent of such a person, concerning matters outside the representation. For example, the existence of a controversy between a government agency and a private party, or between two organizations, does not prohibit a lawyer for either from communicating with nonlawyer representatives of the other regarding a separate matter. Also, parties to a matter may communicate directly with each other and a lawyer having independent justification or legal authorization for communicating with a represented person is permitted to do so. Communications authorized by law include, for example, the right of a party to a controversy with a government agency to speak with government officials about the matter.

[2] Communications authorized by law also include constitutionally permissible investigative activities of lawyers representing governmental entities, directly or through

investigative agents, prior to the commencement of criminal or civil enforcement proceedings, when there is applicable judicial precedent that either has found the activity permissible under this Rule or has found this Rule inapplicable. However, the Rule imposes ethical restrictions that go beyond those imposed by constitutional provisions.

[3] This Rule applies to communications with any person, whether or not a party to a formal adjudicative proceeding, contract or negotiation, who is represented by counsel concerning the matter to which the communication relates.

[4] In the case of an organization, this Rule prohibits communications by a lawyer for another person or entity concerning the matter in representation with persons having a managerial responsibility on behalf of the organization, and with any other person whose act or omission in connection with that matter may be imputed to the organization for purposes of civil or criminal liability or whose statement may constitute an admission on the part of the organization. If an agent or employee of the organization is represented in the matter by his or her own counsel, the consent by that counsel to a communication will be sufficient for purposes of this Rule. Compare Rule 3.4(f).

[5] The prohibition on communications with a represented person only applies, however, in circumstances where the lawyer knows that the person is in fact represented in the matter to be discussed. This means that the lawyer has actual knowledge of the fact of the representation; but such actual knowledge may be inferred from the circumstances. See Terminology. Such an inference may arise in circumstances where there is substantial reason to believe that the person with whom communication is sought is represented in the matter to be discussed. Thus, a lawyer cannot evade the requirement of obtaining the consent of counsel by closing eyes to the obvious.

[6] In the event the person with whom the lawyer communicates is not known to be represented by counsel in the matter, the lawyer's communications are subject to Rule 4.3.

Model Code Comparison

This Rule is substantially identical to DR 7-104(A)(1) except for the substitution of the term "person" for "party."

Rule 4.3 Dealing with Unrepresented Person

In dealing on behalf of a client with a person who is not represented by counsel, a lawyer shall not state or imply that the lawyer is disinterested. When the lawyer knows or reasonably should know that the unrepresented person misunderstands the lawyer's role in the matter, the lawyer shall make reasonable efforts to correct the misunderstanding.

Comment

[1] An unrepresented person, particularly one not experienced in dealing with legal matters, might assume that a lawyer is disinterested in loyalties or is a disinterested authority on the law even when the lawyer represents a client. During the course of a lawyer's representation of a client, the lawyer should not give advice to an unrepresented person other than the advice to obtain counsel.

Model Code Comparison

There was no direct counterpart to this Rule in the Model Code. DR 7-104(A)(2) provided that a lawyer shall not "[g]ive advice to a person who is not represented by a lawyer, other than the advice to secure counsel. . . ."

Rule 4.4 Respect for Rights of Third Persons

In representing a client, a lawyer shall not use means that have no substantial purpose other than to embarrass, delay, or burden a third person, or use methods of obtaining evidence that violate the legal rights of such a person.

Comment

[1] Responsibility to a client requires a lawyer to subordinate the interests of others to those of the client, but that responsibility does not imply that a lawyer may disregard the rights of third persons. It is impractical to catalogue all such rights, but they include legal restrictions on methods of obtaining evidence from third persons.

Model Code Comparison

DR 7-106(C)(2) provided that a lawyer shall not "[a]sk any question that he has no reasonable basis to believe is relevant to the case and that is intended to degrade a witness or other person." DR 7-102(A)(1) provided that a lawyer shall not "take . . . action on behalf of his client when he knows or when it is obvious that such action would serve merely to harass or maliciously injure another." DR 7-108(D) provided that "[a]fter discharge of the jury . . . the lawyer shall not ask questions or make comments to a member of that jury that are calculated merely to harass or embarrass the juror. . . ." DR 7-108(E) provided that a lawyer "shall not conduct . . . a vexatious or harassing investigation of either a venireman or a juror."

Rule 6.1 Voluntary Pro Bono Public Service

A lawyer should aspire to render at least (50) hours of pro bono public legal services per year. In fulfilling this responsibility, the lawyer should:

(a) provide a substantial majority of the (50) hours of legal services without fee or expectation of fee to:

(1) persons of limited means or

(2) charitable, religious, civic, community, governmental and educational organizations in matters which are designed primarily to address the needs of persons of limited means; and

(b) provide any additional services through:

(1) delivery of legal services at no fee or substantially reduced fee to individuals, groups or organizations seeking to secure or protect civil rights, civil liberties or public rights, or charitable, religious, civic, community, governmental and educational organizations in matters in furtherance of their organizational purposes, where the payment of standard legal fees would significantly deplete the organization's economic resources or would be otherwise inappropriate;

(2) delivery of legal services at a substantially reduced fee to persons of limited means; or

(3) participation in activities for improving the law, the legal system or the legal profession.

In addition, a lawyer should voluntarily contribute financial support to organizations that provide legal services to persons of limited means.

Comment

[1] Every lawyer, regardless of professional prominence or professional work load, has a responsibility to provide legal services to those unable to pay, and personal involvement in the problems of the disadvantaged can be one of the most rewarding experiences in the life of a lawyer. The American Bar Association urges all lawyers to provide a minimum of 50 hours of pro bono services annually. States, however, may decide to choose a higher or lower number of hours of annual service (which may be expressed as a percentage of a lawyer's professional time) depending upon local needs and local conditions. It is recognized that in some years a lawyer may render greater or fewer hours than the annual standard specified, but during the course of his or her legal career, each lawyer should render

on average per year, the number of hours set forth in this Rule. Services can be performed in civil matters or in criminal or quasi-criminal matters for which there is no government obligation to provide funds for legal representation, such as post-conviction death penalty appeal cases.

[2] Paragraphs (a)(1) and (2) recognize the critical need for legal services that exists among persons of limited means by providing that a substantial majority of the legal services rendered annually to the disadvantaged be furnished without fee or expectation of fee. Legal services under these paragraphs consist of a full range of activities, including individual and class representation, the provision of legal advice, legislative lobbying, administrative rule making and the provision of free training or mentoring to those who represent persons of limited means. The variety of these activities should facilitate participation by government lawyers, even when restrictions exist on their engaging in the outside practice of law.

[3] Persons eligible for legal services under paragraphs (a)(1) and (2) are those who qualify for participation in programs funded by the Legal Services Corporation and those whose incomes and financial resources are slightly above the guidelines utilized by such programs but, nevertheless, cannot afford counsel. Legal services can be rendered to individuals or to organizations such as homeless shelters, battered women's centers and food pantries that serve those of limited means. The term "governmental organizations" includes, but is not limited to, public protection programs and sections of governmental or public sector agencies.

[4] Because service must be provided without fee or expectation of fee, the intent of the lawyer to render free legal services is essential for the work performed to fall within the meaning of paragraphs (a)(1) and (2). Accordingly, services rendered cannot be considered pro bono if an anticipated fee is uncollected, but the award of statutory lawyers' fees in a case originally accepted as pro bono would not disqualify such services from inclusion under this section. Lawyers who do receive fees in such cases are encouraged to contribute an appropriate portion of such fees to organizations or projects that benefit persons of limited means.

[5] While it is possible for a lawyer to fulfill the annual responsibility to perform pro bono services exclusively through activities described in paragraphs (a)(1) and (2), to the extent that any hours of service remained unfulfilled, the remaining

commitment can be met in a variety of ways as set forth in paragraph (b). Constitutional, statutory or regulatory restrictions may prohibit or impede government and public sector lawyers and judges from performing the pro bono services outlined in paragraphs (a)(1) and (2). Accordingly, where those restrictions apply, government and public sector lawyers and judges may fulfill their pro bono responsibility by performing services outlined in paragraph (b).

[6] Paragraph (b)(1) includes the provision of certain types of legal services to those whose incomes and financial resources place them above limited means. It also permits the pro bono lawyer to accept a substantially reduced fee for services. Examples of the types of issues that may be addressed under this paragraph include First Amendment claims, Title VII claims and environmental protection claims. Additionally, a wide range of organizations may be represented, including social service, medical research, cultural and religious groups.

[7] Paragraph (b)(2) covers instances in which lawyers agree to and receive a modest fee for furnishing legal services to persons of limited means. Participation in judicare programs and acceptance of court appointments in which the fee is substantially below a lawyer's usual rate are encouraged under this section.

[8] Paragraph (b)(3) recognizes the value of lawyers engaging in activities that improve the law, the legal system or the legal profession. Serving on bar association committees, serving on boards of pro bono or legal services programs, taking part in Law Day activities, acting as a continuing legal education instructor, a mediator or an arbitrator and engaging in legislative lobbying to improve the law, the legal system or the profession are a few examples of the many activities that fall within this paragraph.

[9] Because the provision of pro bono services is a professional responsibility, it is the individual ethical commitment of each lawyer. Nevertheless, there may be times when it is not feasible for a lawyer to engage in pro bono services. At such times a lawyer may discharge the pro bono responsibility by providing financial support to organizations providing free legal services to persons of limited means. Such financial support should be reasonably equivalent to the value of the hours of service that would have otherwise been provided. In addition, at times it may be more feasible to satisfy the pro bono

responsibility collectively, as by a firm's aggregate pro bono activities.

[10] Because the efforts of individual lawyers are not enough to meet the need for free legal services that exists among persons of limited means, the government and the profession have instituted additional programs to provide those services. Every lawyer should financially support such programs, in addition to either providing direct pro bono services or making financial contributions when pro bono service is not feasible.

[11] The responsibility set forth in this Rule is not intended to be enforced through disciplinary process.

Model Code Comparison

There was no counterpart of this Rule in the Disciplinary Rules of the Model Code. EC 2-25 stated that the "basic responsibility for providing legal services for those unable to pay ultimately rests upon the individual lawyer. . . . Every lawyer, regardless of professional prominence or professional work load should find time to participate in serving the disadvantaged." EC 8-9 stated that "[t]he advancement of our legal system is of vital importance in maintaining the rule of law . . . [and] lawyers should encourage, and should aid in making, needed changes and improvements." EC 8-3 stated that "[t]hose persons unable to pay for legal services should be provided needed services."

Rule 6.2 Accepting Appointments

A lawyer shall not seek to avoid appointment by a tribunal to represent a person except for good cause, such as:

(a) representing the client is likely to result in violation of the Rules of Professional Conduct or other law;

(b) representing the client is likely to result in an unreasonable financial burden on the lawyer; or

(c) the client or the cause is so repugnant to the lawyer as to be likely to impair the client-lawyer relationship or the lawyer's ability to represent the client.

Comment

[1] A lawyer ordinarily is not obliged to accept a client whose character or cause the lawyer regards as repugnant. The lawyer's freedom to select clients is, however, qualified. All lawyers have a responsibility to assist in providing pro bono publico service. See Rule 6.1. An individual lawyer fulfills this responsibility by accepting a fair share of unpopular matters or

indigent or unpopular clients. A lawyer may also be subject to appointment by a court to serve unpopular clients or persons unable to afford legal services.

Appointed Counsel

[2] For good cause a lawyer may seek to decline an appointment to represent a person who cannot afford to retain counsel or whose cause is unpopular. Good cause exists if the lawyer could not handle the matter competently, see Rule 1.1, or if undertaking the representation would result in an improper conflict of interest, for example, when the client or the cause is so repugnant to the lawyer as to be likely to impair the client-lawyer relationship or the lawyer's ability to represent the client. A lawyer may also seek to decline an appointment if acceptance would be unreasonably burdensome, for example, when it would impose a financial sacrifice so great as to be unjust.

[3] An appointed lawyer has the same obligations to the client as retained counsel, including the obligations of loyalty and confidentiality, and is subject to the same limitations on the client-lawyer relationship, such as the obligation to refrain from assisting the client in violation of the Rules.

Model Code Comparison

There was no counterpart to this Rule in the Disciplinary Rules of the Model Code. EC 2-29 stated that when a lawyer is "appointed by a court or requested by a bar association to undertake representation of a person unable to obtain counsel, whether for financial or other reasons, he should not seek to be excused from undertaking the representation except for compelling reasons. Compelling reasons do not include such factors as the repugnance of the subject matter of the proceeding, the identity or position of a person involved in the case, the belief of the lawyer that the defendant in a criminal proceeding is guilty, or the belief of the lawyer regarding the merits of the civil case." EC 2-30 stated that "a lawyer should decline employment if the intensity of his personal feelings, as distinguished from a community attitude, may impair his effective representation of a prospective client."

Index